I0887329

Research, Reference Service, and Resources for the Study of Africa

Research, Reference Service, and Resources for the Study of Africa has been co-published simultaneously as *The Reference Librarian*, Numbers 87/88 2004.

Research, Reference Service, and Resources for the Study of Africa

Deborah M. LaFond, MLIS
Gretchen Walsh, MLS
Editors

Research, Reference Service, and Resources for the Study of Africa has been co-published simultaneously as *The Reference Librarian*, Numbers 87/88 2004.

Routledge
Taylor & Francis Group
New York London

Research, Reference Service, and Resources for the Study of Africa has been co-published simultaneously as *The Reference Librarian*™, Numbers 87/88 2004.

First published 2004 by The Haworth Press, Inc.

This edition published 2012 by Routledge
605 Third Avenue, New York, NY 10017
2 Park Square, Milton Park, Abingdon, Oxon OX14 4RN

Routledge is an imprint of the Taylor & Francis Group, an informa business

Copyright © 2004 Taylor & Francis

All rights reserved. No part of this book may be reprinted or reproduced or utilised in any form or by any electronic, mechanical, or other means, now known or hereafter invented, including photocopying and recording, or in any information storage or retrieval system, without permission in writing from the publishers.

Notice:
Product or corporate names may be trademarks or registered trademarks, and are used only for identification and explanation without intent to infringe.

Cover design by Jennifer M. Gaska.

Library of Congress Cataloging-in-Publication Data

Research, reference service, and resources for the study of Africa / Deborah M. LaFond, Gretchen Walsh, editors.
p. cm.
"Co-published simultaneously as The reference librarian, numbers 87/88, 2004."
Includes bibliographical references and index.
ISBN 0-7890-2508-6 (alk. paper) – ISBN 0-7890-2509-4 (pbk. : alk. paper)
1. Africana libraries–Reference services. 2. Libraries–Special collections–Africa. 3. Africa–Research. 4. Africa–Library resources. I. LaFond, Deborah M. II. Walsh, Gretchen. III. Reference librarian.
Z675.A55R47 2004
026.96–dc22

2004014896

ISBN 13: 978-0-7890-2509-8 (pbk)

Research, Reference Service, and Resources for the Study of Africa

CONTENTS

ABOUT THE EDITORS

Deborah M. LaFond, MLIS, is Reference Librarian and Social Science Bibliographer for Africana Studies, Communication, Educational and Counseling Psychology, Psychology, and Women's Studies departments and programs at the University at Albany, State University of New York since 1996. Ms. LaFond was formerly a Reference Librarian at the University of California Berkeley (1987-1996). She has co-authored two previous articles; one on diversity in collection development, and an article discussing European Union sources, and survey results on librarian's use of government documents in bibliographic instruction.

Gretchen Walsh, MLS, has been Head of the African Studies Library at Boston University since 1977. Involved in African studies since 1964, she has taught English and French in Nigeria and served as librarian for several USAID projects focusing on the Sahel. Author of numerous articles on Africana librarianship, her most recent book was *Media in Africa/Africa in the Media: An Annotated Bibliography.*

Introduction

Gretchen Walsh
Deborah M. LaFond

The main themes of these essays are clearly stated in the title: Africa and reference service. Reference, of course, is the main interest of readers of this journal. Africa may seem a peripheral, rather exotic topic for most readers. An examination of reference service in terms of research *on* Africa and libraries *in* Africa, however, can provide new insights.

Library service, particularly reference, is in a period of rapid and radical change and development in the United States. Advances in information technology and transformation of resources for research have changed the way librarians work and greatly altered the expectations of researchers at all levels. The important question is whether all of these developments have actually improved the research process, and if libraries are doing the right things to ensure successful research.

Africa is relevant to Americans, no matter how distant or exotic it may seem. Not only do 12.9% of Americans trace ancestry back to Africa, all Americans benefit from the petroleum imported from Africa (18% of America's imports, as you will see in Angel Batiste's paper in this volume), and Americans of all races and backgrounds incorporate African culture into their own–sometimes without being fully aware of the source. The local Starbucks features Kenyan and Ethiopian coffee; the candy bar you consume with that cup of java contains chocolate and peanuts from West Africa; a night out may include dancing to Afropop, or the African inspired rhythms of jazz or Brazilian Samba; even blue-

[Haworth co-indexing entry note]: "Introduction." Walsh, Gretchen, and Deborah M. LaFond. Co-published simultaneously in *The Reference Librarian* (The Haworth Information Press, an imprint of The Haworth Press, Inc.) No. 87/88, 2004, pp. 1-4; and: *Research, Reference Service, and Resources for the Study of Africa* (ed: Deborah M. LaFond, and Gretchen Walsh) The Haworth Information Press, an imprint of The Haworth Press, Inc., 2004, pp. 1-4. Single or multiple copies of this article are available for a fee from The Haworth Document Delivery Service [1-800-HAWORTH, 9:00 a.m. - 5:00 p.m. (EST). E-mail address: docdelivery@haworthpress.com].

http://www.haworthpress.com/web/REF
© 2004 by The Haworth Press, Inc. All rights reserved.
Digital Object Identifier: 10.1300/J120v42n87_01

grass has borrowed the banjo from Africa. More recent events continually keep Americans aware of Africa: your doctor, cab driver, or library tech may be a recent African immigrant; war, famine, and other disasters keep Africa in the headlines, balanced somewhat by the diplomacy of Kofi Annan, or the quiet, almost unnoticed democratic elections in several nations, and small victories in health and economic development at the grassroots level.

Despite connections with Africa, even despite the interest in Africa that Walsh's paper hypothesizes from available statistics, students and other researchers often begin their queries without adequate background knowledge to develop successful research strategies. They need research assistance. It is also important for American librarians to understand the conditions and challenges of their African colleagues. Africa is a continent with many problems. The fact that Western media overemphasize these problems does not make them any less serious. The role that African libraries–and librarians–can play in research and development for Africa *in* Africa is not well understood or supported by either African governments or foreign donor agencies.

The librarians who contributed papers to this volume are a diverse lot–not only in gender, nationality, and ethnicity, but also in the length of their experience, nature of their work, and the library populations they serve. Their papers are equally diverse, but within the broad themes, their papers have sub-themes that unify them despite their very different topics and approaches. These sub-themes are:

- Overcoming obstacles and solving problems: the settings may be U.S. libraries or African libraries; the problems may be access to information; teaching American students to do research on Africa; overcoming colonial legacies or dealing with gender and class bias.
- Responsibility: the need to help students become successful researchers; to provide sufficient and accurate information about Africa; to aid in development of libraries in Africa; to promote understanding between the peoples of the U.S. and of Africa. All examine the responsibility of librarians to both patrons and Africa, and all address the ways that librarians can and do act in fulfilling that responsibility. They also place reference service in a larger context. Good reference service depends on the quality and content of the library collection, depends on a wide range of technical services, and takes place in an environment of ever-advancing information technology that is changing the very nature of research.

- Partnership and cooperation for mutual benefit
- Activism

Walsh, Frank-Wilson, and Batiste are all writing about working with American researchers. Walsh synthesizes some 30 years of library experience to draw attention to shared responsibility for research access: how decisions of authors and publishers, as well as indexers and librarians, affect the ways researchers can find information. She also looks at particular problems caused by different orthographies and terminologies particular to African names and topics, and summarizes the work of the Africana Librarians Council. Frank-Wilson's paper describes the long tradition of a credit-bearing course on library research methods for African studies at Indiana University. The overview of the course traces the history and evolution of reference and research tools and the training needs of students and faculty. Batiste pulls together an impressive array of online business information on Africa, and touches on two primary themes in this volume: the current and potential importance of Africa in the world economy, and the difficulties encountered by researchers looking for specific information about Africa.

Limb's paper looks at the changes that advances in information technology have made in reference service, particularly how librarians interact in the new community of scholars made possible by electronic discussion lists. He also focuses on partnerships between American and African librarians and the mutual benefits of such liaisons. Conteh-Morgan goes beyond a theoretical consideration of libraries' influence on research and intellectual trends, advocating greater activism. Her experience in dealing with African women writers both as a teacher and a librarian provides her with a rich perspective. Noting that the choices librarians make have an impact on what researchers find, Conteh-Morgan emphasizes the librarian's role in selection of research topics through encouraging students to look beyond the traditional canon. Nosakhere's paper describes a cooperative project between a U.S. university and a new university in Cote d'Ivoire. She looks both at the issues in developing a library collection from the ground up, and at the experience of U.S. exchange students in Cote d'Ivoire. The project required a sharply focused examination of the potential reference needs of the Ivoiren students and selection of tools that would most fully suit their needs.

Darch's paper, with its intriguing title, turns a critical and analytical gaze on collection development policies and philosophies, and how they subtly influence research parameters. He raises questions about the origins and legitimacy of "area" studies, particularly African studies, and most particularly about the utility of "African" studies in Africa. His are not simple questions, but are not as far removed from an American librarian's day-to-day reference desk experience as one might think. African studies librarians are frequently asked "Why just the continent, why not the diaspora as well?" or "Why is African economics shelved separately from all other economics?" In libraries, logistical decisions can have unexpected results.

LaFond's paper also focuses on libraries within the higher education context in Africa, examining a wide range of factors that mitigate for, or against, successful research outcomes for students and scholars in Africa. Observations made within Africa, reported in her paper, describe the complex nature of donor influence, as well as the resilience of librarians, students, and scholars in the process of mapping out democratic educational reform. She argues that librarians are important partners in re-vitalizing libraries and publishing within Africa which could encourage democratic self-determination, leadership, and prevent brain drain.

It is our fortune as editors to have encountered such variety. All of the papers highlight possible research topics that may be of interest to students from Africa and those who study Africa. The editors hope you will find this collection to be thought-provoking and encourage further scholarly inquiry and discussion.

PART I: AFRICAN STUDIES IN THE UNITED STATES

"Can We Get There from Here?" Negotiating the Washouts, Cave-Ins, Dead Ends, and Other Hazards on the Road to Research on Africa

Gretchen Walsh

SUMMARY. This introduction to Africana reference describes the populations of researchers, the kinds of questions they ask, and how librarians–both specialist and generalist–may respond. It explores issues in "known-item" searches, including name authority and access to material in collected works and series. Choices made by authors, publishers, in-

Gretchen Walsh is affiliated with the African Studies Library, Boston University, 771 Commonwealth Avenue, Boston, MA 02215 (E-mail: gwalsh@bu.edu).

[Haworth co-indexing entry note]: " 'Can We Get There from Here?' Negotiating the Washouts, Cave-Ins, Dead Ends, and Other Hazards on the Road to Research on Africa." Walsh, Gretchen. Co-published simultaneously in *The Reference Librarian* (The Haworth Information Press, an imprint of The Haworth Press, Inc.) No. 87/88, 2004, pp. 5-96; and: *Research, Reference Service, and Resources for the Study of Africa* (ed: Deborah M. LaFond, and Gretchen Walsh) The Haworth Information Press, an imprint of The Haworth Press, Inc., 2004, pp. 5-96. Single or multiple copies of this article are available for a fee from The Haworth Document Delivery Service [1-800-HAWORTH, 9:00 a.m. - 5:00 p.m. (EST). E-mail address: docdelivery@haworthpress.com].

dexers, librarians, and researchers themselves have an impact on topic searches. Terminology for African languages, ethnic groups, place names, and topics cause problems for novice researchers, but library policy decisions can also impede access. Errors of all kinds–minor or major–can block access to information. The speed of electronic desktop publishing seems to have encouraged reduced care with proofreading, indexing, and verification of quotations and citations. The need for accurate information about Africa is great, but the market for publications and electronic resources focused on Africa is relatively small. This low market share can result in less coverage of Africa in indexes and reference tools. Despite the difficulties encountered in researching Africa, researchers and the librarians who assist them benefit from the tools, services, and initiatives of specialist Africana librarians and from a number of commercially produced resources. *[Article copies available for a fee from The Haworth Document Delivery Service: 1-800-HAWORTH. E-mail address: <docdelivery@haworthpress.com> Website: <http://www.HaworthPress.com> © 2004 by The Haworth Press, Inc. All rights reserved.]*

KEYWORDS. Africa, Africana Librarians Council, African Studies Association, reference functions, name authority, contents notes, analytics, access, keywords, subject headings, search strategies, indexing, full-text searching, terminology, cataloguing, errors, citations, indexes

WHO WANTS TO KNOW WHAT? THE QUESTORS, THE QUEST AND THE GUIDES

- "What is the population of Dar es Salaam? What was it in 1950 and 1900?"
- "My team is representing Namibia in the Model UN. What is that country's stand on global warming?"
- "What's being done about HIV/AIDS in Cameroon?"
- "I'm doing a paper on the Igbo people and my teacher said you'd have some stuff."
- "I'm preparing a proposal to introduce solar cookers to villagers in Burkina Faso. I need information on solar cooking and heating in Africa, and also material on gender roles in rural Burkina."
- "*It Takes a Village to Raise a Child* is supposed to be an African proverb. What language? What people?"
- "Like, do you have anything on African drumming?"

These are typical of the questions fielded daily by the staff of the African Studies Library (ASL) of Boston University. As a specialized department within the university library system, a major component of ASL's mission is to help researchers find the information and scholarship on Africa that they need. We are well equipped to do so. ASL is one of the oldest African studies libraries in the United States, with a collection of over 200,000 volumes, an array of electronic resources, and a staff of three librarians and two paraprofessionals who have among them expertise in African studies based on a combination of academic background, on-the-job experience, and continuing education.

Africa Is Not Just for Specialists

Questions similar to those in the introduction could be posed to any reference librarians at academic and public libraries nationwide, or formed into searches on the Web and electronic information resources by the researchers themselves. It is probably impossible to measure the extent of research on Africa in the U.S., but several figures suggest that a considerable number of people have an academic or personal interest in learning about Africa. The African Studies Association (ASA) http://www.africanstudies.org, the main professional organization of Africanist scholars, has 2,202 individual members belonging to 510 institutions and organizations worldwide. About 85% of these members reside in the United States. There are 489 institutional subscribers to ASA publications. The Association of African Studies Programs listed 55 U.S. institutions as members as of 1993 on its Web site: http://www.africanstudies.org/asa_aasp.html. The *International Directory of African Studies Research* (Baker 1994) included 115 U.S. institutions. The *Directory of African and Afro-American Studies* (Rana 1987) lists 388 universities and colleges offering courses on Africa and its diaspora. Based on these figures, it is reasonable to speculate that during any academic year there could be tens of thousands of students nationwide taking Africa-related courses and writing papers on African topics.

This estimate does not include pre-college students and non-academic researchers, whose numbers could be extensive as well. All institutions receiving federal Higher Education Act Title VI funds as national resource centers for Africa (eleven in 2002–see http://www.ed.gov/offices/OPE/HEP/iegps/nrc.html) have outreach programs that promote and facilitate the study of Africa in the public schools and the community, and develop curriculum materials and lesson plans. Other institutions have similar programs without this federal assistance. Clearly, anyone might have questions about Africa, and any librarian may get a question about Africa at the reference desk, whether or not they have specialized resources on Africa.

Where Are the Specialist Librarians and What Do They Do?

The Africana Librarians Council (ALC) (http://lcweb.loc.gov/rr/amed/9asa.html) of the African Studies Association is the major professional organization for specialist Africana librarians and, increasingly, librarians who have responsibilities for multiple subjects including Africa. Its approximately eighty members represent thirty libraries nationwide, primarily those with major research collections on Africa. Although many specialist librarians provide reference service and develop research tools on Africa, the principal duty for Africana librarians has been collection development. They focus particularly on scholarly, government and commercial publications from Africa, whose acquisition requires a great deal of attention. Thus, even at these institutions, the specialist Africana librarians may only be responsible for collection development, with reference service provided by more generalist staff. Boston University's African Studies Library is somewhat unusual: each staff member has responsibility for some combination of collection development and management, reference service and bibliographic instruction, cataloging, and Web page development. However, even though specialist Africana librarians may not provide direct reference service, they have been extremely active in creating reference and research tools such as bibliographies on a wide array of topics, and guides to Africana collections in libraries and archives.

Are Bibliographies Obsolete?

These service activities came under some scrutiny at the conference held on the 40th anniversary of the ALC, the proceedings of which have been published as *Africana Librarianship in the 21st Century: Treasuring the Past and Building the Future* (Schmidt 1998). In the section on reference and bibliographic instruction, Tom Johnsen, Social Science Librarian at the University of Bergen (Norway), advanced the idea that these narrow, tailor-made bibliographies no longer provide a useful service to researchers, since the major databases do a better job of guiding researchers to books and articles on their topics. He maintained that Africanist librarians should concentrate on teaching researchers how to use the major databases, and devote more energy to making available online the catalogs of those archives and library collections that are still only accessible in card catalogs or local computer systems. He also called on librarians to advocate for the digitization of the documents in those collections to expand access to scholars unable to visit the collections (Johnsen 1998: 67). While most of the audience agreed with Johnsen's second point, his assertion that major databases "do the job better" raised some controversy, with several librarians protesting that general indexes did not serve Africanist researchers well enough, and special bibliographies were a necessary service (Coelho 1998: 79).

Researchers Need More Help Than They May Realize

Specialists, generalist librarians, and end users all depend on tools designed to provide access to information in libraries and on the Web, including OPACs, databases, and search engines. How well do those tools work? How much information and scholarship on Africa is really accessible to researchers distant from the specialized collections? Indeed, how much information within those specialized collections is readily accessible to researchers? Can Web research on Africa substitute for library research? This paper will explore these questions by examining aspects of library and information service that affect successful research on Africa and describing some of the problems peculiar to African resources.

Library catalogs do not provide sufficient access to specialized materials in the collection. Some analyses indicate that over 90% of the information and scholarship in articles, works in series, essays in edited volumes, and the contents of collected works remain elusive (Tyckoson 1997: 11). If these works are not accessible in library catalogs, and are not in major databases, then specialized bibliographies may be the only way that they will ever be found. Moreover, the nomenclature and terminology particular to the study of Africa cause difficulties for searchers using both indexes and library catalogs. Researchers new to Africanist topics need help in sorting out African personal names, terms for languages and ethnic groups, and geographic terms to use in search strategies.

My own experience has indicated that currently available electronic indexes and full-text resources are not sufficient for serious research on Africa for two reasons:

- They leave uncovered and inaccessible vast amounts of information and scholarship that are produced and published outside the

"mainstream." African publications are especially poorly represented.
- Even for the resources covered, access is limited to terms used in the title or text, or to subject headings and descriptors. For African topics, there are numerous problems involved in matching search query terms to terms on the index.

Successful response to reference questions like those sampled in the beginning of this essay depends on several factors:

- The information exists in some published format, and is available for use.
- The researcher or librarian can construct a search that is designed to yield available information.
- The information sources have been made sufficiently accessible for search and discovery through cataloging, indexing, or other means.

Does the Information Exist?

The first factor depends on the output of the publishing industry and the collection development policies and strategies of libraries. Judging from the discussions at meetings and in professional literature, specialized African studies libraries have focused mainly on collection development and the difficulties of obtaining sufficient information and scholarship about Africa, particularly works published in Africa.

Sometimes the information sought has not been published or released, as in these cases:

- "I've based my dissertation on housing development in Accra on data from the 1974 census. My advisor says these figures are too old since it's now 1990, and insists that I use data from the 1984 census. But you don't have it." ASL didn't own it because it had not yet been published, six years after the census was taken. The advisor was skeptical, although we provided the student with confirmation that the census was not yet published. Fortunately vital sections were finally published just in time for this fellow's thesis deadline.
- "I'm doing an exposé of the practices of diamond companies in South Africa regarding apartheid. Where can I find all the secret stuff they don't put in their annual reports?" This student wanted

information that could only be obtained through intense investigation in South Africa. Unless someone had already done such an exposé, he would find little in the library to document unreported corporate activities. In this case we had to advise the student to change his topic.

Even if the information is published, it may not be readily available in the U.S. This is particularly a problem in certain fields–medicine, for example. Few of the major Africana libraries collect medical journals and books; few medical libraries collect materials published in Africa. Thus scholars who consult tools like *African Index Medicus* and *Quarterly Index to African Periodical Literature* (http://lcweb2.loc.gov:8081/asian/qsihtml/qsihome.html) are often frustrated in their quest for the articles they find cited. As collections of rare and sometimes unique materials, Africana libraries provide enormous resources for scholarship, as long as researchers can find the materials those libraries have available on their shelves.

Search Strategies

The second factor, constructing the search, comprises much of the work of any reference librarian:

- identifying the most appropriate research tools and learning their use;
- using those skills to find answers to questions;
- teaching library users the skills needed to make them self-sufficient researchers.

In ASL and other Africana libraries, the resources available include all of the mainstream reference tools and databases, as well as both a large specialized reference collection and a very substantial collection in the stacks, augmented by the staff's "gray cell database," the accumulated experience of many similar research questions. ASL staff used all of these resources to respond to the questions quoted in the introduction.

- The student who needed the population of Das es Salaam had spent an hour looking for "a quick Internet source." It took ten seconds to get the latest edition of *Africa South of the Sahara* off the reference shelf and find the current population. For historical figures we had to go to the main collection.

- There was no direct information on Namibia's stand on global warming, but the Economist Intelligence Unit's Web site (a subscription service) and other economic and environmental sources provided enough background for the model UN team to make an educated guess.
- To locate information on HIV/AIDS in Cameroon and other countries, we used a combination of Medline and *African Index Medicus*. There's a great deal of information on HIV/AIDS in Africa in general, and on some specific countries, but Cameroon is one of the less studied areas.
- The student seeking "stuff" on the Igbo people needed to do some basic reading, starting with the *Encyclopedia of African Peoples* and going on to the OPAC to identify and consult the many books on the Igbo in the collection. He also needed to know that *Igbo* can also be spelled *Ibo*.
- For solar cookers and gender roles in Burkina Faso, we advised a combination of searching the OPAC (knowing that we had collected in both "appropriate technology" and women's issues), subscription indexes such as *Contemporary Women's Issues*, *Environmental Knowledgebase Online*, and *PAIS*, and the Web. We also suggested that the researcher contact some intermediate technology NGOs directly, and found a few helpful directories for him.
- The origin of the proverb "It takes a village . . . " had been a topic on several Africanist and anthropological discussion lists, and their logs proved helpful. (See, for instance, http://www2.h-net.msu.edu/~africa/threads/#Proverbs.) We have a large collection of African folklore and proverbs, but there are few indexes. There was no definitive answer, although several proverbs voiced similar philosophies.
- As for drumming, we had several works in the reference collection (*Garland Encyclopedia of World Music: Africa* and several bibliographies), many works in the stacks, and suggestions for Web sites and local World Music record stores.

Generalist librarians without a specialized collection would be more likely to start with WorldCat and the major databases to look for answers for these questions. User satisfaction with the answers found would depend on the depth of information needed for the research project and the ability of the user to recognize and evaluate the material he finds. Interlibrary loan or visits to Africana libraries might also be necessary.

Teaching research skills to library users has always been difficult. A bibliographic instruction video I saw early in my library career illustrates the way many students begin research: a student enters the library, glances around, pulls open and pushes closed a few catalog drawers (it was *really* long ago), and finally responds to the librarian's friendly "May I help you?" by asking, "Got any books on writers?" In the course of a patient and kindly interview, the student's paper topic emerges: an analysis of the appearance of ghosts in Shakespeare's plays.

The way that students and scholars do research has changed in many ways because of the revolutionary developments in information technology in recent years. Term papers now fit more comfortably into the student's life style. No need to go to the library–just log on to the Internet, download what you find, and write the paper without leaving your room. It can be done while eating, drinking, listening to music, and talking to your friends, all behaviors frowned upon in most libraries. However, Barbara Fister's recent article in the *Chronicle of Higher Education*, "Fear of Reference," indicates that students' research skills have not improved since that long ago video. She observes that students find it embarrassing to ask a research question of a reference librarian, but seem very comfortable with and trusting of the Internet.

> They will blithely e-mail a total stranger with outrageous requests. ("Hi, Jacques, I'm writing a paper on deconstruction, but your book is sort of confusing. Could you explain exactly what you mean by *difference*? Thanks. P.S. It's due Wednesday.") (Fister 2002: B20)

Her hypothetical student's message to Jacques Derrida is comical, but not unlike some I've seen on discussion lists. A student beginning research on a new topic may not know and understand the terminology of the field, including how to formulate questions and select sources. That's part of what they come to college to learn. As Fister points out,

> Experienced researchers constantly use filters they aren't even aware of. In my own field, I know enough context that I can reject inappropriate sources almost instantly and seize a promising lead when I see it. But if I had to find information in an unfamiliar discipline, I wouldn't know a core journal from a marginal one, a tantalizing clue from a dead end. We ask our students to make such choices all the time, without realizing how much being able to

choose wisely depends on a knowledge base they lack and experiences they haven't had. (Fister 2002: B20)

In ASL, we frequently respond to a question like that of the student doing a paper on the Igbo or looking for information on drumming by asking the classic "reference interview" questions: "What do you already know?" "What kind of project are you working on?" Sometimes the general question has masked a very specific need, such as "What caused the ethnic flare-up between Hausa and Igbo in Northern Nigeria in 1967?" or "I need to repair my Yoruba talking drum. What kind of skin is traditionally used as the head?" Other times such questions are really as general as they first seem, particularly when they are papers for some of the introductory African studies courses like "Peoples and Cultures of Africa," which requires each student to select an African people and do a paper on its traditions and current status. A student would have to look at many resources for this project. Part of ASL's reference service is to help neophyte students select topics about which enough information has been published to make a paper feasible.

Shared Responsibility for Access to Information: If Someone Writes It, Will Students Find It?

This third factor is the main focus of this paper. Success in finding information and scholarship on Africa does not depend solely on the skill of the searcher. For the individual scholar, academic research may seem to be a solitary, lonely pursuit, whether she is sifting through volumes of decades-old journals in the stacks or surfing the Web. In fact, successful research depends on the combined (if not always cooperative) efforts of widely dispersed people, often unknown to one another, including: authors, publishers, indexers, catalogers, reference librarians, as well as the researchers themselves. Decisions, policies, and practices of any of these many actors affect the success of research. All of those involved in the process should be aware of the effects of their own and others' actions. Reference librarians need to be acutely aware of all potential interactions, so they can solve problems for researchers.

Unfortunately, while new technologies have opened information horizons for so many people, the deceptive ease of these technologies threatens to cut off the learning process that develops good researchers. Instead of opening and closing catalog drawers in the library, where an alert librarian can intervene with some guidance, a student now is likely to sit in her room, tap a flawed search into her computer, and either fail completely or retrieve incomplete or inappropriate information. That student may well blame the "system" or assume that the information does not exist, but never question her own research skills and strategies. Reference librarians must do all we can to reverse the tendency for students to bypass much-needed reference assistance, and we must do all we can to make all of their research tools work for them, with or without our guidance.

KNOWN-ITEM SEARCHING: ARE OPACs AND DATABASES ADEQUATE ROADMAPS?

When the researcher has an author's name, the citation for a book or article, or is looking for information on a specific person, geographic location, ethnic group or event, the search should be easy and the results both predictable and reliable. Unfortunately, that's not the case. That trusting researcher may be as successful as the hapless out-of-state driver looking for a street address in Boston, where different streets may have the same name, where a street may change names at one intersection, only to change again farther along, where street signs are rare, and where locals will give a stranger directions to "turn left on Dot Ave," when they are referring to Dorchester Avenue.

What's in a Name?

Authors may use pseudonyms; two authors may have the same name; an author may change names during her lifetime, or may use different forms on different works. In many ethnic contexts, "first" and "last" names are not employed as they are in English. When names are rendered phonetically or transliterated into the Roman alphabet, there are variations in spelling. In libraries, all of these situations are resolved into a coherent and consistent name authority file that integrates all forms of author name, with the goal of having all works by the same author together in the catalog.

The Library of Congress' name authority database is usually considered the ultimate authority, but most libraries also have their own local files. Research for name authority involves determining a sufficient number of distinguishing details, such as birth date, death date, middle initial(s), and full form of all names. Additional information may be necessary to distinguish the author from others of the same name, and is always useful to support the record. This information might include academic degrees, with institution and dates, or other achievements. The cataloger may consult other published works of the author, noting in particular any biographical information included in the front matter or notes. Biographical reference sources are frequently helpful. Sometimes there is no information to be found; sometimes sources provide conflicting information. In these cases more rigorous detective work is necessary.

Pseudonyms and Nicknames

Indexes usually provide access only by the name on the piece. Alexander points out that in searching for works by or about an author who uses a pseudonym, researchers need to know and use both forms to catch all relevant citations (Alexander 2001: 230). How would a researcher discover that all names below refer to one African writer, and how would she gather together a bibliography of all of this writer's works?

Makuchi
Juliana Abbenyi
Juliana Sam-Abbenyi
Juliana Nfah-Abbenyi
Nfah Makuchi

In response to a query on H-Africa for fiction on a particular theme, J. Abbenyi recommended "Makuchi's story 'American Lottery.'" (Abbenyi 2002). "Makuchi" did not turn up any entry in our catalog (which turned out to be a glitch that we have subsequently fixed), but a search on the LC authority file revealed that Juliana Makuchi Nfah-Abbenyi writes under the name of "Makuchi." Evidently the author had recommended her own work. Cross-references specified in the authority file will lead the researcher to Nfah-Abbenyi from Makuchi and Abbenyi in a library catalog. In the *MLA Bibliography*, a search on either Makuchi or Abbenyi yields the citations to the same two articles with the author noted as Nfah-Abbenyi, Juliana Makuchi. In addition, Abbenyi also yields a dissertation by Juliana Sam-Abbenyi. All three works have similar topics, and it seems safe to assume that Juliana Sam-Abbenyi and Juliana Nfah-Abbenyi are the same person. Checking the title of the dissertation (*Gender in African Women's Writing: (Re)Constructing Identity, Sexuality, and Difference*) on OCLC provides the information that Nfah Makuchi was the maiden name of Juliana Sam-Abbenyi, but there is no mention of Sam-Abbenyi on the LC authority record. There is little chance that any researcher could depend on finding all of the works of this writer if all he knew was one form of her name.

Return to Laughter is a novel featuring an anthropologist studying a West African village. The author is anthropologist Laura Bohannan, who wrote it under the name of Elenore Smith Bowen. There are records in the LC authority file for both names. A title search on OCLC yields 12 entries for the title: five under Laura Bohannan and seven under Elenore Smith Bowen. The five under Bohannan have a title statement for Bowen with the note "(pseud.)" or "i.e., Laura Bohannan." Only two of the seven entries under Bowen indicate that it is a pseudonym. How would a researcher know to look for academic works by the author of this novel? He wouldn't, unless the edition of the novel or the record in his library included both names for the author.

Authors often use nicknames or variant forms of their names on their works. These Nigerian authors appear on title pages as:

- Pai Obanya
- Jinmi Adisa
- Akin L. Mabogunje

Obanya's actual name is Pius Augustine Ikechukwu Obanya, but according to a biographical note in a collection of essays in his honor, he is "popularly known to his friends and associates as 'Pai.'" In the library catalog, he is entered as "Pai Obanya," with cross-references from his full name. Adisa is entered in library catalogs under his full name, Folajinmi, with a cross-reference from his nickname, Jinmi. However, Mabogunje's name is in the authority file under his nickname, Akin, with cross-references from his full name, Akinlawon. Indexes would simply use the form on the piece. Since the surnames are fairly distinctive, at least to those used to English names, a researcher might be sure of finding them searching only on the last name. One can never be sure, though.

One Author or Two?

One important function of the name authority file is to sort out authors with the same name. For instance, there are three authors named John Harris in our catalog who have written on Africa. They are differentiated by middle initials or birth dates. John Harris is a common American or English name, and one might suspect that there could be two or more authors at work. But surely B. O. Oloruntimehin and Benjamin Olatunji Oloruntimehin are the same author? No–there are two contemporary Nigerian authors writing on similar topics with the same last name and same initials. Name authority work has sorted them out in the OPAC.

In other cases, the same name appears on two works that are so dissimilar that it seems certain that there are two authors with the same name. However, Betty A. Marton wrote both *Revitalizing African Libraries* and a biography of Reuben Blades; Emmanuel Dongala of Cameroon is a mathematician as well as a poet and novelist; Ghanaian physician Aku Ampofo has written volumes on traditional medicine, but is also a sculptor with art books to his credit. The authority file can make this clear.

Different Names, Same Author

Authors change their names for a variety of personal reasons. Catalogers attempt to establish one form of a name, based either on the name used in a preponderance of published works, or the preferred form as indicated by the author. Thus the works of Africanist scholar Adelaide Cromwell will be found under the maiden name she now uses, not either of her former married names Hill or Gulliver.

When the president of Zaire (now the Democratic Republic of Congo) changed his name from Joseph-Desiré Mobuto to Mobuto sese Seko in an "authenticity campaign" in 1972, he insisted that all Zairian citizens do the same. When he fell from power, many people changed their names back again. For example:

- Congolese writer Jimi Yuma was formerly Yuma Jumaini. He changed his name to James Yuma when he emigrated to the U.S. and studied for a doctoral degree. When he published a volume of short stories, he used the name Jimi Yuma. The last is the name he prefers, and the name under which he is entered in the library catalog.
- A noted Congolese political scientist is now entered in library catalogs as Georges Nzongola-Ntalaja, although through the years of Mobuto's "Authenticity" regime in Zaire he used only Nzongola-Ntalaja. In indexes, the surname Nzongola will bring up all forms for Georges Nzongola-Ntalaja, but Nzongola, G (or Georges) will not.

The researcher has to know all variations of the name in order to find all of the author's works, and that isn't easy.

Form of Name and Use of Initials

Some style manuals call for authors' initials only in citations, and some indexes require that form for search entries. British authors frequently use only initials. The social historian M. G. Smith is an example. His full name, Michael Garfield, clarifies his catalog record, but a glance at any library catalog under "Smith" demonstrates the extent of potential confusion. Browsing the results of a search in *Anthropological Literature* for Smith, M. yields citations for Smith, M. G., Smith, Michael G. and Smith, Michael Garfield. Most of the citations were for Smith, Michael Garfield, illustrating the enhancement that Harvard's Tozzer Library has provided for the database. However, there was no referral from the search on the name that appears on most title pages (M. G. Smith) to the form used for most entries. A search on *Sociological Abstracts* on these three variations yields citations for Smith, M. G., and Smith Michael G., but not Michael Garfield Smith.

Sometimes middle initials intended to clarify potential conflicts in the catalog can be confusing. Roy Willis, a distinguished and prolific anthropologist, usually uses no middle initial on his works, but the catalog authority lists him as Roy G. Willis. An unwary student may miss him. *Anthropological Literature* has citations for both the forms Willis, Roy, and Willis, Roy Geoffrey, with no reference between the two lists. *Sociological Abstracts* has citations for Willis, Roy, Willis, Roy G. and Willis, Roy Geoffrey. A researcher who does not already know all forms of an author's name may not find all of his/her works in any of the indexes.

Inversions and Changes

Catalogs and indexes usually invert authors' names for alphabetization. This assumes universality of the Western firstname-lastname pattern, but that pattern is far from universal. Amharic names in Ethiopia consist of a given name and a patronymic, which only refers to the individual's father. It is the given name that identifies the individual. The Ethiopian economist Alemseged Tesfai would be addressed by his friends as Alemseged, and more formally as Mr. Alemseged, but never as Mr. Tesfai. His son would have a given name and the patronymic Alemseged. This author's name is entered in the catalog as Alemseged

Tesfai, with no inversion and no comma, with a cross-reference from Tesfai, Alemseged. A cataloger or indexer unfamiliar with Amharic name conventions may wrongly invert names. To complicate matters, some Ethiopians and other Africans whose form of name should not be inverted decide to transpose the order of their names while they are in the U.S. to avoid the endless confusion and problems with entries in the telephone book and on student and employment records.

Other ethnic groups use patronymics. In the 1970s, the Kenyan author James Ngugi changed his name to Ngugi wa Thiongo. The "wa" designates "son of." The name is correctly entered as Ngugi wa Thiongo, with no inversion and no commas. The pattern does not always hold true, especially if the person uses a European first name, such as Daniel arap Moi, current president of Kenya, whose name is entered as *Moi, Daniel arap*.

Transliteration and Variant Spellings

Two of the major languages spoken in Africa, Arabic and Amharic, use non-roman writing systems. The Amharic syllabary has been used for other Ethiopian languages, and Arabic script is used to write Hausa and other languages. Personal names in Arabic or Amharic writing systems may be transliterated into the Roman alphabet in a variety of ways. LC has designated a standard transliteration table for each of these systems, but names have appeared in publications in a confusing array of variations:

- The name of the Egyptian Nobel Laureate appears on most of his American editions as Naguib Mahfouz, but the LC authority record for his name is Mahfuz, Najib. In indexes, one must do a search by both forms to get all citations by or about him.
- The name of the Libyan head of state appears in publications variously as Khadafy, Kaddafi, Gaddafi, al-Qadhafi, with his first name spelled Moamer, Muammar, or other variations. The LC authority record for his name is Qaddafi, Muammar. Subject or author searching in indexes is difficult because there are so many ways his name may have been spelled in articles.

The name Muhammed is very common in Islamic societies in Africa and elsewhere. There are many variations in form and spelling–25 according to Bertelson (http://filebox.vt.edu/users/bertel/Africana.html).

Certain individuals are most commonly identified in the literature, and for the most part in the LC name authority file, with a particular spelling. For instance, Morocco's king from 1906 to 1961, Mohamed V, for whom a major university has been named. Some authors of reference books have attempted to impose consistency:

> Many rulers' names, especially Arabic ones, are transliterated into Roman Script. I have been uniform in my spellings of Muhammad (at the expense of Mahomet, Mohamed, etc.). . . . (Stewart 1989: xix)

However, this can make it much harder, if not impossible, for researchers to find an author or historical figure in OPACs or indexes.

This problem is not limited to African names. Alexander outlines the problems researchers encounter in the *Modern Language Association Bibliography*. Names with variant spellings (she uses the examples of Feodor Dostoevsky/Fedor Dostoevskii and Leo Tolstoy/Lev Tolstoi) also have entries under all variations, making it difficult for readers using the more common forms (Alexander 2001: 231-232). There's no getting around it, researchers have to learn the variations and use them in searching for works.

There are other problems besides names transliterated from another writing system. When a standard orthography was developed for Nigerian languages, certain sounds that occurred in those languages but not in English were indicated by special diacritical marks. In Yoruba, a dot below certain letters changes the sound. For instance, a dot under an "o" changes the sound from "oh" to a rounder sound closer to "aw." This causes enough problems in typesetting, and even in computer-generated fonts, but the decision to render the "sh" sound in some Yoruba words as an "s" with a dot below is especially confusing. The Nobel Laureate Wole Soyinka's name is pronounced Wole "Shoyinka," and researchers who have heard the name spoken aloud but have not seen it in writing will spend time fruitlessly looking for "Shoyinka" in the catalog. There will be no cross-reference guiding the researcher to the proper spelling, although he will find some works by other authors named Shoyinka who have elected to spell their names with an "sh." Similarly, people familiar with southern African languages pronounce the name of Lesotho as "Lesutu," since the "th" represents an aspirated "t," not the usual "th" sound of English. There are always pitfalls in research on Africa.

Corporate Authors

Corporate authors include names of nations, government bodies, organizations, and businesses. The changes imposed by AACR2 made some of the more arcane rules of entry more comprehensible to library users. It is no longer a demonstration of one's professional acumen to know that the Institute of Development Studies at England's University of Sussex is entered under "Brighton." The entry is now: *University of Sussex, Institute of Development Studies*, with cross-reference from *Institute of Development Studies*. However, many Africa-related corporate bodies are still troublesome. Names of countries have changed, sometimes more than once. For example:

- Gold Coast became Ghana (1957)
- Upper Volta became Burkina Faso (1984)
- Southern Rhodesia became Rhodesia (1964), became Rhodesia-Zimbabwe, became Zimbabwe (1980)

Countries have split and recombined, such as:

- Ethiopia became Ethiopia and Eritrea (1993)
- Federation of Nyasaland and Rhodesia (1953) became Malawi (1964), Zambia (1964) and Zimbabwe (1980, with several intervening names, as shown above)

Place names within countries have changed:

- Salisbury became Harare (1982)
- Lourenço Marques became Maputo (1976)
- Fort Lamy became N'djamena (1973)

For place names, and by extension corporate author names including place names, LC authority work is bound by the decisions of the U.S. Board of Geographic Names, which are now available on its Web site, *Geonet* (http://164.214.2.59/gns/html/). Those decisions are sometimes slow in the making, with the result that a new name may be used extensively in the literature before the Board officially establishes it. Once the new name is established, catalog rules try to make sense of these changes, by using cross-references with information and dates, but indexes and bibliographies usually enter whatever is on the work as the author. The NISC Biblioline indexes *African Studies* and *South African*

Studies (http://www.nisc.com) yield results for author searches under both Rhodesia and Zimbabwe, with no apparent duplication.

Sometimes the very standards used to establish geographic names result in a heading that makes research more difficult. The case of Biafra highlights this problem. In 1967 the eastern region of Nigeria seceded from the federation and formed an independent state called Biafra. In the ensuing civil war, relief posters showing starving children in the secessionist state aroused public sympathy in the U.S. and Europe. The name Biafra was widely recognized, even by people who knew little about Africa.

However, the U.S. never recognized the nation of Biafra. Therefore, the Board of Geographic Names did not certify its name so it was never designated as a corporate author or subject heading by LC. Eventually Biafra lost the civil war and was reincorporated into Nigeria. During its existence, however, its government published numerous documents, and hundreds of books and articles were written about Biafra. Library catalogs list those works under the author *Eastern Nigeria*, even when the document cataloged is *Proclamation of the Republic of Biafra*. The Library of Congress and others concerned with the accuracy of terms do not always take into consideration how researchers are likely to look for information. The effect of decisions about country names when they are used as subject headings or descriptors in library catalogs and indexes is discussed in another section.

Commissions of inquiry are often referred to in the literature by the name of the chair of the commission, although they are entered into library catalogs under the name of the commission. Thus, the report of South Africa's Commission of Inquiry into Labour Legislation is often referred to as the Wiehahn report, and the Commission of Inquiry into Matters Relating to the Coloured Population Group is known as the Theron Commission. Added entries in the alternate title or alternate author fields may provide access in the library catalog, but not always. South Africa's Commission of Inquiry into the Mass Media is frequently referred to as the "Steyn Commission," which causes some confusion, since a title search on OCLC or WorldCat using "Steyn Commission" will yield the *Goldstone Commission Reports on the President Steyn Gold Mine*. A search on the name of the chair of the Mass Media Commission, M. T. Steyn, yields only the *Supplementary Report*. The main report can be found only by title, *Report of the Commission of Inquiry into the Mass Media*, or the author, South Africa. Commission of Inquiry into the Mass Media.

The official language of most African countries is the former colonial language, although many also designate a local language as well. Government publications in these countries are produced in one or the other official language, and sometimes in both languages. Catalog records will use as the author the name of the issuing agency as it appears on the title page, with an alternate author field if two languages are used on the title page, or if there are two title pages.

Of the seven African nations opting to use a local language as the official language, six use Arabic, and the seventh, Ethiopia, uses Amharic. Both of these languages use a non-Roman writing system, so the names of the government agencies designated as corporate authors are transliterated for catalog records and so established in the name authority file. The transliterated corporate author name is used even if the work cataloged is in English or French. Thus the Bank of Morocco, which issues an *Annual Report* in English, is entered as *Bank al-Maghrib*, the Central Bank of Egypt, with several serial publications in English, is entered as *Bank Al Markazi Al Misri*, and the many English language publications of Ethiopia's Central Statistical Office are entered under the corporate author *Ethiopia. YaStatistiks taqlay sehfat bet*. Widenmann points out that former Africana cataloger at Northwestern University, David Michener, termed the practice ". . . correct but inconvenient" (Widenmann 1989: 41). The items mentioned as examples are published in English and have the corporate author identified in English on the title page. Most library catalogs will refer researchers from the English term to the Arabic or Amharic, but less experienced students are often puzzled or annoyed by the cross-reference screen. Authors citing these agencies' publication will very likely use the English version in their citations.

Besides difficulties for researchers caused by language and cataloging rules, changes in name of government agencies make tracing its publications difficult.

Sometimes the change is based on governmental reorganization, but sometimes it's just careless typesetting. Kenya's change from Ministry of Education, Science and Technology to Ministry of Education and Human Resource Development may not affect government functions very much, but it does affect library catalogs. Widenmann points out that sometimes the cover of a government report (which had perhaps been printed in bulk a year or two earlier) carries one ministry name, and the title page carries another (Widenmann 1989: 41). Francophone nations tend to design covers and title pages so that it is difficult to determine which is the body primarily responsible for the publication.

"You Can't Get There from Here": The Effects of Policy and Technology on Access

Could researchers find these citations in library catalogs or major indexes?

- Wole Soyinka's play *Dance of the Forests*
- "American Lottery" in *Your Madness, Not Mine*, by Makuchi
- Brian Warner. "Traditional Astronomical Knowledge in Africa," in *Astronomy Before the Telescope*, edited by Christopher Walker.

For articles in collected essays, monographic series, and serials with distinctive titles for some or all issues, access depends on policies and decisions of library staff, as well as the degree to which researchers know how to use the catalog and other research tools. Access to library collections has always been limited by the technology available. In the card catalog environment, tremendous limitations were placed on access points because of the difficulties and expense of producing and filing cards. Works in collections suffered greatly. Author/title information about the contents of a collection of essays might have been placed in a "contents note" on the catalog card, and was thus at least available to the lucky researcher who came across that card set. When card catalogs were converted to online catalogs, those contents notes became access points if they were input to the MARC 500 (notes) field. Unfortunately, access is not always straightforward.

In an examination of methods used to include contents in a catalog record and the effects of several of those methods on retrieval, Hoffman (2000: 7-9) demonstrates some of the complexities and the ramifications of cataloging policies and decisions. The MARC field for notes has several sub-fields. If the contents note goes into one of those sub-fields, an individual title can be retrieved by a keyword search, but not a title search. Soyinka's play *The Dance of the Forests* appears in the first volume of his *Collected Plays* (1973). A keyword search retrieves the play, but a search for the play's title does not. A different sub-field allows access by title, keyword, and author/title, but has a peculiar problem: if the note reads ***The** Dance of the Forests*, the title can only be retrieved if the search phrase begins with "The." If the record suppresses the article, the title can only be retrieved *without* the article. If the collected works are by the same author, inclusion of the contents in the 740 field (added title entry) will provide full access.

False Economy Contributes to an Information Crisis

Hoffman (2000) proposes a cataloging strategy that would solve the problem of access to works in a collection. Unfortunately, his solution depends on the library's commitment to providing access. The cost of providing full access to the contents of collected works is considerable, both in staff time and computer resources. Budgets are tight. Many administrators may opt to invest more heavily in commercially produced databases. However, without access to the contents of works, much of the library's collection, representing an enormous amount of scholarship, not to mention investment of library funds, may be hidden from view and not likely to be used in research. Indexes may pick up some of the articles, but certainly *not* all. Cataloging backlogs make production of new records more of a priority than painstaking addition of access points. As Hoffman points out, inertia is a strong force (Hoffman 2000: 8). It is particularly unlikely that many libraries will opt to provide access retrospectively to collected works, especially in specialized and "exotic" areas of study.

Databases do not provide access to "everything." Collected works are not routinely indexed in the major services, and are thus hidden from the researcher's view. Leonhardt comments on the need to include contents notes in the catalog record:

> Newly published books may come with tables of contents [in the catalog record], usually at a cost and worth it too, but that leaves millions of other volumes waiting to be described more fully. Undiscovered treasures have no value until they are in the hands of the right reader at the right time. (Leonhardt 2000: 13)

Older scholars with major Africana collections at their disposal may continue to browse shelves and dig out these "treasures," but researchers who are trained to depend on electronic resources and scholars at a distance from specialized Africana collections will have a harder time. This is a major part of the crisis in information services about Africa.

What about the titles in the introduction to this section?

- When the short story "American Lottery" was recommended in response to a query on the H-Africa discussion list, the entire message read: "Makuchi's story, 'American Lottery' in *Your Madness, Not Mine*." How easily could a researcher find the story? Since the book title was supplied, it was easy. The story title is in the contents note in the OPAC, so a keyword search would work. The author's name provides some interesting examples of problems, as discussed earlier.

- Brian Warner's article "Traditional Astronomical Knowledge in Africa," in *Astronomy Before the Telescope*, edited by Christopher Walker, was suggested in another H-Africa discussion (Gottschalk 2001). Would this be found in a library catalog? Not unless a library supplied additional access locally. The OCLC/MARC record has no contents note, and only a single subject heading: *Astronomy–History*. The article could not be found in searches of Web of Science, using the search terms "astronomy" and "Africa," or in anthropology indexes.

Monographic Series

What are a researcher's chances of finding these titles published in monographic series in a library catalog, WorldCat, or an index?

- *African Hunter-Gatherers: Persisting Cultures and Contemporary Problems*
- *Symbolic Categories and Ritual Practice in Hunter-Gatherer Experience*
- *Fetiches II: Puissance des Objets, Charme des Mots*
- *Chefs et Rois Sacrés*
- *Sorcellerie, Societés Secretes et Sacrifice chez les Wuli de Cameroun Occidental*
- *Sectes, Cultures et Societés: Les Enjeux Spirituals du Temps Present*

The odds are not very good.

Library policies and procedures for the treatment of monographic series don't always put real or anticipated needs of researchers above expediency. Some series are classed separately with a series added entry. Classing separately provides the best access for researchers, as long as there is also access by the series title, with accurate holdings notes. Most often chosen for series that cover varied topics, this option may require original cataloging for many or all titles. A series of working papers, which are not widely distributed and are often short and very specialized, are most likely to need original cataloging, and are thus most likely to be put in a backlog. These papers, however, can represent cutting edge research and as such should receive high priority, instead of languishing in a backlog with little access beyond keyword in the title.

Other series are classed together, with or without analytics (author/title records with subject headings) for all or some of the volumes. If such a series is indexed elsewhere, library staff may feel justified in relying on that access rather than providing analytics in the catalog. This can be a mistake.

Shemberg's article, "From Citation to Piece in Hand: The Search for Efficiency in Accessing Monographic Series" (Shemberg 1997), illustrates the difficulties for researchers when the description of a journal in an indexing service differs from its description in a library catalog.

Shemberg notes many problems:

1. Inconsistency in cataloging treatments due to human error.
2. Dual numbering systems on the source.
3. Local decisions over time and in multiple branch libraries to catalog item as a serial, a monograph, or both.
4. Whether or not the field containing the series is indexed.
5. Citation differences in the electronic indexes.
6. Ways in which articles are cited in references.
7. Screen display (Shemberg 1997: 180).

The titles listed above illustrate these problems. *African Hunter-Gatherers: Persisting Cultures and Contemporary Problems* and *Symbolic Categories and Ritual Practice in Hunter-Gatherer Experience* are numbers 26 and 27 respectively of the series *African Study Monographs Supplementary Issue* (a supplement to the journal *African Study Monographs* published in Kyoto). Of the 38 libraries indicating ownership of the supplements on OCLC, only five have individual catalog records for No. 26, and only four of those five have individual records for No. 27. The journal and supplements appear to be indexed only by the *Bibliography of Africana Periodical Literature Database* (http://www.africabib.org/africa.html), although *Africa Study Monographs* is on the list of journals indexed "selectively" by *Anthropological Literature*. The works used as examples were not found in *Anthropological Literature*. Despite the breadth and quality of its scholarship, access to *African Study Monographs Supplements* is minimal. Thus, the articles would be found in Bibliography of *Africana Periodical Literature Database*, but otherwise, they are hidden from researchers, only to be found if the researcher can go to the shelves and browse, or comes across a citation in another article or a specialized bibliography.

The other titles listed above have similar problems. *Systèmes de Pensée en Afrique Noire* is a monographic series showing ownership by

33 libraries on OCLC. Of recent titles, nine libraries have separate catalog records for Volume 12, *Fetiches II: Puissance des Objets, Charme des Mots*, and Volume 10, *Chefs et Rois Sacrés*. The latter volume appears to have two editions, one with a date of 1987, the other 1990. Two additional libraries have separately cataloged the 1990 edition. *Francis*, a database of international humanities and social sciences, with strong coverage for French scholarship, has indexed *Systèmes de Pensée en Afrique Noire*, but one must search by keyword in title (which means using French words) or by their assigned subject headings, most of which are assigned in French with English translations. A trial search on No. 7, *Sorcellerie, Societés Secretes et Sacrifice chez les Wuli de Cameroun Occidental*, using the term "sorcery" was unsuccessful, although the title had been indexed. "Sorcellerie" would have worked, but the English translation of the French subject heading was "witchcraft," not "sorcery."

The final example, *Sectes, Cultures et Societés: Les Enjeux Spirituals du Temps Present* is actually *Cahiers des Religions Africaines* 27-28 (53-56), a special issue published in 1993-1994. Of the 62 libraries holding the periodical title in OCLC, ten have cataloged this issue with a separate record. Individual titles are fairly common for this periodical, and the number and configuration of libraries cataloging any of them separately varies. Our own holdings are sketchy–we have Volume 4-22, and Volume 27-28, but this holdings statement may not really indicate gaps in receipt. The special issues usually have not only distinctive titles, but also very distinctive covers that do not incorporate the journal title. The journal title may appear elsewhere on the work–on the spine, or occasionally in the front matter of the work, but it is easily overlooked. We have caught some issues whose serial title had not been noticed before they were processed as monographs. We may have missed others. Some of the issues "missing" could actually be sitting on the shelves, cataloged as monographs without a series tracing. Since the publisher has not issued a list of special issues, we have been unable to cross check for individual titles to correct our holdings statement.

As long as the parts of an unanalyzed series are on publicly accessible shelves, there is a chance, however slight, that some researchers will find useful items by browsing, even if indexes and the catalogs fail them. But more and more libraries, virtually bursting at the seams, are putting parts of their collections in off-site storage. How will researchers find those gems when there is no catalog access and browsing the shelves is not possible? Why have a book at all if it is rendered invisible? And why, in an "information age" of rapid access to some bits of information, do we so severely limit access to this scholarship?

Conferences

Conferences are important and rich sources of scholarship and information, but papers presented in their sessions can be among the most elusive of resources. The problems with conferences fall into several categories:

- Proceedings are not always published. If published, proceedings may not include all papers, and sessions such as roundtables or discussions may not be included.
- Finding proceedings in a library catalog can be difficult.
- Individual papers may not be accessible either through library catalogs or indexes.

It Wasn't Published–But It's Cited Anyway

Because it is the premier academic organization for the study of Africa in the U.S., the papers read at the annual meetings of the African Studies Association contain a wealth of information and theory. From 1960 until 1995, those papers were collected and offered for sale, either individually or as a set. Most major Africana libraries bought the sets, either in paper or in space-saving microfilm, which was offered beginning in the 1970s. Although supply of the annual meeting papers was considered an important service by libraries and scholars, the cost of producing the sets was not offset by sales. In 1996, the Association experimented with new technology, and offered the meeting papers on CD ROM. However, the new format did not catch on, and sales dropped even lower. The ASA decided to stop providing papers at all. The Africana Librarians Council of ASA has urged the Association to revive the collection and sale of ASA conference papers, but these efforts have so far been unsuccessful. The service had proven costly for the Association, and there seemed to be little interest among the members for distribution of papers.

However, these papers–now unavailable to libraries–are often quoted or listed in other scholars' bibliographies. When a researcher was investigating the role of women in planning transportation in Africa, the African Women's Bibliographic Database (http://www.africabib.org/women.html) yielded some ideal citations–but since they were ASA papers, they are not available. This is the case with many conferences. All too frequently, conference papers are cited in other scholarly writing, but are not published. Style manuals such as *The Chicago Manual of Style*, give instructions for citing unpublished materials, including papers read at conference. However, when an author bases his point on someone's unpublished work, he is frustrating anyone who wishes to consult the sources from which he draws his scholarship. Scholarship that depends on unpublished papers and verbal presentations is hard to verify, and especially ill-serves students.

Finding Conferences

Citation format for conferences in indexes and bibliographies often differs markedly from the format used in library catalogs. Determining if the library has the proceedings or finding holdings on OCLC or WorldCat can be difficult. Bangalore and Carter's *Guide to Searching the Bibliographic Utilities for Conference Proceedings* (1994) goes a long way to demystify the way that library catalogs deal with conferences. They outline the six forms MARC records for proceedings might take, depending on whether or not the conference has a name, and where that name appears in the published proceedings (Bangalore 1994: 3). For instance, most students would not think of looking for a conference by doing an author search on: "International Conference of Ethiopian Studies (3rd: 1966: Addis Ababa, Ethiopia)." The title of this conference is *Proceedings*. If an established body holds a conference, that body appears as author, as in:

> Author = International Council on Archives. East and Central Africa Regional Branch.
>
> Title = *2nd general conference: proceedings, Nairobi, 8th to 9th May, 1972.*

If the conference has a distinctive name, that name is usually entered as the title, as in: *Ethiopian studies: proceedings of the sixth international conference, Tel-Aviv, 14-17 April 1980*, edited by Gideon Goldenberg. This conference can also be found in our catalog under the "alternate author," "International Conference of Ethiopian Studies (6th: 1980: Tel Aviv, Israel)," the pattern noted above, as well as under the editor, Goldenberg.

Understanding cataloging practice helps if the researcher knows the name of the conference or the proper form of the convening body. It does not help in finding conferences held on any particular subject, and if a student comes in armed only with a note from a professor about a half-remembered paper at a "conference on democratization in Africa held at Johns Hopkins a couple of years ago . . . ," reference librarians despair and the student may be out of luck. The *Directory of Published Proceedings. Series SSH: Social Sciences Humanities*, an annual publication, may provide some help.

Finding Papers

Researchers most frequently are looking for information on their topic in any format and will want access to the specific information in individual papers rather than the broad themes of the conferences which might be accessible through the title or subject headings. How likely is it that researchers will find these papers?

> "Niger Delta Petroleum Systems, Nigeria," in *Petroleum Systems of South Atlantic Margins, an outgrowth of the AAPG/ABGP Hedbert Research Symposium Rio de Janeiro, Brazil, November 16-19, 1997.*
>
> "Returning to the Path": The use of Iboga(ine) in an Equatorial African Ritual Context and the Binding of Time, Space, and Social Relationships, in *Ibogaine: Proceedings of the First International Conference.*

Practically nil.

Individual conference papers are only occasionally listed in a contents note, usually only when the proceedings have been formally published. The paper on petroleum in the Niger Delta may well be of interest to anyone studying the environmental problems of this region, but the catalog record for this symposium provides only one subject heading: *Petroleum–Geology–South Atlantic Ocean–Congresses*, and there is no contents note. The paper did not show up in searches of several indexes.

Ibogaine is an alkaloid used in the treatment of heroin and other drug addiction, and is derived from a plant in Cameroon, locally named *iboga*. The paper on ritual use would be of interest to anthropologists, but again, there was no contents note in the catalog record, and the subject heading is simply "Ibogaine–Congresses," with no reference to the ethnographic aspect, nor, in fact, to drug treatment. A search of indexes, both medical and anthropological, failed to yield this paper.

Northwestern University's Melville J. Herskovits Library of African Studies made an enormous contribution to Africanist researchers with their *Africana Conference Paper Index*. The print edition, published by G. K. Hall in 1982, was a rich resource, but frustratingly hard to use. The online version (http://www.library.northwestern.edu/africana/links.html), is now available through the library catalog, and is a tremendous improvement. Researchers can search for papers by author, title, conference title, and keyword. It does not include, however, either the petroleum or ibogaine conference used as examples.

Do libraries provide access to all–or even to enough–of the information contained in their collections? That question is by no means limited to arcane and exotic issues particular to African names and terminology. The catalog provides only limited access to titles of works contained in serials or in collected works. Indexes provide access to only a fraction of those hidden resources. Researchers willing to browse shelves can only explore the shelves open to the public, not those in storage facilities. It's a gloomy picture, but one that can still be changed, if library administrators are willing to commit the resources needed to make their collections fully accessible.

TOPIC SEARCHES: "I KNOW WHAT I WANT TO FIND, BUT NOT WHERE IT IS OR HOW TO GET THERE"

Many researchers, particularly students, use a subject or topic search to begin their research. They may use a subject search in the OPAC, but are more likely to use a keyword search in the OPAC, indexing services, or Web search engines. Whatever tools they elect to use, their success will depend both on two factors:'

- How well they formulate the query.
- How well the creators of the tools used have provided access points.

Most reference librarians see as their main purpose the teaching of students and other library users how to formulate successful search strategies, no matter how user-unfriendly or user-indifferent a system might be. Many reference librarians also have responsibility for selecting, creating, and advocating for subject access and reference tools that are designed with users in mind. Fulfilling those responsibilities means that reference librarians need to understand how OPACs and bibliographic databases work. Catalogers, indexers, and database creators have primary responsibility for making information accessible to the library users, and to succeed they need to understand how researchers look for information.

> The work of catalogers appears not to have a direct impact on patrons; however, a quality catalog is the library's most important reference tool and effective reference depends upon it. If access points are incorrect or incomplete, library materials become essentially impossible to find. (Carver 2002: 168)

Computers have enabled full-text indexing using every word in an abstract or the entire article. This capability vastly increases recall (the number of items retrieved) but can often negatively affect precision (the number of items retrieved that are actually relevant to the topic researched). Precision can be enhanced by use of Boolean operators and mechanisms in the system such as expansion of a word to include plural, possessive, and adjectival forms. Mali can thus be expanded to catch Malian, but would also retrieve terms like *mali*gnant and *Mali*bu if the search is not made more precise. However carefully one crafts a search, no computer can differentiate among the multiple meanings of some words. Konovalav uses the example of *mercury*, which can be "a metal, a Greek deity, a car, a planet or Queen's soloist" in his article "Cataloging As a Public Service" (Konovalov 1999: 26). In an African example, a search in a biological or agricultural database for the country Niger will also bring up *aspergillus niger*, a fungus affecting peanut plants. Some of these references will, of course, pertain to the country Niger, since peanuts are its main cash crop. However, a few serendipitous hits do not justify the frustration of an ambiguous search strategy. If too many irrelevant citations are retrieved, the research process slows down.

"Why not give our users an uncluttered search page like Google?" asked one colleague in a staff-wide discussion on designing a new Web page. Many reference librarians feel that the structure of the catalog and its controlled fields and vocabulary needlessly frustrate researchers.

They prefer a "simpler" interface, one that more closely approximates the way people look for information. No system of subject access can duplicate the potential thought processes of every user. Nor should it. Every user deserves the opportunity of learning how to do research. The skills gained learning from mistakes help researchers to recognize dead ends before wasting time pursuing them, and to develop variations on the search strategy as one goes along. These are valuable lessons to apply throughout one's career and life. The most successful researcher will be able to take advantage of a well-constructed index, and will also be able to cope with inferior indexes, thus getting the most possible out of both. It is our responsibility to teach those information-finding skills.

Teaching researchers to use any and all tools available, no matter how badly constructed, does not shift the responsibility for successful research entirely from the library to the researcher. Libraries are not excused from the need to provide access to all parts of their collections, and to construct that access in ways that are comprehensible to users. Anything less is false economy verging on malpractice.

In an article critiquing the *MLA International Bibliography*, Harriet Alexander comments on the assumption that full-text searching is the solution for all research problems:

> Perhaps the worst problem lies . . . in the concept held by those who engineer and produce the databases that simply computerizing a database–whether it is a bibliography, index, or full-text–is always going to create a better method of retrieving relevant material. What can be ignored is the fact that much record enhancement may be required to allow for better retrieval in a computerized environment. (Alexander 2001: 228)

Cataloging and indexing staff provide that enhancement, but they don't always know how researchers use the catalog and what connections will work best for them. Authors and publishers should also give more thought to how their work may be found once it is published. Researchers need to examine their own expectations and assumptions, sharpen their skills and learn to evaluate information when they find it. Reference librarians evaluate and select information sources, can identify flaws, and sometimes lobby for changes. Once they understand the problems, they can deal with researchers' questions and prepare research guides.

Keyword Searches and Their Problems

The title may be about something–but what? (Germano 2001: B11)

The scholarly author usually concerns herself with the strength and validity of her scholarship, the process of finding a publisher, the hopes of well-placed favorable reviews, and the effect of the publication on prospects for tenure and promotion. *How* the book or article will find its way into the bibliography of a student's research paper is seldom on the author's mind as she writes and prepares the manuscript for publication, but it should be. With the advent of full-text word searching, words in title and abstract are vital components of information retrieval, and the choices made about those words can mean the difference between retrieval and oblivion.

> There was once a time when erudite editors and bibliographers organized indexes to articles based on their awareness of the contents. Now the shibboleth is "keyword," which is a word that is actually part of the title. The computer is not expected to interpret or enhance the available information. An article about Mamluk Egypt that contains no relevant words at all (Mamluk, Egypt, the name of a particular sultan, some dates) is exceedingly unlikely to be reeled in by such an online search . . . (Henige 2002a: 64)

Reference librarians take great care to teach researchers to do effective word searches. Editors and peer reviewers take far less care to inform authors how to use words in the title and abstract to enhance retrieval. The title of a book or article should be both its distinctive identification and a principal indicator of its subject matter, but publishers and authors also want the title to catch the eye of a bookstore browser. In his discussion of academic publishing, William Germano (2001a: 37-42 and 2001b: B10-11) examines the process of selecting a good title for books. He touches on the importance of titles in the research process:

> Librarians, booksellers, Web searches and electronic bibliographies all demand that an academic book be findable. (Germano 2001b: B10)

In online searching, the researcher chooses words or phrases to be matched in the searchable fields of the database. Although controlled vocabulary descriptors and subject headings are still used, most researchers expect to find what they need by free-text searching. As Alexander indicated in her article on the *MLA Bibliography*, researchers share responsibility with indexers and catalogers for successful use of a controlled vocabulary. The researcher must use a thesaurus and learn correct terms, and the indexer or cataloger must learn the terminology of the discipline and select as descriptors the words most likely to be used by researchers. With free-text searching, most of the responsibility rests with the author. If the title is not descriptive, the searcher may never retrieve it. Writers in the sciences seem to have few problems writing descriptive titles, e.g.,

- *Land Use and Soil Conservation in Parts of Onitsha and Owerri Provinces*
- *River Blindness in Nangodi, Northern Ghana: An Hypothesis of Cyclical Advance and Retreat*
- *The Lobster Fisheries in the Republic of South Africa and Namibia, 1975-76.*

All of these titles make clear the probable content of the works, and have words in the title that should be caught on a keyword search. On their own, however, even these might have some problems. Combining "land use" and "Nigeria" might not retrieve the piece on Onitsha and Owerri. A searcher would have to use "river blindness" as well as "onchocerciasis" to yield the work on Ghana. The piece on lobsters might not be found with a broader "marine fisheries" search, although "fisheries" alone would work. Even with very descriptive titles, a search that depends only on words in the title may not be entirely successful.

Terminology Changes Over Time

Straightforward titles can present other problems for online searching. Terminology in all fields changes over time. William Allan's 1964 classic work on agriculture in Africa, *The African Husbandman*, is not likely to be found in a title keyword search by students unfamiliar with older agricultural terminology. Likewise, the title of Robert Chambers' *Settlement Schemes in Tropical Africa* used standard terms for the 1960s, but now "settlement schemes" is an unfamiliar and ambiguous phrase for many students. Sometimes the title is descriptive, but too grand and broad to describe accurately the real subject of the book. *Environmental Leadership in Developing Countries* sounds like a book of potential interest to Africanist scholars, but its subtitle: *Transnational Relations and Biodiversity Policy in Costa Rica and Bolivia* dispels that illusion.

More Image Than Information

If descriptive titles can present problems, the imaginative titles favored by writers in the social sciences and humanities can be real mysteries. Henige observes,

> In my library I see the spines of scores of books in a week with titles that tell me nothing about the contents. . . . . When there is no telling sub-title, the author is begging for anonymity and is all too likely to receive it. (Henige 2002a: 64)

Germano uses Barbara Tuchman's best-selling *A Distant Mirror: The Calamitous Fourteenth Century* as an example of a phrase that could be used to describe practically anything. In his hypothetical title, *A Distant Mirror: Life in a Nineteenth Century Sudanese Village*, the subtitle indicates the subject of the book, but

> Some editors worry that on-line search engines might fail to consider a subtitle, which would mean that your book wouldn't turn up if a browser were looking for books on Sudan. Any catalogue or bibliography short on room or ambition might list only a title, not a subtitle, making the subject of your book hard to determine. (Germano 2001c: 41)

Titles are not protected by copyright, which means that several books may easily have the same title. An Africa-related example is the title of Padraig Carmody's recent work on Zimbabwe: *Tearing the Social Fabric: Neo-Liberalism, Deindustrialization, and the Crisis of Governance in Zimbabwe*. In a scan-title search on OCLC, I put in "tearing the social fabric," and came up with two titles, Carmody's work and an MA thesis: *Tearing the Social Fabric: Architectural Space as Representation and Metaphor in Photographs and Drawings*.

Some authors do take indexing and research access into account when devising titles. Marc Sommers' *Fear in Bongoland: Burundi Refugees in Urban Tanzania* is an example. The author wanted to appeal to a broad audience and used "Fear in Bongoland" to catch general interest. ("Bongoland" is the name used in Burundi for Dar es Salaam, the largest city in Tanzania.) In a discussion of this paper, Sommers, a research fellow at BU, told me he insisted on this main title, even to the point of rejecting an offer from one publisher who was interested in publishing the book but wanted to change the title. However, in devising the subtitle, he deliberately chose words that he thought would be used in searching for the topics covered in his book (Sommers 2002: personal communication).

Those Devilish Details

Sometimes the publisher or author can cause confusion when the title on the title page differs from the title on the cover. For example, the second edition of *Black–Woman–Worker* by Fatima Meer carries a cover title of *Black–Women–Workers*. Another work, *Mabangalala: The Rise of Right Wing Vigilantes in South Africa* has on the cover: *Apartheid's Private Army: The Rise of Right Wing Vigilantes in South Africa*. The catalog records for these works provide the cover title in the MARC 740 field for alternate title, so that searching by either title will be successful. If the catalog record does not include the cover title in an indexed field, such works could elude the researcher looking for the title that appeared on the cover. Paperback covers are often removed for library bindings, so that even browsing the shelf would be fruitless.

Discrepancies in titles can be much more misleading in journals. Catalogers tend to examine books very carefully to include all relevant information; indexers do not necessarily crosscheck the cover, table of contents, and head of title. *Africa*, a standard journal for Africana collections, has taken to listing the themes of its articles on the front cover. For instance, the cover of *Africa* 71(3) published in 2001 announces three themes for its six articles:

- "Time Off: The New Access to Old Pleasures"
- "Probing Identity's Depths and Shallows"
- "Debating 'Reserves' and Degradation."

These theme headings appear nowhere else in the issue, neither on the table of contents page nor in the body of the journal. It is unlikely that they would be used in indexes, but they could well be given to students by faculty (e.g., "look at that article on 'Time Off' in a recent issue of *Africa*"). A more serious problem is that some of the article titles themselves are paraphrased on the cover. Dorothea E. Schulz' article "Music Videos and the Effeminate Vices of Urban Culture in Mali" is listed on the cover as "How Women Enjoy Pop Songs in Mali." The title in the Table of Contents ("Music Videos . . .") was used in the several indexes where the article was found, but the title from the cover could easily be given as a reference by a professor, leading to frustration for student and librarian alike. In ASL's collection, as in many other libraries, the journal cover is discarded when the volume is bound, removing any reference to that cover title and thus any possibility of serendipitously matching the article to a citation that used the cover title.

These anomalies are confusing enough to the researcher who is able to browse the journal, but how does the indexer deal with these ambiguous situations? It doesn't matter which is the "real" title–cover, table of contents, or head of article. What does matter is whether the article can be located using a citation. The only way to be sure is to cite all forms of the title, wherever they occur. Some journals print their table of contents on the front and back covers. If those covers are removed for binding, researchers and ILL staff must rely on correct title and page number information to find the article in the body of the issue. If the title found there differs from the citation, it may not be perceived as the article sought. Conversely, if the index uses the title from the article's first page, a searcher checking only the table of contents might conclude that the article requested is not in the issue cited, and the search will be unsuccessful, even though the book was actually in hand.

Do Subject Headings Help?

Success in free-text searching of title, abstract, or full text in an index and in doing a title or keyword search in a library catalog depends a great deal on the choice of words by author and publisher as well as on the decisions of libraries and indexers on formatting and indexing the records. If no words in the text match the words chosen as search terms, the search will fail.

Since subject headings in a library catalog are controlled vocabulary, they leave less to chance than capricious titles. However, for subject headings to be successful search tools, researchers must understand how they work, and catalogers must apply them accurately. The bottom line is that subject headings provide good access only if researchers use them, and if the citations they lead to actually contain the information sought. Most OPACs now allow word searches on the entire record, so that researchers do not have to be so careful in matching the correct form of subject headings. In a card catalog, one had to know that West Africa was entered as Africa, West. In the first generations of OPACs, many, but not all, such inversions could be found with a search on the natural word order. The latest generation of OPACs makes searching even easier. Subject headings still provide important access points, and the rules governing their use are by no means obsolete or arcane.

Catalogers responsible for developing new subject headings and revising older ones must be familiar with the field of knowledge and the terminology used both currently and in the past. An examination of catalog records for some of the works used as examples for choice of words in titles indicates that subject headings can aid research, but are no guarantee of success.

Land Use and Soil Conservation in Parts of Onitsha and Owerri Provinces

Agriculture–Nigeria
Physical geography–Nigeria
Soil conservation–Nigeria

The title and the subject headings combine to provide good access. *Land use* is also a valid subject heading, and could have been used.

River Blindness in Nangodi, Northern Ghana: An Hypothesis of Cyclical Advance and Retreat

Onchocerciasis

This single subject heading supplies a term not provided in the title, and should give the researcher reasonable access. *Ghana* does not appear as a subject heading, however, and would be an access point only if the single subject heading was combined with a word search.

The Lobster Fisheries in the Republic of South Africa and Namibia, 1975-76

Lobster fisheries–South Africa
Lobster fisheries–Namibia

The subject headings simply duplicate the information in the title. The work would be retrieved with *fisheries* as a word or subject search, but not if *marine fisheries* was used.

The African Husbandman

The best subject headings are on the MARC record for the 1977 reprint:

Agriculture–Africa
Land use–Africa
Traditional farming–Africa

Other records in OCLC have subject headings that give less access:

Africa–Economic conditions (too broad for the subject of the book)
Traditional farming (with no geographic location)

The title, as noted before, is unhelpful for computerized searching. This work is unlikely to be retrieved in a search, and would be used in student research only if it is recommended or appears in a specialized bibliography.

Settlement Schemes in Tropical Africa: A Study of Organizations and Development

Agricultural colonies–Africa

This single subject heading is clearly outdated, and the title, as noted earlier, also uses terminology not likely to be familiar to students today, although it was a standard term when the book was written in 1969. *Land settlement* and *Land tenure* would be better choices as subject headings to provide access to this work for today's researchers.

Fear in Bongoland: Burundi Refugees in Urban Tanzania

Refugees, Hutu–Tanzania–Dar es Salaam–Social conditions
Hutu (African people)–Relocation–Tanzania–Dar es Salaam
Hutu (African people)–Urban residence–Tanzania–Dar es Salaam
Dar es Salaam (Tanzania) –Ethnic relations
Dar es Salaam (Tanzania)–Economic conditions
Dar es Salaam (Tanzania)–Social conditions

This is an excellent example of changes in cataloging style and content since catalogs have been computerized. Six or more subject headings are now much more common than they used to be, when the "rule of three" stipulated that three subject headings could usually describe any book (and produce only three cards to file).

Subject headings have grown in number and changed in character over the past several decades. Changes have occurred both because computerization has made editing of subject headings in catalogs much easier and because major social, scientific and political changes worldwide have changed the words used to describe objects and phenomena. If subject headings are to fulfill their purpose–to guide researchers to useful works in the collection–the terms used must reflect the vocabulary of the researchers.

Geographic Terms

Some changes to subject headings reflect changes in geo-political names. For these, the U.S. Board of Geographic Names is the accepted authority of the Library of Congress, as it is for geographic names used as corporate authors. Former names of nations are not used as subjects. Works on the *Gold Coast* will be found under the subject *Ghana*; *Northern Rhodesia* under *Zambia*, etc. This can be very confusing to researchers. For instance, a 1931 publication of the Gold Coast Census Office has the subject headings *Ghana–economic conditions*, and *Ghana–census*, even though the author is "Gold Coast Census Office." Martin Wight's work *The Gold Coast Legislative Council*, in the series *Studies in Colonial Legislatures*, has the subject heading *Ghana–politics and government–to 1957*, even though prior to 1957 the name *Ghana* referred only to an ancient kingdom in West Africa.

Bias in LC Subject Headings?

As noted earlier, when the Eastern Region of Nigeria seceded from the Federation in 1967, the United States did not recognize Biafra as a sovereign nation, so the U.S. Board of Geographic names did not establish it as a valid name. Although Biafra was used widely in writings about the area and its people, libraries did not use the name as an author or as a subject heading. However, a valid subject heading had been established for a secessionist state in U.S. history. *Confederate States of America* is an established subject heading, along with *United States–History–Civil War, 1861-1865*. Sanford Berman asserts that the difference in treatment is based on racism because the leaders of the Biafran rebellion were black, while the leaders of the Confederacy were white (Berman 1993: 109-110). Whatever the basis of the decision on Biafra as a subject heading, it's too bad that a more convincing argument was not made to use the name Biafra. The subject heading *Nigeria, Eastern* does the researcher a disservice, leading him to a large body of works with only a portion directly related to Biafra. Widenmann reports that David Michener, cataloger for Northwestern University's Herskovits Library, used Biafra as a subject heading and corporate author, but notes that few libraries give their catalog departments this much discretionary power (Widenmann 1989: 41). Some databases, such as ERIC, use Biafra as a descriptor; most rely on use of the name in title or abstract.

LC does change subject headings in response to a variety of pressures and appeals on the part of activists. One such change that was particularly welcome to Africanist scholars and librarians was the change from [ethnic name] (African tribe) to [ethnic name] (African people), e.g., *Ndebele (African tribe)* is now *Ndebele (African people)*. Widenmann notes that the ALC made the suggestion to the Library of Congress, along with eight other "most desired" changes, but it was still nine years before the recommendations were implemented (Widenmann 1989: 45).

Language, the principal medium of any culture or society, is layered with meanings and subtext so that even the most straightforward-seeming terms can become controversial, and subject headings in a library catalog are as capable of offending as any other terms in any other venue. In the introduction to *Subject Cataloging: Critiques and Innovations*, Sanford Berman describes the purpose of the collection of essays:

> . . . To pinpoint what's wrong with current subject cataloging, demonstrating why it often doesn't 'work,' and sometimes transmits undesirable messages. (Berman 1984:1)

Twenty years later, librarians still have to be aware of the multiple "messages" that subject terms may carry, but must always keep foremost the principle that subject headings are intended to aid research, not instruct the public in terminology or the concepts it represents, nor to correct misconceptions and change attitudes. It's not easy, though, to define the line between developing terms that one thinks will work best as subject headings for researchers, and developing terms that express one's own views or a particular political/ideological approach. It is often up to the reference librarian to assist researchers in understanding the structure of established terms, and in devising a search strategy with the greatest chances of success.

While some students already have a specific topic by the time they start research, many come in to the library looking for material on a broad concept such as ethnic conflict in Africa and need to find examples to use as case studies. Biafra is a good example of ethnic conflict. What search strategy would lead a student to the topic and material on it?

The first problem encountered is that *ethnic conflict* is not used extensively as a subject heading. Searching for *ethnic conflict* as a subject yielded only 17 entries, and only one on an African country. A keyword search using "ethnic conflict" yields 281 entries, with numerous entries on Africa or African nations. Results were similar for the same searches on WorldCat.

Use of related terms such as *ethnic relations* or *conflict management* yields more potential entries. None of these works is on Biafra, although the secession of Biafra and the resulting civil war were among the first widely publicized examples of ethnic conflict in Africa. It would seem to be a casebook study for any student wanting to do a paper on ethnic-based conflicts in Africa, but a student would have to know about it before beginning a search in the OPAC.

During the civil war in Nigeria, press coverage used the term genocide to describe the treatment of Igbos in northern Nigeria in the months preceding secession, but none of the books on Biafra have this subject heading. The only use of *genocide* as a subject heading for works on Nigerian events is for two books on the treatment of the Ogoni in the 1990s. The only way that students will be guided to Biafra as an example of ethnic conflict and genocide in Nigeria is by a suggestion from library staff or their professors.

Our hypothetical student is still looking for an example of ethnic conflict in Africa. Perhaps she has heard of the Ogoni because of the publicized support of such commercial enterprises as the Body Shop (http://www.thebodyshop.com/web/tbsgl/values_dhr.jsp). A key recent book for a paper on the Ogoni would be Ike Okonta's and Oronto Douglas' *Where Vultures Feast: Shell, Human Rights, and Oil in the Niger Delta*. However, that student would not find it using the subject headings *Ogoni*, *genocide* or *human rights*, even though the words "human rights" appear in the title, and one of the largest sections in the index is for the Movement for the Survival of the Ogoni People (MOSOP), and the passages indexed describe mass killings of Ogonis. Rather, the subject headings are:

Petroleum industry and trade–Corrupt practices–Nigeria–Niger River Delta.

Petroleum industry and trade–Environmental aspects–Nigeria–Niger River Delta.

Shell International Petroleum Company, Ltd.

I brought up this example at a recent meeting of the ALC's Cataloging Committee. Several colleagues looked into it, and provided the rationale for the subject headings according to established rules and precedent. The subject headings describe the book correctly enough, but do not provide any access to a student looking for examples of ethnic-based conflict in Africa. A student researching the topic would only find this book if a teacher or advisor had recommended it, or if it had appeared in a specialized bibliography.

African Language and Ethnic Names

Any research involving African ethnic groups and languages is complex, no matter what search terms are used. There are nearly 2,000 languages spoken in Africa, with a corresponding number of ethnic groups. The names of those languages and ethnic groups used by the people themselves are frequently quite different from the names used by outsiders. If the English call their European neighbors German, the French call them Allemand, and they call themselves Deutsch, then it should be no big surprise that the Fula people of West Africa are known variously as: Fellani, Foulah, Foulb, Ful, Fulah, Fulahs, Fulani, Fulbe, Fulfede, Fulfulde, Peul, and Peulh.

When a student begins research on the Fula, the OPAC will guide him to books in the collection, regardless of what term he first uses for the search. However, if he goes to indexes such as *Anthropological Index Online* and *Anthropological Literature*, he will have to use several forms of the name to catch all references. With *Anthropological Index Online* Fulani yielded 11 references, and Peul yielded 4 different ones. *Anthropological Literature* yielded 146 for Fulani, and 41 for Peul.

Another problem for searchers is that some languages, particularly the Bantu family, use prefixes on a root word to indicate an individual, a group, or the language. Use of these prefixes has been inconsistent in studies of African peoples and languages. One study may refer to kiSwahili, another to Swahili. LC subject headings have been established to provide consistency in searching, but are themselves inconsistent from one language to another. For instance, some subject headings omit the prefix, as in *Swahili language* instead of kiSwahili and *Zulu language* instead of isiZulu, but others keep it, as in *Kinyarwanda language* instead of Rwanda or Runda, as it is sometimes called in the literature.

All of these features make looking for works about an African language difficult. But if a researcher is trying to find works *in* an African language, he can run into a complete dead end. The language of publication is not commonly used as a subject heading, since the purpose of cataloging is to provide researchers with terms describing the subject matter. However, ASL, like many other Africana libraries, collects material in most African languages mainly as examples of the language. The books are collected to be used as readers for students of the language, or for linguistic research. The subject matter, be it cattle raising, latrine building, romance, or murder mystery, is often of secondary interest. What we want to give our users is a subject heading for the language. LC subject headings do not accommodate this strategy easily. ASL has used the pattern *[language name]–Readers*, and *[language name]–Texts*, although this is not actually the correct use of the subject heading *Readers* or *Texts*. To find the AIDS prevention comic book published in Lesotho in the Sotho language (*Bacha malaeneng: comic ka bacha le AIDS*), one would have to go through the rather tedious process of a subject search on *AIDS Disease*, then limit by language. There is another problem. In order to limit by language, one would have to know that the code for Sotho is "sso," or find it under "Southern Sotho" in the list of languages. There is no subject heading that could be used to indicate that this is a Sotho language reader.

Works of fiction, until recently, have not been given subject headings. This makes fiction in African languages very difficult to find. For instance, a student or teacher looking for Swahili readers would probably never pull up the BU Libraries' copy of the Swahili translation of Hemingway's *The Old Man and the Sea* (*Mzee na bahari*) if it weren't for guides prepared by ASL staff. It could be found on an author search limited to Swahili. Unless she already knew that a work of Hemingway's had been translated for East African readers, a researcher would be unlikely to use this strategy.

Searching by subject or author and limiting by language as a strategy, difficult as it is, to find African language readers could be made completely impossible in some libraries, if they choose an option offered by Innovative Interfaces, Inc. and undoubtedly other library system providers. III's installation default is a list of selected languages for the "limit by language" feature so that researchers are offered only the "most commonly sought" languages. We only learned of this situation when a patron attempted to limit by a language not on the list. In the staff discussion that ensued, it became clear that researchers preferred the full list of languages and it was restored.

Limiting a search by language cannot find all works in Swahili or any other language. If the OPAC can be programmed to search on the MARC language code, researchers will have greater chances of finding all works in a given language, if, of course, the language code has been correctly supplied. For some languages there is a further problem: until recently many African languages had no individual codes, but were grouped into "bucket codes" for a larger linguistic grouping, such as "Niger-Congo, Other" and "Sub-Saharan Africa (Other)," which made works in the languages designated by those codes nearly impossible to retrieve (Widenmann 1989: 53). The Library of Congress is now much more receptive to subject headings and codes for "lesser spoken" African languages when they are submitted by ALC members. Some libraries, Northwestern University in particular, have opted to put African language material into their collections with "collection level records: a call number showing location" (not necessarily a classification number), a "main entry" in square brackets, e.g., *[Bamileke language publications]*, and a geographic code and subject heading in the form *Bamileke language–texts* (Widenmann 1989: 53). This practice at least affords some degree of access to such materials.

Variations in the orthography of African languages as used in academic writing can cause problems for research on specific persons. The epic of Sundiata, ruler of the empire of Mali in the 13th century, is a case in point. The name is spelled several ways in the literature: Sunjata, Sundiata, Soundiata, Son-Jara. The subject heading for the oral epic, which has been published in many forms, is *Epic of Son-Jara*. However, the subject heading for the historical figure is *Keita, Soundiata, d. 1255.* The subject heading for the ethnic group is *Mandingo (African people)*, although terms used in academic writing on the group include Mande and Mandekan, as well as Mandingo. The heading for the language is *Mandingo language*. In indexes such as the *MLA Bibliography* and *Francis*, one must use all forms of the names or both the person and the language/ethnic group to be sure of catching all relevant citations.

Can One Word Say It All?

Broad subject headings may seem to be a good choice for catalogers who are trying to describe general works, but those broad terms tend to render those books nearly invisible no matter what specific information they may contain, particularly when the title is also general. *Africa*, the enormously useful collection of essays on African history and current conditions edited by Phyllis Martin and Patrick O'Meara, has only one subject heading: *Africa*. Both of our library's copies of the third edition (1995) are on permanent reserve, repeatedly used as required reading for one or more classes. There is a contents note on the OCLC record for the first edition, which would provide some access to the contents, but the note is omitted from the record of the third edition. This book is recommended for class readings, but invisible in the catalog. How would a student find it other than its appearance on a reading list?

Another case is *New Guinea Tapeworms and Jewish Grandmothers: Tales of Parasites and People*, a popular work on parasites that contains several chapters relevant to Africa. The MARC copy provides two subject headings: *Biology* and *Parasitic Diseases–popular works*. Contributed copy on OCLC provides a contents note in the 505 notes field and four subject headings, although none give any better clues about the topics covered. OCLC copy for another edition uses only the subject heading *Biology*. Who will ever find this work, whatever topic they may be researching?

Sometimes an index can help in providing access to information contained in books when the subject headings fail. In a non-African example, a student came to the general reference desk seeking books (not journal articles) that discuss walking on hot coals in India. The librarian tried checking through *India–Description and Travel*, but quickly saw that would be fruitless. He then tried a database, Expanded Academic Index, found a citation to *Net of Magic: Wonders and Deceptions in India*. The subject headings were *Magic–India–History*, and *Magic Tricks–India–History*. The search on *Expanded Academic Index* simply used the terms "India" and "walking" and "coals" and provided the key to success.

Many library systems now allow a keyword search on the entire record, which aids retrieval enormously. But even this doesn't help if no subject headings are applied at all. Only recently have works of fiction been given subject headings, mostly in public library catalogs. Autobiography is also given short shrift. Yet, for African studies, novels and autobiography make powerful teaching tools, as evidenced by Jean Hay's compilation *African Novels in the Classroom.*

> First, Western students with little or no first-hand experience of African societies will pick up a vast array of information from reading a novel, including such details as what houses and cities and villages look like; what a meal might consist of; what kinds of work people do; how leisure time might be used; how a prosperous government minister, a hard-working peasant, or a call girl might dress or behave; but perhaps most important of all, they will absorb many clues about relationships–the extended family in its urban and rural permutations, the bonds of conflicts between workers, or the varying relationships between the sexes, between officials and peasants, black and white, young and old. (Hay 2000: 2-3)

But how does a teacher find novels that illustrate the situation and points she wants to cover in the course? Not in the catalog.

Can libraries or indexing services provide sufficient access for all kinds of research and information needs patrons may bring to them? Probably not. Certainly no library can be expected to provide subject access in such detail as to describe the eating habits of characters in novels so that a researcher could find examples of the symbolism of cuisine in African novels. For such projects, scholarly communication remains an important component of research, particularly electronic discussion lists such as H-Africa. All participants in the research process–researchers, authors, publishers, indexers and librarians–have to consider research access as part of their responsibility.

"ALL FOR WANT OF A HORSE SHOE NAIL": SMALL MISTAKES CAN CAUSE BIG PROBLEMS

> For want of a nail, the shoe was lost
> For want of a shoe, the horse was lost
> For want of a horse, the rider was lost
> For want of a rider, the battle was lost
> For want of a battle, the war was lost
> For want of a war, the kingdom was lost
> –All for the want of a horse shoe nail.

–Caedmon recording, *Mother Goose*, 1958

Academic research on Africa contributes to a better understanding of Africa throughout the community and may help shape economic and foreign policy on the national level. Unfortunately, despite its importance, research on Africa can be thwarted by simple human error. Advances in information technology have enormously increased the power of researchers to cast their searches broadly as well as to dig more deeply into the resources available, but the technology is for naught if the input to the databases is flawed or incomplete.

Errors Can Derail Access

Typographical errors happen all the time; who hasn't, for instance, sent out flyers urging students to visit the library's research "Web sties"? When typographical or other errors interfere with access, however, the result is research failure, not merely embarrassment. Errors in catalog records can effectively render invisible important information in items owned by the library. The researcher must also be careful keying in searches. A human reader may understand what you *meant* to type, but the computer reads it letter by letter.

Input Errors Affect "Known-Item" Searches

- "Untied States" entered as a search on Google brings the message "Did you mean *United States*?" as well as a few hits, e.g., http://news.fws.gov/articles/ProposalWouldReintroduce.html ("Proposal Would Reintroduce Migratory Whooping Cranes to Western Untied States")
- "Ehiopia" instead of "Ethiopia" on OCLC yields the record for *Ehiopians and the Houses They Live In*, with one library listed as holding this erroneously entered title. The record for the correct title shows holdings in eleven libraries, but researchers doing a title search at the library with the flawed record would not find the book in their own collection.
- While writing the section on "known-item searches" for this paper, I was puzzled when a keyword search using "strong and breed" did not yield the citation for *Totem Voices: Eight Plays from the Black World Repertory*, a collection that included Wole Soyinka's *The Strong Breed.* This should have been an excellent example of the contents note (505 MARC field) providing access to titles in a collection. Eventually I noticed the typographical error in the contents

note: "The *stong* breed/Wole Soyinka." The record had been downloaded from OCLC with the typo. The OCLC record has since been corrected, but our record retained the typo until I alerted catalog staff to the problem. (In the process, I also found a record with "Stong Brook, NY" as the place of publication.)

Because the title page is the chief source of information for a printed book, *AACR2* specifies that catalogers should transcribe it as it appears, including any inaccuracy or misspelled words. The cataloger can use one of three ways of indicating the correct spelling: inserting the word "[sic]" after the error; inserting missing letters, in square brackets, when this is appropriate; or adding "i.e." followed by a correction, all in square brackets. Bowman points out the "inherent conflict between the requirement that the title-page should be transcribed accurately and the purpose of the catalog, namely to allow users to find items that they are searching for" (Bowman 2001: 40). The following examples illustrate some of the problems in retrieval:

- The OPAC record for *Perpsectives [sic] on Regional Co-operation from South Africa's Mass Democratic Movement* indicates the error with *[sic]* in the 245 (title) field and provides the correct spelling in the 740 (alternative title) field.
- In the record for the title *General Smuts Exposes the Folly of Neutrality; Speech in the Senate of the Union Parliament at Cape Town on January 30th, 1940*, the imprint date reads "1939 (sic)." Although the discrepancy between the dates in the title and the imprint would not impede access, without the "(sic)," a researcher would be hard pressed to determine which date was correct. One assumes that the original cataloger did the research necessary to determine the correct date and mark the incorrect one.
- In the collection *Africa and the Successor Generation: Summary Report and Papers Presented at the 10th Anniversary Meeting of the Africa Leadership Forum*, one paper has the title: "Agriculture in Subsaharan Africa, Backbone or Archilles (sic) Heel?" Because the title appears in the 505 (notes) field rather than a title field, a correct title is not supplied in the 740 (alternate title) field. A word search on the terms "agriculture and Africa" will bring up the record, but if a professor sends a student to find "the paper that called agriculture Africa's Achilles' heel," the student is doomed to failure.

Indexes of journal articles do not always correct or otherwise indicate typographical errors.

- The Swedish environmental journal *Ambio* listed in its Table of Contents an intriguing article: "Lessons from Twenty-five Years of Conversation and Seven Years of Research Initiatives in the Kondoa Highlands of Central Tanzania" (*Ambio* v. 28 no. 5, August 1999). Noticing the title, I wondered if development professionals were finally confessing that they talk much and do little. The title at the head of the article turned out to be "Lessons from Twenty-five Years of *Conservation* . . . "–not "conversation." Would a researcher find the article doing keyword search on "Tanzania and conservation"? *General Science Full Text* cites this title with the correct spelling, so that search would work. However, anyone using the same search strategy on *Environmental Knowledge Online* would be foiled. It cites the title with "conversation."
- "The Case of the Wrong Campbell": *Review of African Political Economy* #42 (1988) lists Horace Campbell as the author of an article that was actually written by John R. Campbell. This error came to light when Boston University's Africana cataloger researched name authority to distinguish the John R. Campbell who wrote the book she was cataloging from others in the catalog. She tracked down an article he listed as "forthcoming in *Review of African Political Economy*" in the bibliography of the work being cataloged. Rather than verifying the author's name, the article in *Review of African Political Economy* caused confusion because the author was identified as Horace–not John R.–Campbell. Correspondence with Horace Campbell finally established that Horace and John were not the same person, and that the attribution in *Review of African Political Economy* had been an error. BU has amended its journal copy with the correct name, but indexes, including *Bibliography of Africana Periodical Literature Database* (http://www.africabib.org) and *Africa Bibliography 1989* cite Horace Campbell as the author. Researchers looking for the work cited in John Campbell's bibliography would fail to find it in those indexes with an author search, even though the article itself had indeed been indexed.

Name authority is plagued with typographical errors:

- E. *G*. Egner appears as the author on the cover of a working paper, but E. *B*. Egner appears on the title page. Which is the typo? LC name authority has established E. B. Egner as the author's name.
- The author's name on the title page reads Mohamed Lyes Mesli, but both the cover and the biographical note reads Mohamed Elyes Mesli. Based on information on other works by this author, the name is established as Mohamed Elyes Mesli. This may be a variation in Romanization rather than a typo.
- There are two LC name authority records for one author: Tibaijuka, Anna Kajumulo and Kajomulo-Tibaijuka, Anna. Our cataloger noticed the anomaly and alerted LC staff, who corrected the record, using Tibaijuka, Anna Kajumulo. The OCLC record is now correct for all of her works, but the libraries that had already downloaded the erroneous record may not have updated their OPACs.

Assumptions based on partial information or faulty memory can lead researchers astray:

- "The case of the posthumous interview." The editor of a German collection of papers on the Algerian author Frantz Fanon wanted an author to include commentary on Fanon's meeting with Che Guevara in Algeria in 1964. Even when told that Fanon had died in 1963, the editor insisted that the meeting had occurred, referring to an interview with Che Guevara in the December 26, 1964 issue of the Algerian magazine *Revolution Africaine*. The interviewer in the German translation (Guevara 1989: 185-190) was identified as Fanon. The researcher checked the magazine's actual text, and the byline on the article identified the interviewer as Fanon's widow, Josie Fanon. The German translation had omitted the first names, using only the surnames Fanon and Guevara to identify each speaker. The failure of the German publication to fully identify the interviewer had created a research Twilight Zone. If the editor of an academic publication was misled, how many students' papers may have cited Frantz Fanon's posthumous meeting with Che Guevara?
- A student and her teacher were once irate that we didn't own, and couldn't find nationwide, a work by Samir Amin. Although they only had a partial title, a series of keyword searches yielded the work they wanted. It was in our collection, and the author's name was Galal Amin, not Samir Amin.

Information Technology Is Not Fool-Proof

Small errors in the way data is input to a record can cause major problems with searching or display of records. One keystroke can make a big difference.

- During the discussion on the "limit by language" option on our OPAC, one staff member complained that when he looked for works in German by Paul Tillich, he found German to English translations along with the German language publications. Catalogers recognized the problem–the 041 (language code) had been filled in as *engger*, which would cause the work to show up on a list limited to works in German, instead of *eng|ger*, which indicates a work translated into English from German. The entries for Tillich were corrected, and a catalog department supervisor advised staff to be on the lookout for other such problems.
- The International Standard Book Number (ISBN) and International Standard Serial Number (ISSN) are intended to be unique identifiers for books and serials. Some electronic indexes now offer a direct link from a citation in the database to the entry for the journal title in the library's catalog, but because ISBNs and ISSNs are long strings of digits, it's all too easy to mistype one without noticing, even if input is checked. This link works by the computer matching the ISSN in the citation to the ISSN in the catalog record. An error on either side will cause a mismatch. Reference librarians need to advise students to double check negative results in the OPAC, not just go straight to an interlibrary loan form, or to discard the citation in frustration because they need the information immediately. Students don't always listen to advice, and they are frequently using the indexes without help at any point from a reference librarian.
- As described earlier, full-text searching has several inherent flaws rooted in its dependence on the computer matching words character by character, while humans think of words as things and concepts. Even more problems are caused by the errors derived from conversion of older printed pages into digital text by means of optical character recognition (OCR). Nicholson Baker, ever on the lookout for a problem, describes searching for the term "modem life" in JSTOR, and getting citations dating back to 1895. The computer had "recognized" *modern* as *modem* (Baker 2001: 71). One has to suspect that Baker set up this particular "discovery" (is

"modem life" a real term?), but Baker's motives do not mitigate the reality of the problem.

- When I showed a student how to use the *Bibliography of Africana Periodical Literature Database* (http://www.africabib.org/) to find articles on the Dan, a people of Cote d'Ivoire, we came up with hundreds of hits–far more than I would have expected. Most turned out to have the letters *dan* embedded somewhere in the title (e.g., Su*dan*, etc.) and the limitation to country name didn't help. When I notified the compiler of the index of the problem, he was able to find the two programming errors and fix them–but wondered how many researchers had hit the same problem without reporting it.

Mistakes in Reference Works: Why Don't They Do It Right the First Time?

Accuracy is particularly vital for reference works and bibliographies. Most authors of reference works are competent and reliable, but far too many works display the effects of careless research, writing, editing, or proofreading that can mislead students and cause great harm. Few publishers now provide any editing or proofreading. Manuscripts are to be submitted camera-ready, and it's up to the author to make sure that everything is as it should be. After working on a manuscript, the author-proofreader tends to see what was meant, not what was actually typed. A few slips in the process of cutting, moving, and pasting can result in bizarre sentences and weird sequences of text. Even a conscientious author can let serious errors slip through. Some authors don't seem to check their work at all.

When a publisher asked me to review the manuscript of a large bibliography on Nigeria prior to their decision to publish, I noted the following errors, among many others:

- A book that had been advertised in a publisher's catalog as "forthcoming," but had never been published, was listed with a full citation, including publication date.
- Entries for the 1953 population census of the three regions of Nigeria (Northern, Eastern, and Western) were not listed under the correct author: *Nigeria. Dept. of Statistics*, nor even under each separate region, but all under *Nigeria, Northern* as the corporate author.

- John Ogilby's *Africa: Being accurate description of the regions of Aegypt, Barbary, Lybia, and Billendurlgerid, the land of Negroes, Guinee, Aethiopia, and the Abyssines: with all the adjacent islands* was listed as "Obilby, John. *Africa*. 1670." The typo in the author's name would render an author search fruitless, and the distinctive title was reduced to a single word that would not be likely to yield the actual citation with a title search.

The bibliography needed a great deal of work, but the publishers decided to produce it "as is," with a caveat in the introduction. This may absolve them from liability, but doesn't help the students using it for research.

The quality and credibility of an academic work depends as much on attention to details as it does on the originality of the author's ideas and the thoroughness of her research. Robert McHenry, former editor in chief of the *Encyclopedia Britannica*, warns:

> The conviction that details, by definition minor, don't matter is gradually penetrating and perverting all of publishing, up to and including academic publishing. (McHenry 2002: B5)

After providing several disheartening examples of errors, he asks,

> Can it be that they [university presses] need reminding that an error can falsify the author's intent and meaning? That it stands on the page, there at every rereading, which is something that ought to happen regularly to any good book? And do the buyers and readers of serious books need reminding that they are ill served by slipshod editorial practice? (McHenry 2002: B5)

Reviewers of reference books have a difficult task. Librarians reviewing a reference work will usually pay most attention to its utility and construction, basing their remarks on issues of what questions this work might answer, and how easily a researcher could find specific pieces of information. Unless they are knowledgeable of the particular topic, they might not question the authority and accuracy of the information presented. Walford offers as a basis for good reviewing the criteria used by the British Library Association to judge annual awards for outstanding reference works and bibliographies.

1. The authority of the work and the quality and kind of the articles or entries.
2. The accessibility and arrangement of the information.
3. The scope and coverage.
4. The style.
5. The relevance and quality of the illustrations.
6. The quality of the indexing.
7. The adequacy of the bibliographies and references.
8. The up-to-dateness of the information.
9. The physical presentation.
10. The originality of the work (Walford 1982:167).

In 1989, the ALC culminated numerous discussions on this topic by publishing "Guidelines for Compiling African Bibliographies" (Henige 1989), which included a call for review organs "to treat reference works at least as critically, if not more critically, than non-reference works" (Henige 1989: 13). These guidelines are the basis of judging the biannual Conover-Porter Award, presented by the ASA for the best reference work or bibliography published during the previous two years. The ALC guidelines are echoed and updated by the Reference and User Services Association's "RUSA Guidelines: Guidelines for the Preparation of a Bibliography" (RUSA 2001: 115-117). Walford also refers to Ken Kister's list of qualities needed for a good reviewer:

1. Ability to write clearly, succinctly and sometimes quickly.
2. A thorough and comparative knowledge of reference materials and their make-up, characteristics and uses.
3. An objective stance.
4. An honest and independent spirit (Kister 1979, quoted in Walford 1982: 169).

Do such guidelines actually influence authors and publishers to produce high quality reference works, and reviewers to look at them critically for accuracy as well as utility? Not consistently enough. Two examples illustrate my concerns.

Stewart, John. *African States and Rulers: An Encyclopedia of Native, Colonial, and Independent States and Rulers Past and Present*. Jefferson, NC: McFarland, 1989.

The second edition was published in 1999. I reviewed the first edition in *Choice* (Walsh 1989). David Henige reviewed the second edition in *History in Africa* (Henige 2001c). Stewart provides incredible detail, for example, exact dates for the kings of Daniski in West Africa in the 15th century, and the names of all the Sultans of Gobir from c. 1100 to 1742. Where did he get all this information? There were no notes to the individual entries, and Stewart's preface does not inspire confidence:

> By far the most valuable source for compiling this book was the writer's own notes taken in the 1970s and based on hundreds of direct African and European sources. Because the writer had no idea, a decade ago, that this research would ever turn up in published book form, the vast majority of these on-the-spot documents and oral sources are now unable to be credited accurately. (Stewart 1989: xx)

The author assures readers that the bibliography (a slim two and a half pages) corroborates those notes. It does not. Even though a reliable book of this genre would be used all the time, I had to give it a "not recommended" assessment in the review; this was not a work I could send students to with any confidence. The publisher was incensed by this review and complained to the editor of *Choice*, impugning my credentials while failing to counter any of the criticisms, or to provide more substantial credentials for the author. He noted that *Library Journal* and other library media had given the book glowing praise. None of the authors of the reviews I read had any expertise on Africa, and had probably praised the book because it looked useful.

The positive reviews may have contributed to the publisher's decision to bring out a second edition ten years later. When David Henige reviewed the 1999 edition in *History in Africa*, the longer academic review format allowed him to make more specific criticisms of factual errors and dubious assertions, and also to provide essential context of African historical scholarship. He found the bibliography shockingly inadequate, and comments on the author's dependence on the resources at his disposal at a university library with no African studies collection, with no mention of visits to specialized collections or ILL (Henige 2001c: 401). He notes that the one review published at the time he wrote his was favorable (Henige 2001c: 402).

James S. Olson. *The Peoples of Africa: An Ethnohistorical Dictionary.* Westport, CT: Greenwood Press, 1996.

> The short review in *Choice* (Azzolina 1996) says "it is hard to imagine a more complete dictionary than this one," while a longer review in *International Journal of African Historical Studies* (Beidelman 1997) concludes that the author has "no glimmer of awareness" of the central historical issues in African studies. Olson gives citations for many entries, but they are not reliable. At least one author's name is misspelled, and some entries cite references that do not confirm the assertions made. Again, this is not a work I–or most other Africana librarians–would send students to for basic ethnographic information. The ALC, in fact, is formally objecting to its inclusion on a list of "authorities" for LC subject headings.

Inferior reference works may receive good reviews because the reviewer has too little knowledge of the subject matter, because editors discourage negative reviews, or because it is too difficult to document criticism of a work in the 200 words allotted to reviews in library media such as *Choice* and *Library Journal*. Henige points out that scholarly journals, which allow much longer assessments, rarely review reference works (Henige 2001d: 28-29). Even if a substantial review appears in a scholarly journal, it is often too late to influence purchase decisions in libraries. Most libraries receive books from approval and blanket order plans in advance of the appearance of scholarly reviews. By the time the academic journal publishes the review, the book is probably already on the shelf.

Budget constraints usually limit the number of reference works purchased on specialized topics. While BU's African Studies Library may have several dozen reference works dealing with a narrow African topic such as West African literature, a more general collection probably has only a handful to cover all topics continent-wide. Thus, the selector for the specialized collection can afford to make a few mistakes in choosing reference works, since other works can fill in the gaps. If an inferior reference work is chosen for a general collection, it is not as likely to be replaced or supplemented. The selector would, of course, want "the best," but may not be well served by reviews in making his selection.

Many authors seem to feel it's possible to write a reference book on a topic simply on the basis of personal interest, or that it's possible to compile a bibliography on any topic, regardless of personal knowledge at the outset of the project. Authors of reference books I have reviewed and found to be inferior have had "interesting" credentials. The author of *African States and Rulers: An Encyclopedia of Native, Colonial, and Independent States and Rulers Past and Present* has written works on the moons of the solar system, Antarctica, the British Empire, and Italian film. The author of *The Peoples of Africa: An Ethnohistorical Dictionary* has written works on John Wayne, Vietnam, sports in America, the New Deal, the Alamo, Native American civil rights, Cuban Americans, and U.S. economic history. A reviewer or selector would do well to look carefully at the credentials of the author, and examine the sources on which an African reference book is based.

It's not easy to write a reference work. An assignment I accepted to write 1,000 words on libraries in Africa for the *Encyclopedia of Sub-Saharan Africa* was a nightmare. The editors wanted to include description of the medieval libraries of Arabic manuscripts in Timbuktu and other West African cities, with commentary on their present condition; the same had to be done for Ethiopian manuscript collections. Government, church, and other archives needed coverage, as did public libraries in the colonial regimes and their influence on future writers and statesmen as well as ordinary citizens. Differences in colonial policies concerning libraries were important to note; university libraries, school libraries, training for African librarians, and regional library associations were all too important to be overlooked. Only when these topics had been covered could I get started on my own special interests: the "book famine" and its solutions, the role of information technology in African libraries, and international library cooperation. The outline alone adds up to 10% of the allotted words, allowing only a sentence or two to skim the surface of each topic.

Publishers and editors may begin a project in good faith, but encounter problems beyond their control. The *Encyclopedia of Sub-Saharan Africa* took several years to complete, during which time the original publisher was absorbed by a larger company and that company by a conglomerate. Academic writers are notorious for ignoring deadlines and pursuing their own agendas. Delays and defaults by contributors increase expenses, raising the cost of the book and potentially reducing the market share.

One has to wonder sometimes how some reference books are conceived. I received not long ago an invitation to write 5,000 words on Africa for a projected three volume set: *From Ice Age Symboling to the Internet: An Encyclopedia of Graphic Communication*, a work dealing with the history of the technologies associated with writing and book production. Since this was far from my area of expertise, even if I fully understood what was wanted, I declined, and recommended a more qualified colleague. That person also declined. The editors wrote back that they were having great difficulties finding anyone to write the section on Africa, and that they would probably have to exclude Africa from the work.

This project may be of dubious merit and utility, but the publishers' experience is still of interest. In follow-up correspondence, the editors said they had contacted 40 Africanist scholars over a period of five years, with few replies. Two authors had agreed to write, but in the end failed to produce articles. The editors were clearly on a low budget, since they were offering no remuneration to authors. If the book comes out, one criticism may well be the neglect of Africa in its coverage–despite their efforts. This is an irresolvable dilemma: bad coverage or no coverage at all. It makes one appreciate the good reference works all the more.

Using Parts of the Book for Research

Because of the interdisciplinary nature of African Studies, researchers may be casting wide nets, consulting many works on more general topics in the hopes of finding relevant information within them. When librarians can find few citations for a student's specific topic in the OPAC or other databases, our advice is often "Try going broader. See if there's a chapter or section in a general work." Finding those sections without reading the entire book can be more difficult than it should be. Not only students have problems; serious scholars are assumed to have read broadly in their areas, and to recall what they have read, but when it comes to locating the exact citation needed to support an assertion, the senior scholar may have as hard a time as a student exploring a new topic. Ideally, an academic book has a structure that aids readers in finding the particular topics it covers. Henige notes:

> . . . the act of effective readership has become much more complex. With increasing interdisciplinarity and the sheer volume of volumes, research often takes the form of dipping into works that appear to be of marginal interest, looking for just a few points, even one only, sometimes hoping to find them, sometimes not. In this environment, the index that provides optimal access is nothing less than *de rigueur*, whoever accomplishes it. (Henige 2002b: 242)

Despite this increased need, the practice of indexing academic books seems to be declining; only 55 to 82 per cent of 20th century non-fiction works are indexed (Henige 2002b: 231).

Without a back-of-the-book index, information within a book becomes much harder to find. Even when there is an index, errors can render it useless. More than once I've seen an index that provides page or item references to entries in the text that have no connection to the index term. Usually this means that the text may have been revision #12, but the index was still referring to version #11. Years after acquiring the book, we discovered that a particularly useful bibliography in the ASL collection on health in Africa had skipped Nigeria in the indexing–making any entries on this important country invisible unless the researcher scanned the entire work.

Anyone who has done back-of-the-book indexing knows the problems involved. Geographic and personal names are easy enough, but creating descriptors for topics and concepts becomes murky. One takes terms from the text, adds broader or alternate terms, and then tries to see the draft index the way a researcher might. But should one design the terms for the expert or the novice? Is alphabetical order a sufficient finding aid, or is a hierarchical subject arrangement better? Creating an index requires the author to step away from her position of expert and to look at the work the way a reader/researcher would. The American Society of Indexers has posted its *Indexing Evaluation Checklist* (http://www.asindexing.org/site/checklist.shtml) with guidelines for indexers aimed at making indexes useful for readers.

Another strategy that librarians often recommend is "Find a few good books or articles and look at the works the author refers to in the bibliography or notes." Good advice–if those notes and references are complete, accurate, and reasonably easy to use. Bibliography and footnote/endnote styles sometimes seem to be designed to impede rather than aid research. In a comic piece for the *Chronicle of Higher Education*, Bauman pokes fun at the multiplicity of styles, but says quite accurately: "Checking sources is becoming impossible" (Bauman 2001: B5). A work may have only notes, no bibliography, so that one must sometimes trace back through multiple notes on the pattern: "Author's last name, *Title*, p. 215-216" to find the full citation. This form is at least somewhat easier than tracing *op. cit.* and *ibid.* back to the first use. Paul Stiff (1997) discusses issues of footnote/endnote design in terms of how readers use books and those notes. He concludes, "Designers just need to think less about designing books and more about designing for reading" (Stiff 1997: 72).

Notes, whether foot- or end-, in whatever format, serve several purposes:

- They attribute quotations and paraphrased passages to the original author, avoiding actual or apparent plagiarism.
- They allow fellow scholars to go to the sources the author used, examine them, and test the author's conclusions.
- They give students the benefit of both a wider list of potential resources for their own papers, and some insights into the research process.

Notes, clearly, are an important part of scholarly publishing. A work's bibliography might be even more important. Henige describes two forms of bibliographies: works cited and works consulted, noting that the latter "could approach a complete bibliography on the subject at hand at a certain time" (Henige 2002a: 77). Like Baumann and Stiff, Henige faults authors who provide only notes–"forcing readers to ferret out citations hidden away in some footnote or another" (Henige 2002a: 77), and noting that citations in notes are often incomplete or wrong.

Some publishers are moving toward supplying notes and bibliographies of books separately on a Web site. Court describes the experience of the University of Toronto Press in this practice, and lists both advantages and disadvantages (Court 2002: 47). The more credible advantages he describes include making the bibliographies searchable, and providing full-text files for some citations. Among the disadvantages are the potential permanence of location (URL), and even the technology itself. Henige notes the same problems of impermanence, as well as inconvenience to the reader, and inaccessibility of the Web to readers in Africa (Henige 2002a: 79-80). Court lists "advantages" that are arguably anything but beneficial. From the publishers' point of view, his first item–low cost–may be enough to sway the decision to go electronic. His assertion that "only a small proportion of a book's readers consult its notes and bibliography" (Court 2002: 47) pretty much dismisses the research process as irrelevant, an odd position for an historian and archivist writing on the policies of a university press (Court 2002: 51). The practice of putting bibliographies and notes in a separate online file may cause problems for researchers. The assumption that few read the notes or consult bibliographies is a much greater threat to scholarship itself.

These larger issues have the potential for major problems in scholarly publishing, but even smaller errors, whether carelessness, citation style, or deliberate misinformation, are still troublesome. Citation styles that call for authors' initials rather than the full name do readers a disservice, as explored in earlier sections. Whatever style is used, the author should determine the correct form of the surname, and spell it correctly. Page numbers are too often left off citations, or only the first page is noted. This keeps a researcher from determining if the work cited is a brief note or a substantial article. It also makes ILL requests far more difficult. The whole title of the book or article is necessary, and if the journal title is abbreviated, a key to those abbreviations should be included (Henige 1989: 12).

No one is immune from mistakes. David Henige, who frequently criticizes authors who fail to include keys to abbreviations, slipped up in his 2001 article "Reviewing Reviewing." He refers to the online review database BCMR, but fails to spell out the title or give a URL (Henige 2001d: 23). The acronym turned out to be BMCR (*Bryn Mawr Classical Review*, http://ccat.sas.upenn.edu/bmcr/), but it took some digging before I was finally able to look at the item he cited.

Researchers will often come to the library expecting to find reports and other publications to which newspaper articles and media broadcasts refer. These may be government documents, articles in medical journals, or findings of research institutes. As Altshiller points out, attributions such as "a study in a medical journal recently reported" are of scant help to readers who want to find the actual article (Altshciller 2002: 70).

Besides the citations and footnotes, accuracy is needed in the actual quotes and paraphrases of the material cited. As an author, it is frustrating to recall a perfect quote to make a point, but be unable to locate the source and confirm the wording. Editors once had fact checkers to follow up on these matters. In ASL, we were once asked to verify a San tale about Mantis and the creation of earth, which Carl Sagan had used in an article scheduled for publication in *Reader's Digest*. Without verification from some source, use of such a folkloric example would be colorful writing, but dubious and perhaps harmful scholarship. To be sure, with folklore, even a published verification of a story or proverb does not guarantee validity since so much depends on how the tale was collected, transcribed, translated, and interpreted. Few publishers do thorough fact checking these days, much less observe the niceties of attributing folk literature.

Ellipses are used to indicate the omission of words, presumably irrelevant or unnecessary for the point being made, in the sentence or passage quoted. They are honestly used to save space and to stay focused on a point, but can all too frequently be used dishonestly. Most readers tend to suspect them in ads for movies quoting reviews. What negatives might ellipses before or after words like "breathtaking . . . ," ". . . astonishing" hide from view? Librarians do not censor, and refrain from labeling works in the collections, but surely we should be pointing out to students the need to be cautious readers. When I was working my way through graduate school by typing theses, one client used a quotation to support an important point. The footnote included not only the citation, but also the parenthetical notice: "The author has added the word 'not' to this sentence." If readers, as Court asserts, do not read the notes, no one would notice that the thesis writer had edited the quote to mean the opposite of the original statement! Henige cites a reviewer who informed readers "the translation of a century-old ethnographic work gratuitously added a word–a word that by itself buttresses a hypothesis by the translator that otherwise lacks robust textual support" (Henige 2001d: 34, 36 [note]).

How much are these matters the concern or the responsibility of reference librarians? The answer depends on the role that libraries and librarians play in teaching students how to conduct research, and that role can differ from institution to institution. Even when librarians are consigned to relatively passive roles, their teaching limited to use of catalogs and indexes, they are still on the front line helping researchers sort out the messes created by scholarly writers who misquote, mis-cite, and ill serve other scholars by other sins of either omission or commission. Henige sums up the scholar's responsibility: ". . . quoting is simply a particularly explicit example of sound scholarship–tangible attention to the small things from which larger things derive" (Henige 2002a: 70). It is the sum total of all of those things, small and large, from typographical errors to deliberate misrepresentation, that can mean the difference between successful and failed research.

GUIDEBOOKS AND TRAVELERS' AID ON THE ROAD TO RESEARCH ON AFRICA

The first four sections of this paper have identified and discussed obstacles to successful research on Africa. Some of these problems are specific to the subject, but many others are more generic, affecting library research on any topic. Despite the dismaying situation described, the prospect is far from hopeless. The Africana Librarians Council (ALC) and other groups and individuals have created many guides and aids for researchers. During its forty-five year existence, the main purpose of the ALC has been aiding research on Africa. Its report, *Opportunities and Challenges in Africana Library Service: A Framework for Cooperation and Development* (http://people.bu.edu/gwalsh/alc-coop.html), describes initiatives that reflect the purposes of the ALC outlined in its By-Laws (http://lcweb.loc.gov/rr/amed/7bylaws.html):

- Provide information related to acquiring resources for those whom the members serve.
- Encourage research and publication with the intent of making Africana resource materials in all formats more accessible.

In its early days, the ALC was more concerned with technical services–collection development and cataloging–than with reference and public services. To a great extent, of course, *all* library service is public service; what goes on behind the scenes is the foundation for reference and research service. Thus the undertakings of the ALC in cataloging and collection development have helped to achieve successful research and reference service.

Cataloging

Many of the problems noted in the previous sections involve cataloging and related issues. ALC's Cataloging Committee has addressed many of these concerns, particularly in subject headings and name authority. Africana catalogers work collectively, through the Committee's "Subject Heading Funnel Project," with the Library of Congress to develop and refine subject headings for African languages, ethnic groups, and other topics. Individual Africana catalogers alert LC to errors and anomalies in authority records for African personal and corporate names. (For reports of these and other accomplishments and projects, see http://lcweb.loc.gov/rr/amed/catcte.html.) The ALC Cataloging Committee has also compiled a directory of persons with African language expertise who can assist with cataloging African language materials, which often languish in backlogs.

Collection Development

The mechanics of collection development are often considered distinct from reference activities, but its product–the collection–is the foundation of research and the reference service that aids it. Without a collection, either on site or reasonably accessible by researchers, no library research could be done. ALC members have made efforts to provide advice on how best to represent Africa in general collections, but their specialized experience can sometimes get in the way. Building a collection on Africa in a large research library is quite a different undertaking than developing a core collection for an undergraduate library. Discussions of collection development at ALC meetings tend to focus on the problems that member libraries–with fairly large budgets–encounter in identifying and acquiring obscure publications from Africa, while a collection officer for an undergraduate library needs to learn what resources could be purchased with the few thousand dollars per year allocated to build a reference and general collection on Africa.

In the 1980s Nancy Schmidt compiled several lists of Africana works recommended for community colleges. These appeared in the *Newsletter* of the Pacific Coast Africanist Association, and were later published in *ASA News* (Schmidt 1986 and 1989). John Howell's 1989 article, "Creating a Standard List Online of Books on African Studies for Undergraduate Libraries and Keeping It Up-to-Date," proposed basing a list on several existing bibliographies, and using the "invisible college" of American Africana bibliographers to keep it up-to-date via computer. The lists he suggested were:

- Paden, John N. and Edward W. Soja. 1970. "Bibliography," volume 3 of *The African Experience.*
- Duignan, Peter. 1971. *Africa South of the Sahara: A Bibliography for Undergraduate Libraries.*
- Hartwig, Gerald W. 1974. *The Student Africanist's Handbook: A Guide to Resources.*
- Gosebrink, Jean Meeh. 1986. "Bibliography and Sources for African Studies," in *Africa* edited by Phyllis M. Martin and Patrick O'Meara (Howell 1989: 115).

The last title is updated by Nancy Schmidt's "Africana Resources for Undergraduates: A Bibliographic Essay" in the 1995 3rd edition of *Africa*, edited by Phyllis Martin and Patrick O'Meara, which is available online: http://www.indiana.edu/%7Elibsalc/african/schmidt.html. Howell notes in his paper that the first three bibliographies on his list were out of date at the time. In the 1980s the Library of Congress published *U.S. Imprints on Sub-Saharan Africa: A Guide to Publications Cataloged at the Library of Congress*. This project was dropped in 1992. While it proved to be of limited use as a selection tool, the lists did demonstrate the extent of U.S. publishing on Africa, averaging some 800 titles annually from academic, commercial, and small presses.

African imprints, especially primary sources such as government documents and newspapers, are an essential component of specialized collections supporting research on Africa. Books and magazines published in Africa should, as much as possible, also be represented in more general collections. One tool to help general libraries identify significant African imprints for their collections is *Africa's 100 Best Books of the 20th Century* (http://www.columbia.edu/cu/lweb/indiv/africa/cuvl/Afbks.html). This was a project undertaken by the Zimbabwe International Book Fair (http://www.zibf.org/), along with associations of African publishers (http://www.africanpublishers.org/). The 100 Best Books site also provides suggestions for librarians and teachers who wish to incorporate African books into their work. The quarterly *African Book Publishing Record* features reviews of African publications, as well as listings of recent publications. *Choice* and several scholarly Africana journals regularly carry reviews of African publications if they are reasonably available in the U.S. Since its establishment, the African Books Collective (http://www.africanbookscollective.com/), a consortium of African publishers, has been the most reliable vendor for African publications. It now has affiliated with Michigan State University Press for distribution. Additional help for libraries wishing to add African imprints to their collections can be found in lists of publishers, dealers, and vendors at sites such as:

- http://www.columbia.edu/cu/lweb/indiv/africa/cuvl/Aflibrarian.html
- http://www-sul.stanford.edu/depts/ssrg/africa/afrbook.html

as well as in several publications by Hans Zell:

- *The African Publishing Companion: A Resource Guide*
- *The African Studies Companion: A Resource Guide & Directory*
- *The Electronic African Bookworm: A Web Navigator.*

Magazines for Libraries includes a section recommending journals from and about Africa for both specialized and more general collections. This list includes journals and annuals that are invaluable reference tools, such as *Africa South of the Sahara*, published by Europa, and *Africa Contemporary Record*, published by Holmes and Meier.

Once an annual publication, the latter has slowed down, so that the current volume covers 1996-1998, and appeared in January 2003. At close to $500 each, these works may be big budget items, but are well worth the cost.

Members of ALC compile an annual list of bibliographies and reference works on Africa for the *African Book Publishing Record.* The African Studies Association's Conover-Porter award for outstanding achievement in Africana bibliography and reference tools was instituted by the ALC and is selected by a committee of ALC members. A list of award winners from 1980 to 2002 can be found at http://lcweb.loc.gov/rr/amed/c-p%20award%201980-02.html, along with procedures for nominations. The newsletter of the Africana Librarians Council, *Africana Libraries Newsletter*, is a forum for sharing information on new works and resources, as well as articles and notices pertaining to ALC activities (http://www.indiana.edu/%7Elibsalc/african/aln/index.html). There are several recent guides to reference works:

- *Reference Guide to Africa: A Bibliography of Sources* by Al Kagan and Yvette Scheven. This is used as a text for some courses on Africana bibliography. It lists and discusses reference works by broad topic and genre.
- *Africa: A Guide to Reference Material*, by John McIlwaine. This compendium arranges works by geographic region and country, as well as broad topic.

Both of these guides are valuable tools for determining what reference works may help with research, and can be used to build a reference collection, even though many items mentioned are now out of print.

An initiative of Ken Lohrentz, Africana bibliographer at the University of Kansas, may prove to be a model for outreach from Africana libraries to more general libraries. With funding from the Title VI grant, Lohrentz held a regional Africana collection development conference in April 2002. This meeting resulted in the establishment of MPALA, the Mountain-Plains Region Africana Libraries Association. Its objectives include sharing information on Africana references sources and other information resources, building collections cooperatively, and improving shared access. A description can be found on the University of Kansas African Studies Web site: http://www.ku.edu/~asrc/resources/atc/newsletter/Newsletter%20spr%2002/africana%20library.htm.

What Reference Books Should Be Written?

The lists described above indicate that many reference works on Africa have been published and many are still available. Are there enough? Do the works available meet the needs of students and other researchers? Many reference works, while of high quality, are out of date, and new editions or treatments of the topic have not been published. The ALC has compiled a list of over twenty works (http://lcweb.gov/rr/amed/bibpr.html) that need updating. This list, published in *ASA News* (Schmidt 1993), includes both general works and books on specific topics published from the 1960s through the 1980s. It does not address the question of what additional works might be needed, but have never been written.

Publishers are usually attentive to what librarians say they want by way of reference works, since libraries are their principal customers. But specialist African studies libraries comprise a market too small to have much clout. The figures in the first section of this paper supported the hypothesis that thousands of students nationwide might be doing research on Africa, but the numbers of institutions totaled only a few hundred. Even if every institution or organization with an interest in Africa had a library with a generous budget for reference works on Africa–and they do not–the market would still be small by most standards. Hans Zell, a noted publisher of reference works and bibliographies on Africa whose books have won many Conover-Porter awards for excellence, has frequently voiced his concern over low sales, most recently in an e-mail exchange on the Africana librarians' listserv. In a January 2002 message, he noted that Bernth Lindfors' update (1992-1996) of his *Black African Literature in English* bibliography had yet to reach sales figures of 200 copies in the year following production, compared with sales of nearly 700 copies of earlier editions. There are a number of possible reasons for these low sales, but even sales of 700 copies might not attract most major publishers to an African reference project.

Reference Works Online

Publishers of print reference works are concerned about competition with online resources, and many are converting print works to online products to satisfy what is seen as a market trend. Ideally these two formats should complement each other, rather than compete, since each has its advantages for researchers. There are several good guides to online reference sources for Africa:

- Stanford University's *Africa South of the Sahara*: http://www-sul.stanford.edu/depts/ssrg/africa/ency.html
- Peter Limb's *Africa from A to Z*: http://www.lib.msu.edu/limb/a-z/az.html

Among the online reference sources that are good for basic facts are:

- The Library of Congress' *Country Studies*: http://lcweb2.loc.gov/frd/cs/cshome.html#toc
- The CIA's *World Factbook*: http://www.odci.gov/cia/publications/factbook/
- The State Department's *Background Notes*: http://www.state.gov/r/pa/ei/bgn/

Online reference products are not automatically more desirable or more effective than print resources. "Searchability" can be an advantage, but frequently researchers beginning work on a topic they know little about simply do not know enough to be able to formulate productive searches.

Some reference works that have gone online have actually become less useful for students than they were in print, as least in the experience of ASL. One case is the *Country Reports* and *Country Profiles* published by the Economist Intelligence Unit. The print versions of this extremely expensive series were excellent as an introduction to a country, particularly when read in conjunction with the "Recent History" and "Economy" essays for each country in *Africa South of the Sahara*. The undergraduates–and even more advanced scholars–who sat down and read these overviews then had enough background knowledge to formulate the queries and search strategies needed for further research. The online version is searchable, and designed to respond to keyword queries with a selection of text passages. When students have to devise searches without the requisite background knowledge, they are more likely to fail.

To be sure, the online version does allow researchers to read the full text of the *Country Reports* and *Country Profiles* on the screen. Students who take this option then want to print it out–with the print cost passed from EIU to the student or the library, which has already paid handsomely for the online version. If *Africa South of the Sahara* also goes online, students will have no reliable concise introduction to African countries in print format.

The entries in general encyclopedias can serve as an introduction to some extent, although most of these are also online products, so have the same problem of costly printing by users. Often, however, professors scorn encyclopedias, or outright forbid students' use of them. This seems to be a misunderstanding of the role encyclopedias and other general reference tools can play in providing the background and orientation students need to begin solid research. Professors' scorn can be understood, since many researchers don't fully understand the concept of primary, secondary, and tertiary resources. It's not just students at fault: a consultant preparing an environmental impact statement on oil drilling off the shore of Nigeria once called ASL because he had photocopied a "key article," but had failed to take down the citation. The "key article" turned out to be from the *Encyclopedia Britannica.*

Indexes

When beginning a research project, most students go immediately to databases indexing journal articles, preferably those with full text. Johnsen has asserted that "[t]he big commercial databases, for instance the ISI or the OCLC First Search databases, do the job of covering all the important journals much more comprehensively than any single compiler could ever dream of" (Johnsen 1998: 67). However, several difficulties Africanist researchers may encounter have been discussed earlier, including:

- the quality of the entries
- difficulties inherent in African names and terminology
- the need for sufficient understanding of the topic before a good search strategy can be devised.

Additionally, one cannot simply make the assumption that "all of the important journals" are covered. A significant body of Africanist research is not covered in the major indexes because it is outside the mainstream. Journals and reports published in Africa or by research and other organizations worldwide are not indexed in the major services. Generally speaking, ASL staff will suggest going to specialized indexes first, and then to more general services. Many of these specialized indexes are offered free of charge on the Web.

- *African Periodicals Bibliography Database*: http://www.africabib.org is the database ASL staff direct most users to first. It covers some 300 journals pertaining to Africa, with over 46,000 citations. It is free of charge, easy to use, focused on Africa, and generally covers journals that are in our collection or easily available via ILL. This project, directed by Davis Bullwinkle, director of the Research Library of the Institute for Economic Advancement on the campus of the University of Arkansas-Little Rock, began as an in-house bibliography. This site also features the *African Women's Bibliographic Database*, and a link to *DISA, Digital Imaging Project of South Africa* (http://www.africabib.org/DISA.html), which provides tables of contents and full text for journals from the anti-apartheid struggle.

- The Library of Congress' *Quarterly Index of African Periodical Literature*: http://lcweb2.loc.gov/misc/qsihtml/ covers 300 journals published in Africa that are acquired regularly by the Library of Congress' Nairobi Field Office. This online service complements the print version: *Quarterly Index to Africana Periodical Literature*.
- H-Africa's Table of Contents service: http://www2.h-net.msu.edu/~africa/toc/ provides links to the Web sites of an array of Africanist journals, some of which include tables of contents, and links to the logs of TOCs which have been posted to H-Africa. The list also includes a link to the logs of "TOC: Non-Africanist Journals," postings of articles pertaining to Africa in a variety of journals. This site is not searchable.
- *African Abstracts Online*: http://asc.leidenuniv.nl/library/abstracts/asa-online is the free, online continuation of the print journal. At present the issues are in pdf files, but a browsable product is planned. A searchable database of the journal and its predecessor, *Documentieblad*, is available on the NISC database *African Studies*, described below.
- The NISC databases: *African Studies*, *South African Studies*, and *African Healthline* (http://www.nisc.com/) are subscription-based eclectic collections of databases developed by a wide variety of institutions, including libraries, research institutes, and commercial companies.

Indexes in print format:

- *International African Bibliography*, a quarterly index of books, articles, and papers. It is arranged by geographic area and country, indexed by subject and author.
- *Africa Bibliography*, an annual index of books and articles arranged by subject under geographic divisions. Indexed by author

and subject. Usually contains an essay on African publishing, the book trade, or libraries.

- *A Current Bibliography on African Affairs*, a quarterly index of articles arranged by subject, with an author, subject, and regional index.

ALC has done a comparison of coverage of six print indexes (two of them now online) at http://lcweb.loc.gov/rr/amed/bibcli.html. The indexes include:

- *International African Bibliography*. London: International African Institute, 1971-
- *Quarterly Index to Periodical Literature, Eastern and Southern Africa*. Nairobi, Kenya: Library of Congress Office, 1991- (also online)
- *Africa Bibliography*. Manchester, England: Manchester University Press, 1984-
- *African Studies Abstracts*. London: Hans Zell Publishers, 1994- formerly Rijksuniversiteit te Leiden. Afrika-Studiecentrum: Documentatieblad. (also online)
- *Index of African Social Science Periodical articles*. Dakar: CODESRIA (Council for the Development of Economic and Social Research in Africa), 1989-
- *A Current Bibliography on African Affairs*. Washington, DC: Greenwood Periodicals for the African Bibliographic Center, 1973-

This comparison showed that there was remarkably little overlap among the indexes. Researchers wishing to cover "everything" need to consult as many of these as possible.

Few of the journals covered in these indexes are covered in the large indexing services. This situation is changing, however. Several projects are underway to increase the availability of African journals worldwide by putting them on the Web. One of these projects is sponsored by the International Network for the Availability of Scientific Publications (INASP). *African Journals Online* (AJOL) at http://www.inasp.org.uk/ajol/ provides the tables of contents and abstracts of articles for more than fifty African journals, mostly in the sciences, but also in the social sciences. A pilot project is underway to publish entire journals online. Michigan State University's African E-Journal Project (AEJP) works with African publishers to go online. The first arrangement with Project Muse encountered some problems, and an alternative arrangement is being worked out with Michigan State University Press. Information on this project can be found at http://www.isp.msu.edu/AfricanStudies/asc_side.htm.

Dissertations and Theses

Dissertation Abstracts is an essential tool for doctoral candidates as well as many other researchers. Except for scattered lists of dissertations done on particular topics at individual universities, no comparable service existed for African dissertations until a joint project of the Association of African Universities, the Ford Foundation, and the Rockefeller Foundation developed the Database of African Theses and Dissertations (DATAD) http://www.aau.org/datad/. An ambitious project, DATAD could be a welcome development for African and foreign scholars alike. African scholarship can move into the mainstream and take its rightful place as a primary interpreter of African history and life. Not all research done in African universities, of course, focuses on Africa, and it is perhaps even more important for African scholars with non-African specialties to have wider recognition. DATAD is a subscription database.

Various lists provide access to U.S. dissertations on Africa for those who want either a compilation of theses produced at one institution or simply find it easier to browse a current awareness list of theses pertaining only to Africa. A list arranged by broad topic appears regularly in *ASA News*, compiled by Joe Lauer of Michigan State University. A guide to online and print resources on dissertations worldwide is available at http://www-sul.stanford.edu/depts/ssrg/africa/theses.html.

Access to Collections

Prior to the advent of OCLC, WorldCat and online catalogs, the holdings of library collections were accessible to researchers only by visiting or consulting printed catalogs. Recognizing the need for some guidance for Africanist researchers working far from the major centers for the field, ALC members and others put together some guides:

- Duignan, Peter. *Handbook of American Resources for African Studies*. [Stanford, Calif.]: Hoover Institution on War, Revolution, and Peace, Stanford University. 1967.
- Bhatt, Purnima Mehta. *Scholars' Guide to Washington, D.C. for African Studies*. Washington: Smithsonian Institution Press, 1980.

- Nyquist, Corinne and Leon P. Spencer. *The Lonely Africanist: A Guide to Selected U.S. Africana Libraries for Researchers*. [Los Angeles: African Studies Association, 1984].
- *African Studies Information Resources Directory* compiled and edited by Jean E. Meeh Gosebrink. Oxford: Published for the African Studies Association [by] Hans Zell, 1986.
- Zell, Hans M. *The African Studies Companion: A Resource Guide & Directory* London: H. Zell, 1989.
- *International Directory of African Studies Research*. Edited by the International African Institute; compiled by Philip Baker. London; New York: H. Zell, 1994.

An online guide to Africana libraries can be found at:

- Africa South of the Sahara
  http://www-sul.stanford.edu/depts/ssrg/africa/libs.html

Library Web Sites

The Web sites developed and maintained by Africana libraries not only link to catalogs and guides to their collections, but often provide an array of bibliographies, research tools, and other aids to research. Sites of ALC institutions include:

Boston University African Studies Library
http://www.bu.edu/library/asl/home.html

Includes guides to specialized portions of the print and electronic collections (http://www.bu.edu/library/eresources/eafricanstudies.htm), tutorials and research guides.

Columbia University
http://www.columbia.edu/cu/lweb/indiv/africa/

Includes a guide to Web resources:

(http://www.columbia.edu/cu/lweb/indiv/africa/cuvl/)

and research guides:

- *African Civilizations*
- *International Conflict Resolution*

- *Maps & Power in Modern African History*
- *Swahili Acquisitions at Columbia*

Cornell University John Henrik Clarke Africana Library
http://www.library.cornell.edu/africana/

Includes *Sankofa*, the Africana Library newsletter, and links to related Web sites.

Duke University
http://www.lib.duke.edu/ias/africa/

Includes a guide to African studies resources in the Duke University Libraries, and links to pertinent Web sites.

Harvard University
http://www-hcl.harvard.edu/widener/collections/sub_saharan_africa.html

Tozzer Library
http://hcl.harvard.edu/tozzer/

Howard University Moorland-Spingarn Research Center
http://www.founders.howard.edu/moorland-spingarn/

Includes the Moorland-Spingarn Archives electronic newsletter, *HU ArchivesNet*.

Indiana University
http://www.indiana.edu/%7Elibsalc/african/

Includes links to Web sites, including "favorites" suggested by faculty and students; guides to special portions of the collection, and "*Africana Resources for Undergraduates: A Bibliographic Essay*" by Nancy J. Schmidt, reprinted from Phyllis M. Martin and Patrick O'Meara (eds.), *Africa*. Third edition. Bloomington: Indiana University Press, 1995: 413-434.

Library of Congress African and Middle East Reading Room
http://lcweb.loc.gov/rr/amed/

Includes country guides and links to selected Web sites.

Michigan State University Africana Library
http://www.lib.msu.edu/coll/main/africana/

New York University
http://www.nyu.edu/library/bobst/research/soc/africa/

Contains research guides and links to selected Web sites, arranged in categories.

Northwestern University Melville J. Herskovits Library of African Studies
http://www.library.northwestern.edu/africana/

Contains links to catalogs of specialized materials in the collection, including the electronic poster collection, the Conference Paper Index, the Africana Vertical Index, and the Timbuktu Archives as well as links to selected Web sites and reference resources.

Ohio University
http://www.library.ohiou.edu/subjects/africa/asubmain.htm

Contains guides to materials in the collection, including the depositories of government publications from Botswana and Swaziland.

Princeton University
http://www.princeton.edu/~pressman/africa.html

Contains links to selected Web sites.

Rutgers University
http://www.libraries.rutgers.edu/rul/rr_gateway/research_guides/africana/africana.shtml

Contains a guide to reference works, descriptions of special portions of the collection as well as links to related Web sites.

Schomburg Center for Research in Black Culture (NYPL)
http://www.nypl.org/research/sc/sc.html

Contains exhibits and guides to special collections.

Smithsonian Institution, Warren M. Robbins Library, National Museum of African Art
http://www.sil.si.edu/libraries/nmafa-hp.htm

Includes extensive links to Web sites related to African art.

Stanford University
http://www-sul.stanford.edu/depts/ssrg/africa/africa.html

The Library's site provides guides to Stanford's collection. The librarian, Karen Fung, also created and maintains *Africa South of the Sahara* (http://www-sul.stanford.edu/depts/ssrg/africa/guide.html), the most comprehensive and well-organized guide to Web sites pertaining to Africa.

SUNY-Albany
http://library.albany.edu/subject/africana%5Fmain.html

Includes a monthly list of new titles and links to electronic resources.

University of California–Berkeley
http://www.lib.berkeley.edu/Collections/Africana/

Includes links to selected Web sites.

UCLA
http://www.library.ucla.edu/libraries/url/colls/ssafrica/index.htm

Includes links to selected Web sites.

University of Florida
http://web.uflib.ufl.edu/cm/africana/

Contains research guides to African women writers and a bibliography of theses and dissertations on Africa completed at the University of Florida from 1956 through 2000.

University of Illinois Africana Reading Room
http://www.afrst.uiuc.edu/Library/lib.html

Contains lists of recent acquisitions, numerous research guides (http://www.afrst.uiuc.edu/Library/lib.html#REF), and a list of theses and dissertations completed at the University of Illinois from 1921 to 2000. The Center for African Studies site (http://www.afrst.uiuc.edu/) also contains links to sites useful for research.

University of Iowa
http://www.uiowa.edu/%7Eintl/ACAD/ASP/ASP_libresources.html

The University of Iowa also hosts the *Electronic Journal of Africana Bibliography* (http://sdrc.lib.uiowa.edu/ejab/) which features bibliographic essays and bibliographies on a variety of topics.

University of Kansas
http://www.lib.ku.edu/wantsonref/area.htm#africa

University of Michigan
http://www.lib.umich.edu/grad/guide/guide.php?id=60

University of Pennsylvania
http://oldsite.library.upenn.edu/resources/subject/area/africa/africa.html

Guides to the collections at University of Pennsylvania and links to related sites. The site of the African Studies Center links to extensive research sites for African studies.

Yale University
http://www.library.yale.edu/african/

Contains a variety of guides to Yale collections and to Internet resources on Africa.

Primary Sources: Guides and Full Text

Primary sources are an important part of research for undergraduates as well as established scholars. Frequently "primary sources" are thought of as manuscripts, letters, etc., housed in archival collections, but they can also include newspapers, government documents, and commentary published at the time of an event. Boston University has a tutorial under construction defining types of primary sources for Africanist research, and providing aids for finding materials in library collections and on the Web. It will be available on the African Studies Library Web site when it is complete (http://www.bu.edu/library/asl/home.html).

Africa Research Central (http://www.africa-research.org/mainframe.html) is a gateway to archives, libraries, and museums with important collections of African primary sources. It has a searchable database of primary resource repositories in Africa, and an alphabetic list of repositories in Europe and North America. Links are given for those repositories with Web sites. The Cooperative Africana Microforms Project (http://www.crl.edu/areastudies/CAMP/index.htm) is a major source for primary research materials. Items in the collection can be borrowed via interlibrary loan by members of CAMP or CRL.

Digitization of unique or rare materials makes them accessible to researchers, no matter where they are or what the strengths of their libraries might be. Some of these resources may be offered free of charge, such as the Timbuktu Manuscript Digitization Project, which aims at preserving the manuscripts of the Mamma Haidara library in Timbuktu. The library was featured on Henry Louis Gates' TV special, *Wonders of the African World* (http://www.pbs.org/wonders/fr_e5.htm), and is described on several Web sites, including: (http://www.crl.edu/areastudies/CAMP/collections/timbuktu.htm) and (http://pubweb.nwu.edu/%7Ejhunwick/haidara.html).

Another source for primary text online is the University of Wisconsin's Africana Digitization Project (http://libtext.library.wisc.edu/Africana/). Eight texts of works written between 1526 and 1680 have been digitized. Most of these have been edited and otherwise prepared for the digital format. The text can be searched by keyword.

Newspapers

Newspapers are an important primary source for many kinds of research. This rich source of information, however, makes for a collection that is difficult to manage. Subscriptions are often haphazardly fulfilled; the paper deteriorates quickly, and few African newspapers are indexed to any degree. Many African newspapers are now accessible online, at least for current issues. A particularly useful guide is "Electronic Journals and Newspapers on Africa": http://www.columbia.edu/cu/lweb/indiv/africa/ejournals.html.

The ALC is developing a union list of African newspaper holdings called Afrinul (http://www.crl.edu/areastudies/CAMP/afrinul.htm). Currently the site only lists the holdings of the few libraries that participated in the pilot project, but shortly Afrinul will include newspaper holdings of all North American libraries. There are few, if any, indexes to articles in African newspapers.

Bibliographies

It is probably clear to any reader of this paper that I do not agree with Johnsen's contention that there is no need for special bibliographies for African topics because the big databases do the job better. Students need specialized bibliographies to help them get started, and to get at the books and articles that would not be found with most search strategies because the words used in the title, descriptors, or subject headings did not include the search terms used by the researcher. The real problem is getting those bibliographies to the researchers who need them. Besides book-length works, good bibliographies may be in the backs of scholarly books, published as journal articles, or posted online. They could, in short, be as elusive as the works to which they might guide the researcher. Probably the most complete lists of bibliographies for African studies are those compiled by Yvette Scheven covering more than 20 years of publication:

- *Bibliographies for African studies, 1970-1975*
- *Bibliographies for African studies 1970-1986*
- *Bibliographies for African studies, 1976-1979*
- *Bibliographies for African studies, 1980-1983*
- *Bibliographies for African studies, 1987-1993*

The late John Howell inaugurated an electronic collection of bibliographies and bibliographical essays: *Electronic Journal of African Bibliography*, http://sdrc.lib.uiowa.edu/ejab/. Bibliography projects are regularly announced at the meetings of the Bibliography Committee of the ALC: http://lcweb.loc.gov/rr/amed/bibcte.html.

Surfing the Tangled Web: A Mixed Metaphor for a Mixed Blessing

Librarians and educators alike view with alarm the apparent tendency for researchers at all levels to turn first to electronic resources rather than to a library to find information. Even more disturbing is the assumption of many administrators that this trend signals the end of the need for traditional libraries, leading them to allocate funds accordingly. Some of the ambivalence about the use of the Web in research is reflected in the terms used to describe it. Researchers tend to use the words "Web" and "Internet" interchangeably, and attach different meanings and connotations to the terms than either librarians or computer technicians would assume. Perhaps the most troublesome aspect of muddled terminology is a form of metonymy–a figure of speech in which the container denotes the thing contained. The Web is a *means* of disseminating information, but most people speak of it as if "Internet" and "Web" were the information itself. Because the content of the Web is diverse, including library catalogs, commercially produced bibliographic and informational databases, scholarly writing, and individual postings of all kinds, research on the Web can yield both gold and dross.

The gold is a great benefit indeed to researchers on Africa, particularly when they are distant from specialized library collections. Distance is no longer a constraint. One can sit in Flagstaff, Arizona, and search the catalogs of SOAS, Bordeaux, or the University of Botswana. One can now search WorldCat by author, title, or keyword and get citations from the catalog records of thousands of libraries nationwide and worldwide–more than 32 million records. Government agencies and NGOs can publish papers and reports directly on their Web sites, avoiding the costs of printing and distribution. Thus a great deal of "grey literature" that was once so difficult to obtain is now widely accessible.

The dross to be found on the Web hardly needs description or explanation to reference librarians. Many students, and even some faculty tend to take Web sources at face value without applying any critical analysis at all. Often doing a Google search yields thousands of entries. For example, "Great Zimbabwe" is the name of impressive ruins of large stone structures in Zimbabwe. A Google search yields 11,200 entries when the terms are enclosed in quotation marks to ensure a search for the phrase rather than the words in any position. (Without the quotation marks, the search yielded 1,060,000 results.) While the first dozen or so provide nice photographs and seemingly good text, a check of the site developers indicated a wide range of sources, including a PBS *Nova* transcript, the abstract of an article in the journal *Archaeology*, a site providing information on postcolonial and post imperial literature in English developed by faculty at Brown University and the University of Singapore, papers written by undergraduates at North Park University, and a Unesco report, among many others. Researchers would have to apply careful critical judgment in choosing which sites to mine for information.

The difference between dross and gold may lie in the search techniques and assumptions:

- "I need to find at least one primary source for a paper on Cecil Rhodes. I checked the Internet but couldn't find anything." The student had done her search for primary sources on Amazon.com.

After we made sure she understood what primary sources are, ASL staff worked with her to find works by Rhodes in our collection, and to find books and articles *about* him that were published during his lifetime.

- "I found a citation for a report on Mozambique done by a consultant to the British Department for International Development. Where can I find the report?" The paper was not in WorldCat. We found that the Department for International Development did have a Web site, but did not post their consultant's report. However, a search on Google for the consultant's name (fortunately a fairly unusual one) yielded a directory entry that seemed to be the right person, with an e-mail address in Mozambique. After some correspondence, the consultant sent a copy of the report to the student. This was an excellent example of combining the best of print and Internet capabilities.

All of the concerns described in detail in earlier sections of this paper are of even greater concern for researchers using the Web. Variations in personal and corporate names, the terminology used to designate topics, errors, and decisions about inclusion and coverage can cause trouble for novice or unwary researchers. Additionally, because of the freewheeling nature of the Web, developers of Web sites may have definite agendas that include promoting a point of view or theory, and providing disinformation to support it.

The World Wide Web has become the most popular but least understood means of looking for information for nearly all kinds of researchers. The student described in an earlier section of this paper wasted his time looking for the population of Dar es Salaam on the Web because a print reference work provided the information more quickly. But when a local pastor was looking for information on popular music in Madagascar, a few minutes on the Web got him to a page with a description of musical forms, interviews with popular performers, and photos of musical instruments, whereas our print bibliographies could only yield a few references to articles in journals we did not carry.

Excessive expectations of the Web's capabilities are causing alarm among academics and observers. David Miall comments: "The promise of the new medium has led to inflationary claims, suggesting that the human species is about to burst from its chrysalis into an information utopia" (Miall 200: 1405), and Ciolek cautions: "There are good reasons to believe that the unparalleled flowering and growth of the World Wide Web may ultimately prove to be a curse rather than a blessing"

(Ciolek 1997 http://www.educause.edu/pub/er/review/reviewArticles/32323.html). These comments may exaggerate the situation somewhat, but students are noticeably drifting away from conventional library resources rather than integrating Web resources into a research strategy that includes print resources.

There are several misconceptions about the Web, and while they affect all research, they are especially harmful to research on Africa. In the *Chronicle of Higher Education* Richard Berkman advised: ". . . don't limit your searches to the Web–most of the world's knowledge still remains in print" (Berkman 2000: B9). This is particularly true for African studies. Most information and scholarship about Africa is still only available in print, not as text on the Web. But because of the graphic and multimedia capabilities of the Web, examples of art, music, landscape, and daily life are widely accessible, conveying understanding far more effectively than more academic publications. Students have to come into the library to do real research, and they will have to do so for many years to come. We cannot lure them in simply by criticizing and disparaging the Internet as a research tool, and we won't do it by opening up coffee shops and entertainment centers.

Without doubt, the best guide to Web resources is *Africa South of the Sahara* (http://www-sul.stanford.edu/depts/ssrg/africa/guide.html). This site, developed and maintained by Stanford African studies librarian Karen Fung, has arranged annotated links to sites dealing with Africa into two large sections: "Topics" and "Countries/Regions." It's a gold mine. The *Digital Librarian* page "Africana: Resources on Africa" is also good, although much more scantily annotated. *Africa South of the Sahara* also has a section on evaluating Web resources, with links to sites and tutorials on using the Web and determining if the information found can be used safely.

Electronic Reference

Almost every library now offers an e-mail reference option. At Boston University, the rule that queries are answered only for BU students, faculty, and affiliates is waived for questions pertaining to Africa, which are referred to ASL staff. Most of the library sites listed earlier have similar services. Many libraries also participate in 24/7 reference services.

H-Africa has instituted an "Ask-a-librarian" service. The queries at first came directly to my personal e-mail address at BU, and I gathered a group of volunteers from ALC members to respond to them. It took a while to work out the most efficient logistics and queries still seem to be very general and often unrealistic, on the order of "send me all the information on women in Africa."

The H-Africa list itself functions rather more successfully as a collegial reference service. Frequently one of the librarians subscribing to the list responds to queries with resources and research strategies, and this advice is supplemented with suggestions from academic list members. The Ask-a-librarian service grew out of a professors' query on behalf of a student, which seemed to be bypassing basic library research. It sparked some interesting discussion on research strategies (http://www2.h-net.msu.edu/~africa/ Open "Discussion Logs" and go to November 2002). Non-members can post queries, and some librarians are taking advantage of this option. The history bibliographer at Boston University recently posted a query in hopes of tracking down a quote from Frantz Fanon.

ALC members who subscribe to H-Africa often refer questions from that list to the ALC list, thus broadening the base of expertise responding to the query. ALC members also use their list for the reference queries that stump them. Some ALC members are participating in QuestionPoint, and a recent query that had evidently been made by a publisher looking for the titles of literary works to include in an anthology raised a useful discussion of how these electronic services might be attracting commercial enterprises eager to have research done without the expense of hiring researchers.

Based on a successful pilot project, the Library of Congress' African Section has established an ongoing service to assist scholars. Researchers may select all or any of an array of East African countries for bibliographic updates on works recently cited in the Library of Congress catalog. (See http://lcweb.loc.gov/rr/amed/ for more information.) Many academic libraries operate formal or informal notifications to faculty of new titles received in their fields.

Teaching Africana Research Strategies

Formal courses in African studies bibliography and research strategies are taught at several institutions. Several of these have posted the syllabus and/or course materials on their Web sites:

- University of Illinois: http://alexia.lis.uiuc.edu/course/fall1996/433M.html

- Indiana University: http://www.indiana.edu/~libsalc/african/g732/gen.html
- University of Florida: http://www.uflib.ufl.edu/cm/africana/afs6905.htm

These postings can be useful for reference librarians in determining what resources to recommend or to add to their collections.

While only a few universities offer formal instruction in library research for course credit, most libraries offer tours, orientations, tutorials, and other group instruction. At Boston University we use every group and individual opportunity to teach students and other researchers how to incorporate the Web into an integrated research strategy that will yield good results. We do this in formal tutorials offered in conjunction with the Office of Information Technology each semester, and by posting those tutorials on the library Web sites. We also do library and research orientations tailored for specific courses, both in the library and in the classrooms, depending on the preference of the instructor. Currently we have:

- a general tutorial on Africa
- women in Africa
- peoples and cultures of Africa with an accompanying research guide for information in all formats
- the culture and arts of Africa
- a guide to finding primary and archival resources on the Web.

All of these tutorials can be found on the ASL Web site: http://www.bu.edu/library/asl/index.

Each of these tutorials emphasizes the role of the Web as a gateway to print, electronic, conventional, and other resources. Depending on the sophistication of the class, we touch briefly or at some depth on search strategies used in OPACs and WorldCat, and point out the links to other catalogs on the BU Libraries page (http://www.bu.edu/library/lib.html), and on the *Africa South of the Sahara* site (http://www-sul.stanford.edu/depts/ssrg/africa/libs.html). We always include some discussion of the resources at the Cooperative Africana Microform Project (CAMP), which BU students can borrow via ILL. Non-members of CAMP and CRL should read the information about borrowing these materials at the CAMP Web site: http://www.crl.edu/areastudies/CAMP/index.htm.

CONCLUSION

These are "interesting times" for libraries, with rapidly changing technology and assumptions about information and research. Are we headed for utopia or chaos and doom? The future of research and the libraries that support it depends on the combined efforts of those who produce information and knowledge, those who seek it, and the librarians, library administrators, and information specialists who link the producers with the seekers. While the study of Africa has special qualities and concerns, its future depends on this same combination of actors.

BIBLIOGRAPHY

Works Cited

Abbenyi, J. (2002) [message on H-Africa] March 19, 2002. http://www2.h-net.msu.edu/~africa/.

Alden, Patricia, David Lloyd, and Ahmed I. Samatar, eds. (1994) *African Studies and the Undergraduate Curriculum.* Boulder, CO: L. Rienner Publishers.

Alexander, Harriet (2001) "Searching the MLA International Bibliography: All, Nothing, or Something Between." *Reference and User Services Quarterly* 40(3): 228-233.

Altschiller, Donald (2002) "A Librarian's Plea to Journalists: Give Us a Clue!" *Columbia Journalism Review* 41(3): 70.

American Society of Indexers. *Frequently Asked Questions about Indexing.* http://www.asindexing.org/site/indfaq.shtml.

______. *Indexing Evaluation Checklist.* http://www.asindexing.org/site/checklist.shtml.

Anhang, Abe, and Steve Coffman (2002) "The Great Reference Debate" *American Libraries* 33(3): 50-54.

Ayres, F. H. (2001) "Authority Control Simply Does Not Work." *Cataloging & Classification Quarterly* 32(2): 49-59.

Azzolina, D. S. (1996) "Review of *The Peoples of Africa: An Ethnohistorical Dictionary.*" *Choice* 34(4): 593.

Bade, David (2002) *The Creation and Persistence of Misinformation in Shared Library Catalogs: Language and Subject Knowledge in a Technological Era.* Champaign, IL: Publications Office, Graduate School of Library and Information Science, University of Illinois at Urbana-Champaign.

Baker, Nicholson (2001) *Double Fold.* New York: Random House.

Baker, Philip, compiler (1994) *International Directory of African Studies Research.* 3rd edition. London; New York: H. Zell.

Bangalore, Nirmala S. and Judith A. Carter, eds. (1994) *Guide to Searching the Bibliographic Utilities for Conference Proceedings.* Chicago: Subject & Bibliographic

Access to Science Materials Committee, Science and Technology Section, Association of College and Research Libraries, American Library Association.

Barry, Randall (1987) *African Personal Names*. Memo for comments, Library of Congress. "... will be published in a future issue of *Cataloging Service Bulletin*."

Baumann, M. Garrett (2001) "The Devilments of Style." *Chronicle of Higher Education*. November 9: B5.

Beall, Jeffrey (2001) "Publishers' Errors Make Catalogers [sic]: An Analysis of the Error Indicators *[sic]* and *[i.e.]* in Cataloging." *Cataloging & Classification Quarterly* 32(3) 87-107.

Beidelman, T. O. (1997) "Review of *The Peoples of Africa: An Ethnohistorical Dictionary*." *International Journal of African Historical Studies* 30(3): 671-672.

Berkman, Richard (2000) "Internet Searching Is Not Always What It Seems." *Chronicle of Higher Education*, July 28: B9.

Berman, Sanford (1984) "Introduction: Subject Cataloging: Critiques and Innovations." *Technical Services Quarterly* 2(1/2): 1-2.

______. (1993) *Prejudices and Antipathies: A Tract on the LC Subject Headings Concerning People*. Jefferson, NC: McFarland and Company.

Bertelsen, Cynthia D. (1995) *Issues in Cataloging Non-Western Materials: Special Problems with African Language Materials*. http://filebox.vt.edu/users/bertel/Africana.html.

Bowman, J. H. (2001) "Sic Catalog Syndrome: Title Page Transcription as a Barrier to Retrieval." *Cataloging & Classification Quarterly* 32(1): 39-54.

Brubaker, Jana (2002) "Ambiguous Authorship and Uncertain Authenticity: A Cataloger's Dilemma." *Cataloging & Classification Quarterly* 34(4): 19-30.

Burbules, Nicholas C. (2001) "Paradoxes of the Web: The Ethical Dimensions of Credibility." *Library Trends*, 49(3): 441-453.

Carver, Amy L. (2002) "We Are All Reference Librarians: Using Communications to Employ a Philosophy of access for Catalogers." *College and Research Library News* 63(3): 168-170.

Ciolek, T. Matthew (1997) "Today's WWW, Tomorrow's MMM: The Specter of Multi-Media Mediocrity." *Educom Review* 32(3): 23-26 (http://www.educause.edu/pub/er/review/reviewArticles/32323.html).

Coelho, Jill (1998) "Summary of Discussion on Panel on Reference and Bibliographic Instruction." In: *Africana Librarianship in the 21st Century: Treasuring the Past and Building the Future: Proceedings of the 40th Anniversary Conference of the Africana Librarians Council*. Edited by Nancy J. Schmidt. Bloomington, IN: African Studies Program, Indiana University, 79-80.

Corley, Julie A. (1998) "Can the Web Really Do It All? Perceptions of Historical Research on the Internet." *The Public Historian* 20(1): 49-57.

Cox, Richard J. (2002) "Unfair Use: Advice to Unwitting Authors." *Journal of Scholarly Publishing* 34(1): 31-42.

Court, John P. M. (2002) "Bibliographies and Notes as a Separate Online Publication: A Novel Trend in Support of Scholarly Publishing." *Journal of Scholarly Publishing* 34(1): 43-52.

Dillon, Dennis (2001) "Songs of the Dodo: Information Extinctions, Innovation, and Ecosystem Change." *Journal of Library Administration* 35(3): p. 67-78.

Drabenstott, Karen M. (2000) "Web Search Strategies." In: *Saving the Time of the Library User Through Subject Access Innovation: Papers in Honor of Pauline Atherton Cochrane.* Edited by William J. Wheeler. Champaign, IL: Graduate School of Library and Information Science. 114-161.

Fister, Barbara (2002) "Fear of Reference." *Chronicle of Higher Education* June 14: B20.

Fugmann, Robert (2000) "Obstacles to Progress in Mechanized Subject Access and the Necessity of a Paradigm Change." In: *Saving the Time of the Library User Through Subject Access Innovation: Papers in Honor of Pauline Atherton Cochrane.* Edited by William J. Wheeler. Champaign, IL: Graduate School of Library and Information Science: 7-45.

Germano, William (2001a) "Choosing the Right Title for Your Book." *Chronicle of Higher Education* July 13: B6.

______. (2001b) *Getting It Published: A Guide for Scholars and Anyone Else Serious about Serious Books.* Chicago: University of Chicago Press.

______. (2001c) "Interview." *Chronicle of Higher Education* July 13: B6.

______. (2001d) "Untitled." *Chronicle of Higher Education,* June 22: B10-B11.

Gottschalk, Keith (2001) [Message to H-Africa, 16 Aug 2001] http://www2.h-net.msu.edu/~africa/ Guevara, Ernesto (1989) *Ausgewahlte Werke in Einzelausgaben.* Translated by Horst-Eckart Gross. Dortmund: Weltkreis.

Hauptman, Robert (1999) "Information Ethics." *Choice* 37(2): 261-273.

Hay, Margaret Jean, ed. (2000) *African Novels in the Classroom.* Boulder: Lynne Rienner Publishers.

Henige, David (1989) "Guidelines for Compiling African Bibliographies." *ASA News.* 22(4): 7-13.

______. (2001a) "Being Fair to the Hounds: The Function and Practice of Annotation." *History in Africa* 28: 95-127.

______. (2001b) "Mis/Adventures in Mis/Quoting." *Journal of Scholarly Publishing* 32(3): 123-135.

______. (2001c) "One-Eyed Men in the Kingdom of the Blind." (Review of *African States and Rulers* by John Stewart.) *History in Africa* 28: 395-404.

______. (2001d) "Reviewing Reviewing." *Journal of Scholarly Publishing* 33(1): 23-36.

______. (2002a) "Being Fair to the Hounds: The Function and Practice of Annotation, II." *History in Africa* 29: 63-88.

______. (2002b) "Indexing: A User's Perspective." *Journal of Scholarly Publishing* 33(4): 230-247.

Herring, Susan Davis (2001) "Using the World Wide Web for Research: Are Faculty Satisfied?" *Journal of Academic Librarianship* 27(3): 213-219.

Hoffman, Herbert H. (2000) "Improving Access for Works in Collections." *Technicalities* 20(6): 7-9.

Hoffman, Herbert H. (2002) "Library Practices with NINO." *Technicalities* 22(2): 1, 10.

Howell, John Bruce (1989) "Creating a Standard List Online of Books on African Studies for Undergraduate Libraries and Keeping It Up-to-Date." *Africana Resources and Collections: Three Decades of Development and Achievement* edited by Julian Witherell. Metuchen, NJ: Scarecrow Press: 109-117.

Jackson, Michael Gordon (2003) "The Great Reference Debate Continued–with a Manifesto." *American Libraries* 34(5): 50-52.

Johnsen, Tom (1998) "Africana Librarians on the Information Highway: Do We Need to Reconsider Our Directions?" In: *Africana Librarianship in the 21st century: Treasuring the Past and Building the Future: Proceedings of the 40th Anniversary Conference of the Africana Librarians Council.* Edited by Nancy J. Schmidt. Bloomington, IN: African Studies Program, Indiana University: 66-72.

Khurshid, Zahiruddin (2002) "Arabic Script Materials: Cataloging Issues and Problems." *Cataloging & Classification Quarterly* 34(4): 67-77.

Konovalov, Yuri (1999) "Cataloging as a Customer Service: Applying Knowledge to Technology Tools." *Information Outlook* 3(9): 25-27.

Lam, Vinh-The (2000) "Enhancing Subject Access to Monographs in Online Pubic Access Catalogs: Table of Contents Added to Bibliographic Records." In: *Saving the Time of the Library User Through Subject Access Innovation: Papers in Honor of Pauline Atherton Cochrane.* Edited by William J. Wheeler. Champaign, IL: Graduate School of Library and Information Science: 163-172.

Leonhardt, Thomas W. (2000) "Technical Services in the 21st Century." *Technicalities* 20(5): 1,12-13.

Limb, Peter (2002) "Accessing African Archives, Libraries and Journals: Partnerships, Ethics and Equity in the 21st Century." *African Research and Documentation* 90: 29-41.

Lohrentz, Kenneth (2002) *Regional Africana Library Conference On Reference And Collection Development.* http://www.ku.edu/~asrc/resources/atc/newsletter/Newsletter%20spr%2002/africana%20library.htm.

Marconi, Joseph V. (1976) *Indexed Periodicals: A Guide to 170 years of Coverage in 33 Indexing Services.* Ann Arbor, MI: Pierian Press.

McHenry, Robert (2002) "Where Have All the Proofreaders Gone?" *Chronicle of Higher Education*: B5.

Miall, David (2001) "The Library Versus the Internet: Literary Studies under Siege?" *PMLA* 116(5): 1405-1414.

Morris, Dilys, and Gregory Wool (1999) "Cataloging: Librarianship's Best Bargain." *Library Journal* 124(11): 44-46.

Page, Laverne (2002) "New Directions in Reference and Collections Development in Africana Collections in the United States." *African Research and Documentation* 90: 53-57.

Rana, Hanif M. and John A. Distefano, compilers (1987) *Directory of African and Afro-American Studies in the United States.* Los Angeles: African Studies Association.

"RUSA Guidelines. Guidelines for the Preparation of a Bibliography." (2001) *Reference and User Services Quarterly* 41(2): 115-117.

Schmidt, Nancy J. (1986) "Checklists for Updating Holdings on Africa in Community College Libraries." *ASA News* 19(1): 45-49.

______. (1989) "Checklist for Updating Holdings on Africa in Community College Libraries, 1988 Update." *ASA News* 22(1): 45-49.

______ . (1993) "Bibliographies and Other Reference Works that Need to Be Updated." *ASA News* 26(3): 26-27.

Schmidt, Nancy J., ed. (1998) *Africana Librarianship in the 21st Century: Treasuring the Past and Building the Future*. Bloomington, IN: African Studies Program, Indiana University.

Shemberg, Marian (1997) "From Citation to Piece in Hand: The Search for Efficiency in Accessing Monographic Series." *Library Resources and Technical Services* 41(3): 180-189.

Smith, Linda C. (2000) "Subject Access in Interdisciplinary Research." In: *Saving the Time of the Library User Through Subject Access Innovation: Papers in Honor of Pauline Atherton Cochrane*, edited by William J. Wheeler. Champaign, IL: Graduate School of Library and Information Science: 100-113.

Stewart, John (1989) *African States and Rulers: An Encyclopedia of Native, Colonial, and Independent States and Rulers Past and Present.* Jefferson, NC: McFarland.

Stiff, Paul (1997) "A Footnote Kicks Him: How Books Make Readers Work." *Journal of Scholarly Publishing* 28(2): 65-73.

Tenopir, Carol (2002) "The Web: Searchable, Hidden, and Deceitful." *Library Journal*, 127(12): 36-37.

Tyckoson, David (1997) "The Catalog as Index to the Collection." *Technicalities* 17(1): 10-12.

U. S. Imprints on Sub-Saharan Africa. (1986-) Washington, DC: Library of Congress.

Walford, A. J. (1982) "The Reviewing of Reference Books." In: *Ethics and Reference Services*. Edited by Bill Katz and Ruth A. Farley. New York: The Haworth Press, Inc.: 165-169.

Walker, Kizer, and Barbara H. Kwasnik (2002) "Providing Access to Collected Works." *Cataloging & Classification Quarterly* 33(3-4): 211-224.

Walsh, Gretchen (1989) "Review of *African States and Rulers: An Encyclopedia of Native, Colonial and Independent States and Rulers Past and Present.*" *Choice* 27(2): 294.

______. (1994) "Dynamics of Information for African Studies: The Library and Beyond," *African Studies in the Undergraduate Curriculum.* Boulder, CO: Lynne Rienner: 213-228.

______. (1998) "Africana Reference: The Bumblebee Analogy." In: *Africana Librarianship in the 21st century: Treasuring the Past and Building the Future: Proceedings of the 40th Anniversary Conference of the Africana Librarians Council*. Edited by Nancy J. Schmidt. Bloomington, IN: African Studies Program, Indiana University: 53-59.

Widenmann, Elizabeth A. 1989. "Recent Developments in Africana Cataloging in the United States (1973-1988)." *Africana Resources and Collections: Three Decades of Development and Achievement: a Festschrift in Honor of Hans Panofsky*. Edited by Julian W. Witherell. Metuchen, N.J., Scarecrow Press: 39-61.

Witherell, Julian W., ed. (1989) *Africana Resources and Collections: Three Decades of Development and Achievement: a Festschrift in Honor of Hans Panofsky.* Metuchen, NJ: Scarecrow Press.

Resources Cited

Africa Bibliography (1985-) Manchester, England: Manchester University Press. Annual.

Africa Contemporary Record; Annual Survey and Documents (1961-) New York: Africana Publishing Co. Annual.

Africa South of the Sahara (1971-) London: Europa Publications Ltd.

African Book Publishing Record Oxford, Eng., Hans Zell Ltd.

African Index Medicus. (1993-) Brazzaville: Association for Health Information & Libraries in Africa and WHO Regional Office for Africa. Quarterly.

Bhatt, Purnima Mehta. (1980) *Scholars' Guide to Washington, D.C. for African Studies* Washington: Smithsonian Institution Press.

A Current Bibliography on African Affairs (1962-) Farmingdale, N.Y.: Baywood Pub. Co. Quarterly.

Directory of Published Proceedings. Series SSH: Social Sciences Humanities (1968-) Annual.

Duignan, Peter. (1967) *Handbook of American Resources for African Studies.* [Stanford, Calif.]: Hoover Institution on War, Revolution, and Peace, Stanford University.

Duignan, Peter. 1971. *Africa South of the Sahara: A Bibliography for Undergraduate Libraries.*

Economist Intelligence Unit. *Country Reports and Country Profiles.*

Encyclopedia of Africa South of the Sahara (1997) New York: Scribner's and Sons.

Encyclopedia of African Peoples. (2000) New York: Facts on File.

Garland Encyclopedia of World Music. Volume 1: Africa. (1998) New York: Garland.

Kagan, Alfred, and Yvette Scheven. (1999) *Reference Guide to Africa: A Bibliography of Sources.* Lanham, MD: Scarecrow Press.

Gosebrink, Jean E. Meeh (ed.) (1986) *African Studies Information Resources Directory.* Oxford: Published for the African Studies Association [by] Hans Zell.

Gosebrink, Jean Meeh. 1986. "Bibliography and Sources for African Studies" In *Africa* edited by Phyllis M. Martin and Patrick O'Meara: 381-439.

International African Bibliography (1971-) London, Mansell. Quarterly.

Hartwig, Gerald W. 1974. *The Student Africanist's Handbook: A Guide to Resources.*

Lindfors, Bernth (2000) *Black African Literature in English, 1992-1996.* Oxford: Hans Zell.

McIlwaine, John. *Africa: A Guide to Reference Material.* (1993) London: Hans Zell.

Nyquist, Corinne and Leon P. Spencer. (1984) *The Lonely Africanist: A Guide to Selected U.S. Africana Libraries for Researchers.* [Los Angeles: African Studies Association].

Quarterly Index to African Periodical Literature. (2000-) Nairobi, Kenya: Library of Congress Office, Nairobi, [2000-] continues *Quarterly Index to Periodical Literature, Eastern and Southern Africa.* (1991-1999) Nairobi, Kenya: Library of Congress Office.

Paden, John N. and Edward W. Soja. (1970) "Bibliography" Volume 3 of *The African Experience.* Evanston, IL: Northwestern University Press.

Scheven, Yvette. (1977) *Bibliographies for African studies, 1970-1975.* Waltham, MA: Crossroads Press.

______. (1980) *Bibliographies for African studies, 1976-1979.* Waltham, MA: Crossroads Press.
______. (1984) *Bibliographies for African studies, 1980-1983.* Munich: Hans Zell.
______. (1988) *Bibliographies for African studies 1970-1986.* London: Hans Zell.
______. (1994) *Bibliographies for African studies, 1987-1993.* London: Hans Zell.
Schmidt, Nancy J. (1995) "Africana Resources for Undergraduates: A Bibliographic Essay" in the 1995 3rd edition of *Africa*, edited by Phyllis Martin and Patrick O'Meara.
U. S. Imprints on Sub-Saharan Africa. (1985-) Washington, DC: Library of Congress.
Zell, Hans (1997) *The African Studies Companion: A Resource Guide & Directory.* London: H. Zell Publishers.
Zell, Hans (2000) *The Electronic African Bookworm: A Web Navigator.* Oxford: African Books Collective.
Zell, Hans (2002) *The African Publishing Companion: A Resource Guide.* Lochcarron: Hans Zell Pub.

Web Sites

Africa from A to Z: http://www.lib.msu.edu/limb/a-z/az.html.
Africa Research Central: http://www.africa-research.org/mainframe.html.
Africa South of the Sahara (Stanford University): http://www-sul.stanford.edu/depts/ssrg/africa/guide.html.
African and Middle Eastern Reading Room, Library of Congress: http://lcweb.loc.gov/rr/amed/.
African Books Collective: http://www.africanbookscollective.com.
African E-Journal Project: http://www.isp.msu.edu/AfricanStudies/asc_side.htm.
African Journals Online: http://www.inasp.org.uk/ajol.
African Studies Abstracts Online: http://asc.leidenuniv.nl/library/abstracts/asa-online.
The African Studies Association (ASA): http://www.africanstudies.org.
African Studies Internet Resources (Columbia University): http://www.columbia.edu/cu/lweb/indiv/africa/cuvl/.
Africana Digitization Project: http://libtext.library.wisc.edu/Africana.
The Africana Librarians Council (ALC): http://lcweb.loc.gov/rr/amed/9asa.html.
Africa's 100 Best Books of the 20th Century: http://www.columbia.edu/cu/lweb/indiv/africa/cuvl/Afbks.html.
Association of African Studies Programs (AASP): http://www.africanstudies.org/asa_aasp.html.
Bibliography of African Periodical Literature Database: http://www.africabib.org/africa.html.
Cooperative Africana Microform Project: http://www.crl.edu/areastudies/CAMP/index.htm.
Database of African Theses and Dissertations (DATAD): http://www.aau.org/datad/.
Electronic Journal of Africana Bibliography: http://sdrc.lib.uiowa.edu/ejab/.
H-Africa: http://www2.h-net.msu.edu/~africa.
Howell, John Bruce. (1997) *Guides, Collections and Ancillary Materials to African Archival Resources in the United States*: http://sdrc.lib.uiowa.edu/ejab/1/index.html.
Library of Congress Country Studies: http://lcweb2.loc.gov/frd/cs/cshome.html#toc.

NISC Online: http://biblioline.nisc.com/.

Northwestern University. Melville J. Herskovits Library of African Studies. *Africana Conference Paper Index*: http://www.library.northwestern.edu/africana/links.html.

Opportunities and Challenges in Africana Library Service: A Framework for Cooperation and Development: http://people.bu.edu/gwalsh/alc-coop.html.

Quarterly Index to African Periodical Literature: http://lcweb2.loc.gov/misc/qsihtml.

Schmidt, Nancy J. (1995) "Africana Resources for Undergraduates: A Bibliographic Essay" in the 1995 3rd edition of *Africa*, edited by Phyllis Martin and Patrick O'Meara. http://www.indiana.edu/%7Elibsalc/african/schmidt.html.

Timbuktu Manuscript Digitization Project: http://pubweb.nwu.edu/%7Ejhunwick/haidara.html.

United States. Department of State. *Background Notes*: http://www.state.gov/r/pa/ei/bgn/.

World Factbook. (1981-) Washington, DC: Central Intelligence Agency: http://www.odci.gov/cia/publications/factbook/.

Zimbabwe International Book Fair: http://www.zibf.org/.

Teaching African Studies Bibliography–Information Literacy for 21st Century Scholars

Marion Frank-Wilson

SUMMARY. Indiana University has a long tradition of teaching African studies bibliography. It began in 1964 with Alan Taylor and was taught successively by Jean Meeh Gosebrink, David Easterbrook, Nancy Schmidt, and, for the last four years, by this author. This article discusses developments of the class as they have been implemented over the last four years. In the past, bibliographic tools in African studies disciplines were scarce, and the goal of the class consequently was to introduce the students to those tools. Nowadays, with the proliferation of sources in the field, both in electronic and print formats, the focus of the class has shifted. While various elements of the class have been maintained, the course now has several new elements, primarily in the form of discussion sessions based on the reading of articles and other sources. The focus of the class is no longer on how to find scarce, hidden materials, but rather to develop strategies and techniques to find a wide variety

---

Marion Frank-Wilson is Librarian for African Studies, Main Library E 660, Indiana University, 1320 East 10th Street, Bloomington, IN 47405-3907 (E-mail: mfrankwi@indiana.edu).

Special thanks go to Moira Smith, librarian for Folklore, Anthropology, Sociology and Gender Studies at Indiana University, for reading a draft of this article and making valuable suggestions for improvement.

[Haworth co-indexing entry note]: "Teaching African Studies Bibliography–Information Literacy for 21st Century Scholars." Frank-Wilson, Marion. Co-published simultaneously in *The Reference Librarian* (The Haworth Information Press, an imprint of The Haworth Press, Inc.) No. 87/88, 2004, pp. 97-107; and: *Research, Reference Service, and Resources for the Study of Africa* (ed: Deborah M. LaFond, and Gretchen Walsh) The Haworth Information Press, an imprint of The Haworth Press, Inc., 2004, pp. 97-107. Single or multiple copies of this article are available for a fee from The Haworth Document Delivery Service [1-800-HAWORTH, 9:00 a.m. - 5:00 p.m. (EST). E-mail address: docdelivery@haworthpress.com].

http://www.haworthpress.com/web/REF
© 2004 by The Haworth Press, Inc. All rights reserved.
Digital Object Identifier: 10.1300/J120v42n87_03

of materials ranging from print sources to oral accounts in libraries worldwide. *[Article copies available for a fee from The Haworth Document Delivery Service: 1-800-HAWORTH. E-mail address: <docdelivery@haworthpress.com> Website: <http://www.HaworthPress.com> © 2004 by The Haworth Press, Inc. All rights reserved.]*

KEYWORDS. African studies, bibliography, bibliographic instruction, information literacy

INTRODUCTION

The tradition of teaching African studies bibliography at Indiana University (IU) began in 1964 with Alan Taylor who taught two bibliography classes: "Introduction to the Bibliography of Africa South of the Sahara" (G 732) through the Graduate School, and "Librarianship and Bibliography of Africa South of the Sahara" (L 529) through the Library School (Taylor 1969:5; Kagan 1998:69). The Library School class is no longer offered, but G 732 has been taught ever since. It is now a required class for all master's and doctoral students who take African Studies as a minor. After Alan Taylor left, G 732 was taught successively by Jean Meeh Gosebrink, David Easterbrook, Nancy Schmidt, and, for the last four years, by this author.[1]

This article discusses recent developments of the class as they have been implemented over the last four years. Developments in African Studies at Indiana University and, more generally, in information-seeking behavior in the 21st century, suggested defining the teaching of African bibliography in a wider sense and situating it firmly within the context of scholarly communication in the field.[2]

AFRICAN STUDIES AND AFRICAN STUDIES BIBLIOGRAPHY AT INDIANA UNIVERSITY

In the 1960s bibliographic resources focused on Africa were scarce. Consequently, when Alan Taylor first taught the class, the focus was to identify those resources, and as a term project, the students produced a publishable bibliography thereby contributing to the discipline (Schmidt 1990:20). By the time Nancy Schmidt took over in 1984, the situation had improved somewhat. Students still faced the challenge of identifying Africa-related materials, but more and more sources in various formats (print, audio-visual, microfiche) had been published. It became necessary to teach the students how to evaluate sources and use them effectively for their research and to provide some context for the study of bibliography. In addition to bibliographic overviews, a historical overview of publishing in Africa and a discussion of the role of national bibliographies in African development were included. In class presentations and group discussions, students evaluated resources and at the same time learned about the history of African Studies research. Term papers now were a bibliography on a topic related to their coursework or dissertation (Taylor 1969:6; Schmidt 1990:20).

Clearly, over the course of the roughly 35 years that the class has been taught at Indiana University, it reflected trends and issues in the field of African Studies. It is hardly surprising then that the class has evolved again with recent developments in the discipline.

It is still a 3-credit class, required for all students who have African Studies as a minor. With few exceptions, bibliography classes are not usually offered in the students' main disciplines and generally students are not familiar with systematic bibliographic research.[3] As has been noted in descriptions of other African bibliography classes (Taylor 1969; Schmidt 1990; Kagan 1998), the students' backgrounds vary considerably. Not only do they come from different countries and continents (Africa and the U.S.), but they are at different stages in their studies with majors in disciplines as divergent as political science and literature. Some may be at the master's level whereas others are already in a Ph.D. program; some have done preliminary field research, others have not been to the field yet, etc. Despite these differences, there are similarities. A conversation at the beginning of the class about students' expectations for this class reveals that for the most part they are not familiar with bibliographic tools and the methods of systematic bibliographic research. One of the most often expressed goals is to acquire the skills to develop effective, targeted search strategies for both electronic and print sources. All students need to conduct library research during their time as graduate students, not only at Indiana University but also in Africa during their field research, and later in other libraries–possibly with Africana collections comparable to IU's or, more likely, in libraries with smaller collections. Accordingly, the goal of this class is to teach students the efficient use of research collections at Indiana University, and at other institutions in the U.S. and abroad, as well as during their field research in Africa.

Apart from the specific situation at IU, other considerations played a role in the class' shift. As already stated in Nancy Schmidt's article (Schmidt 1990:20, 22), the proliferation in the publishing of Africa-specific resources, the increasing interdisciplinarity of area studies, as well as the time-constraints of one semester, make it impossible to cover all areas in bibliographic surveys. Not only are the students engaged in interdisciplinary research, their topics nowadays constantly explore new areas of connections, as has been noted in a study by Jane Guyer. In her study, Guyer gives an overview of African Studies in the U.S. since World War II and points out that students are now moving into new areas of studies, such as AIDS, refugees, informal economies, or the environment–and they look at these issues from both social science and humanities viewpoints (Guyer 1996:11). A one-semester bibliography class cannot cover all of these potential areas of study and research, and the students will have to rely on their own bibliographic research. Accordingly, it is no longer sufficient for the course to simply introduce the students to a list of Africana resources. In addition, they must learn the skills to find and evaluate relevant sources on their own.

COURSE DESCRIPTION

In the following paragraphs, I will describe the class as it has been taught since 2001 at Indiana University. While various elements of the class have been maintained (there still are detailed bibliographic surveys for various disciplines and government publications, as well as for general periodical indexes, handbooks, and other general sources), the course now has several new elements, primarily in the form of discussion sessions based on the reading of articles and other sources.

Electronic Resources/Information Technology

Until recently, Africa-specific topics were not well-covered in subscription databases such as Academic Search Premier or Lexis-Nexis Academic Universe. Whereas the majority of resources in African Studies are still only available in print, the ever-growing number of general electronic databases now provide better coverage of some African topics–although their coverage is mainly restricted to American and European publications. Now, there are specialized databases exclusively for African Studies.[4] Consequently, whereas four years ago I dedicated only one class session to electronic sources, this section now takes up the first four weeks of the semester. Those four weeks are spent on various aspects of electronic sources ranging from a discussion of differences between library online catalogs, subscription databases, and information found on the World Wide Web to the teaching of electronic search strategies. While most students are familiar with author and title searches as well as basic keyword searches, they tend to be unaware of advanced subject and keyword searches. An overview of Library of Congress subject headings (Africa-specific) and concepts underlying cataloging rules forms the basis for teaching advanced electronic searching. This information, in fact, plays a role not just with regard to electronic searching but also when looking for print sources. It demonstrates the connection between cataloging and indexing, and how that relates to searching for and finding information. Students find, for example, that for many topics there is a lack of subject headings, which means that regular subject and keyword searches will not retrieve sources for these topics. Students learn that no initial search results do not necessarily mean no publications on a given topic. It simply means that they have to apply some more thorough and imaginative search strategies.

Another common pre-conception is to equate electronic sources with the World Wide Web. Students often have difficulties grasping the difference between sources found on the Web and in subscription databases and library online catalogs. In a practical class session, students are divided into different groups and are assigned a topic to research using various electronic sources and applying the keyword searching techniques they learned earlier. The groups then present their findings and discuss the different kinds of resources they found. This information is further enhanced by a whole class session dedicated to the library's subscription databases. A reference librarian who tailors it to Africa-specific topics teaches this session. Students, for example, are introduced to databases with Africa-specific content (e.g., the NISC database African Studies, Web of Science, etc.), alert services offered by Ingenta and others, table of contents databases, etc.

With the increasing presence of electronic sources in our lives, the skills to evaluate those sources play an important role. Students are not always aware that practically everybody can post information on the World Wide Web and that they have to apply their own quality control. Katrien Polman's article "Evaluation of Africa-Related Internet Resources" gives a good overview of evaluation criteria ranging from criteria similar to those for print sources, to criteria specific to electronic sources, such as authority, credentials of the author, ease of navigation, does the site have original content or merely links to other sites, duration of the site, and frequency of updates (Polman 1998:401-408).

The section on electronic sources concludes with a discussion of information technologies in relation to Africa. Different authors have suggested that new technologies might be a way for Africa to bridge the information gap, whereas others fear that it might actually widen it. There are always several students in the class who have already been to Africa for preliminary research. They and students from Africa usually have their own experiences and viewpoints on the matter, which leads to a discussion involving the whole class.

Center for Research Libraries

While the course has many elements tailored to the specific situation of Africana materials at Indiana University, it is also designed to give students the necessary research skills to effectively find information in other libraries in the U.S. and worldwide. It is important in this respect to introduce them to the Center for Research Libraries. Kenneth Lohrentz's article "Africana at the Center for Research Libraries: A Survey of Collections and Access" serves as an excellent introduction to the holdings of CRL (Lohrentz 1998). A discussion follows about cooperative collection development projects carried out by the Africana Librarians Council, such as the filming of the Senegal National Archives, and the collection of dissertations.

Archives in Africa

Before actually presenting resources, there is a discussion session about issues and debates surrounding the situation of archives in Africa. David Henige's article on "The Half-Life of African Archives" is a required text for this class session (Henige 1989). In his article, Henige describes problems of access and draws attention to the need for more accounts of various African or Africanist archives that would describe holdings, specific practices with regard to copying, etc. (Henige 1989:203). Since most students in the class plan to do field research, this topic meets with a lot of interest, and the discussion is usually lively. Another required reading for this session is a recent discussion thread on archives from the H-Africa listserv. Periodically, the acquisition of an African archive by a European or American library sparks a lively and sometimes heated debate about the appropriation of African national heritages by former colonial powers on the one side, and, on the other, the need to preserve those national heritages for future generations of scholars (African and American/European). The most recent example of such a debate concerned the acquisition of the complete papers of Ruth First (South African anti-apartheid activist) by the Institute of

Commonwealth Studies in U.K. (February 6, 2002 http://www2.h-net.msu.edu/~africa/threads/index.html#Archives). On one side of the debate are scholars who maintain that these materials should stay in their country where African scholars have access, and where they could contribute towards capacity building by having African scholars work on them. Also, by leaving the materials in their home country, scholars from Europe and the U.S. would have been encouraged to come to South Africa, rather than South Africans trying to obtain visas to work on South African papers in the United Kingdom. On the other side of the debate, scholars point out that access to the materials is of utmost importance, no matter where. They point to problems of preservation in many African countries and suggest that the materials might be better preserved elsewhere. Various suggestions have been made to solve this problem, ranging from leaving scanned copies of the materials in the guest country, or leaving the originals and moving the copies, to assisting African countries to preserve their materials. This debate not only introduces the students to the current discourse in the field, but also acquaints them with major scholars and their roles in the debate. Using a discussion which has recently occurred on an electronic listserv also serves the purpose of demonstrating sources for recent/current research.

The class session concludes with a bibliographic overview of sources related to archives in Africa. The chapter on primary sources in Kagan/Scheven's reference guide provides a good survey of sources in that field and is another required reading (Kagan, Scheven 1999:33-46).

Oral Tradition–Oral History

The session on archives in Africa directly leads to another discussion session on storing and accessing African oral tradition. Students read a 1985 article by 'Bunmi Alegbeleye on oral archives in Africa in which he points out that younger Africans rely less and less on oral tradition as a way to pass on cultural information. In fact, Alegbeleye equates each time an old man dies in Africa with the burning down of a library in Europe. He urges the collection of oral data but points out that this collection can only be of value if researchers deposit it in the country where it can be publicly accessed. This article leads to a discussion of the responsibilities of researchers to deposit their findings in the guest country versus the inclination/practice not to make primary research available until it is exhausted for the researcher's publications. It also leads to a discussion about field notes and audio-visual recordings and whether they should be made available to the population of the guest country.

The bibliographic survey for this session includes not only various resources on oral tradition, but also sources on interview technique and etiquette as well as material on working with human subjects. Clearly, it is not possible to discuss any of these issues exhaustively in a single class session. Rather, this session serves to introduce topics which will later be covered in research methods classes or which students will encounter during their preparations for field research.

Librarianship in the U.S. and in Africa

Another topic closely related to the discussion of African archives is librarianship in Africa. As with the other discussion sessions, this one is designed to provide a larger context for conducting research by providing students with information on issues in African librarianship, i.e., collection development issues, cataloging issues, preservation issues, and the like. In some cases, there is information available in the form of articles about collections in African libraries; in other cases, students who have already conducted research in Africa share with the class what they experienced. Several articles and sections of a book on librarianship in Africa are reading assignments and are discussed in class (Alemna 1995; Alemna 1996; Alegbeleye 1988; Alegbeleye 1996). This discussion is followed by an overview of the literature on libraries and librarianship in Africa based on the chapter in Kagan/Scheven's book (Kagan, Scheven 1999:141-156).

Also included in this class session is a discussion of area librarianship in the United States, its history, current practices, and the training of area librarians. This has developed into one of the more popular class sessions, mainly for two reasons. One, it helps students understand libraries and library services and therefore be more effective in their information gathering. But, secondly, with the tight job market in many African Studies disciplines, many students also look at librarianship as a possible course for future study. Students whose research makes work with and in archives a necessity seem to have a natural affinity for library work and are always particularly interested.

Publishing

Lastly, two class sessions are devoted to publishing, both in Africa and the United States. The chapter on "Africa," in Peter Altbach's *International Book Publishing: An Encyclopedia* gives the students a historical overview of publishing in Africa, as well as of current publishing trends on the continent (Altbach 1995:366-423). The chapter is sub-divided into several sections, and the author of the section entitled "Publishing in Africa," Hans Zell, discusses the role multinational publishing houses played in the history of African publishing, particularly with regard to the long neglect of publishing in African languages; and Africa's book-famine in the late 1980s and early 1990s where many university and public libraries have been unable to purchase new books.[5] He also points out the growing trend towards pan-African and collective approaches to deal with problems faced by African publishers. Some of those efforts include the creation of the African Publishers Network (APNET), and the African Books Collective (ABC). ABC is a self-help initiative set up by a group of African publishers in 1989 and handles all aspects of marketing and selling African books in Europe and the United States. For the students in the bibliography class, this is a way to locate and purchase African books outside of Africa.

In keeping with the practical nature of the class, a discussion of publishing in the field of African Studies in the U.S. is also included. I am book review editor for *Africa Today*, a refereed African Studies journal that is edited at Indiana University, and during one of the last class sessions, one of the journal's editors and myself speak to the class about academic publishing. Most students consider careers in academia or other venues where publications are used as a measure of success, and this session is one of the most popular of the semester. We introduce students to selecting the right journal for a particular article, the submission and review process, reviewing books, etc. This is admittedly a topic somewhat removed from a more narrow definition of a bibliography class. However, I believe its inclusion in this class is justified since it helps students become informed and information-literate scholars–which is after all the overall goal of this class.

CLASS ASSIGNMENT

Various class assignments help students become familiar with important sources. They are asked to annotate six sources of their choice. This exercise is usually perceived as useful, and students start exchanging information as and when they discover useful sources. Moreover, students are given four sets of questions for which they have to use sources discussed and presented in class. Other in-class exercises are designed to deepen their familiarity with what has been discussed, e.g., looking for information on the Web and in online databases and comparing the types of information found, evaluating bibliographies, etc.

As in classes taught by previous Africana librarians at Indiana University, students are required to submit an annotated bibliography with bibliographic essay as the final term project. For this project they are free to choose a topic of use to them either for their dissertation or their current coursework. The students are required to write a bibliographic essay introducing their topic, the kinds of sources they include in their bibliography, and a detailed account of limits and scope. The bibliography has to be annotated with more focus on evaluative annotations than before.

CONCLUSION

The goal of this article has been to describe the African Studies bibliography class as it has developed and evolved at Indiana University over the past four years. Whereas the class in the past consisted mostly of bibliographic surveys designed to introduce students to hard-to-find sources in the field, it now places these bibliographic surveys into a larger context of conducting research in African Studies. I believe this development is justified and necessary and can be explained by changes that occurred between 1964 (when the class was first taught) and now. Unlike in 1964, there are now more and better bibliographic tools available.[6] As Nancy Schmidt in her 1990 article pointed out, "Today the course must cover a 'feast' of bibliographic sources in print, microform, online and CD ROM, as well as computerized databanks and depositories of data of scholarly interest throughout the world" (Schmidt 1990:19). This wealth of materials and the increasingly interdisciplinary nature of research conducted nowadays make it impossible to cover the whole field in one semester. Consequently, the focus of the class is no longer on how to find scarce, hidden materials, but rather to develop strategies and techniques to find a wide variety of materials ranging from print sources to oral accounts, as well as sources found in African archives; and, more importantly, to be able to evaluate these sources for their quality and relevance. Moreover, students nowadays are mobile–they will all go to Africa for their research, and they can also be expected to use other libraries around the world. An African Studies bibliography class in the 21st century cannot be restricted to sources in one library, nor can it attempt to present exhaustive bibliographic surveys for any discipline. It has to teach the skill and the knowledge to conduct research on a global scale.

AUTHOR NOTE

Marion Frank-Wilson is a graduate of Bayreuth University in Germany (Ph.D. 1992). Her extensive field research resulted in the publication of *AIDS Education through Theatre* (Bayreuth African Studies Series, Bayreuth, 1995). Other publications include articles on African and English literature, and she is the book review editor for *Africa Today*. She is also editor of the Africana Librarians Newsletter of the Africana Librarians Council of the African Studies Association. Her current research interests are in the fields of African travel writing and electronic publishing/scholarly communication in Africa. She is Librarian for African Studies at Indiana University where she teaches a bibliography class, "Introduction to the Bibliography of sub-Saharan Africa."

NOTES

1. In 1990 Nancy Schmidt published an update on the class, which in 1986 had been upgraded to a required 3-credit class (Schmidt 1990).

2. Besides Indiana University, African studies bibliography is taught in several other places, as described in a 1998 article by Alfred Kagan. His article is based on a question submitted to members of the Africana Librarians Council to find out at which institutions formal African Studies bibliography courses were taught. At the time Kagan's article was written, apart from Indiana University, such courses were only taught at the University of California at Los Angeles and the University of Illinois at Urbana/Champaign. An African Studies bibliography class used to be taught at Michigan State University, but was discontinued in the mid-1980s. Recently, bibliography classes have been offered by the University of Florida and Boston University.

3. Fine Arts, Slavic Studies, and Sciences are among the exceptions.

4. NISC's subscription databases "African Studies" and "South African Studies"; and the free database "AfricaBib.org," developed and maintained by Davis Bullwinkle; this database indexes 325 African Studies journals.

5. The other sections are on "Francophone Africa" by Diana Newton (pp. 373-383), "Kenya" by Henry Chakava (pp. 383-395), "Nigeria" by Victor Nwankwo (pp. 396-414), and "South Africa" by David Philip and Mike Kantey (pp. 415-423).

6. With Kagan/Scheven's *Reference Guide To Africa* we now even have a textbook for bibliography classes.

Africa Business and Economic Resource Index: Selected Internet Resources

Angel D. Batiste

SUMMARY. Increasingly, the global business community is viewing Sub-Saharan Africa as a continent of rich business, trade, and investment opportunities. A major challenge to political and business leaders is access to accurate and time-critical information on business, economic, political, and social developments in the Sub-Saharan African countries. This resource guide will provide an organized collection of major African business and economic information resources available via the Internet. Additionally, it includes an appended selection of information sources available in print format. The information originates from multiple Internet-based sources, including African commercial and government agencies, U.S. commercial and government agencies, and international organizations engaging in economic, business, and trade issues in the Sub-Saharan African countries. *[Article copies available for a fee from The Haworth Document Delivery Service: 1-800-HAWORTH. E-mail address: <docdelivery@haworthpress.com> Website: <http://www.HaworthPress.com> © 2004 by The Haworth Press, Inc. All rights reserved.]*

KEYWORDS. Africa, business, commerce, investment, trade, Internet resources

---

Angel D. Batiste is Area Specialist, African and Middle Eastern Division, Library of Congress, Washington, DC 20540-4821 (E-mail: abat@loc.gov).

[Haworth co-indexing entry note]: "Africa Business and Economic Resource Index: Selected Internet Resources." Batiste, Angel D. Co-published simultaneously in *The Reference Librarian* (The Haworth Information Press, an imprint of The Haworth Press, Inc.) No. 87/88, 2004, pp. 109-149; and: *Research, Reference Service, and Resources for the Study of Africa* (ed: Deborah M. LaFond, and Gretchen Walsh) The Haworth Information Press, an imprint of The Haworth Press, Inc., 2004, pp. 109-149. Single or multiple copies of this article are available for a fee from The Haworth Document Delivery Service [1-800-HAWORTH, 9:00 a.m. - 5:00 p.m. (EST). E-mail address: docdelivery@haworthpress.com].

http://www.haworthpress.com/web/REF
© 2004 by The Haworth Press, Inc. All rights reserved.
Digital Object Identifier: 10.1300/J120v42n87_04

INTRODUCTION AND BACKGROUND

Africa's vast potential in the global emerging market can no longer be ignored. With more than one-tenth of the world's population, the 48 nations of Sub-Saharan Africa have a rapidly growing market of over 700 million consumers offering enormous commercial potential for U.S. exporters. It also offers investors enormous untapped raw materials and natural resources. According to the Department of Commerce, the U.S. exported more to Sub-Saharan Africa in 2000 than to all the states of the former Soviet Union combined, including Russia. Sub-Saharan African countries supply 18% of American oil needs. In 2001, U.S. direct investment in Sub-Saharan Africa more than quadrupled to $3.8 billion.

Since the mid-1990s a number of important measures to improve U.S. economic and commercial relations with the African nations have materialized. In 1994, the Uruguay Round Agreements Act on Africa directed the Clinton Administration to develop a trade and development policy toward Africa and to report on this policy to Congress annually for five years. In 1997, the Administration launched its Partnership for Economic Growth and Opportunity trade initiative, integrating the key objectives of trade incentives for economic reforms underway in the region, enhanced U.S. economic engagement, integration of the Africa region into the global trading system, and support for sustainable economic and social development.[1] In 1998, the administration appointed an Assistant U.S. Trade Representative (USTR) for Africa and a senior advisor for African programs at the Export-Import Bank.[2] In addition, the Administration hosted the first annual U.S.-Sub-Saharan Africa Trade and Economic Cooperation Forum to discuss expanding trade and economic relations between the U.S. and Sub-Saharan African.[3] Symbolically, President Clinton's historic trips to Africa in 1996 and 1998 also transformed U.S. relations with the Sub-Saharan African countries. The visits highlighted Africa's opportunities as well as U.S. support for economic transformations underway in the region.

Complementary to the Partnership Initiatives, a number of legislative proposals have caused greater attention to be given to emerging economic opportunities and U.S. economic relations with the African nations. In May 2000, President Clinton signed the historic African Growth and Opportunity Act (AGOA), an unprecedented trade bill for Africa designed to open the U.S. market to products made in Africa. The bill is the first ever trade and investment legislation on Africa to be considered by the U.S. Congress. It ushers in a new era of U.S. foreign policy in the continent and establishes a new paradigm for the development of closer economic ties between the U.S. and Africa.[4] The AGOA and greater U.S.-Africa trade and commercial partnerships are also strongly supported by the American private sector and the Bush Administration.[5] At the same time, African government and private sector leaders, regional organizations, and multilateral development agencies, such as the African Development Bank Group and the World Bank Group, are establishing policies and multilateral agreements to increase Africa's private economic growth.[6]

A major challenge to the U.S. and global business community becoming important actors in the African business environment is access to credible and time-critical information to make smart, definitive business decisions. The growing demand for up-to-date macro- and microeconomic information about the country-specific economic and industry trends, investment opportunities, and the African private sector is increasing at a prolific rate. At present, access to data dealing with business opportunities and policy issues in the African economies is scattered in multiple data sources. Available bibliographic tools (i.e., accessions lists, book lists, and bibliographic guides) which specifically document African business and financial information sources are far from complete. More importantly, a great variety of 'non-conventional' literature of an ephemeral nature such as unpublished working papers, feasibility studies, research reports, and documents of African government agencies and international organizations seldom comes under bibliographic control and is hard to obtain. On the Web, African business information resources still remain largely invisible and researchers may spend countless frustrating and often unproductive hours. For example, finding out what exists and then trying to obtain access to it typically requires not only a series of research avenues, but a substantial investment of time.

To fill the void that exists where African business and economic information is concerned, and to provide more comprehensive services to researchers looking for information about business and economic trends in the African nations, there is a need to identify and provide improved bibliographic control and access to existing information resources, particularly Internet and Web resources.

COLLECTION SCOPE AND AUDIENCE

This *Africa Business and Economic Resource Index* will organize and provide access to selective sources of business information on the

African countries that are available on the Internet. The sampling of information resources have been identified and evaluated for the ongoing development of a selected centralized resource or 'portal model' of relevant Africa-focused business, trade and investment information resources. In its first version, the *Index* will focus on providing access to African business and financial Internet information resources primarily at the continental and sub-regional levels.[7] Coverage includes general business directories, financial, legal, and market information, industry analysis, basic country economic and statistical data, business and industry news, stock and currency exchanges, and specialized business journals. Priority will be given to Internet resources which provide substantial sources of information on African business topics frequently required by specialized researchers–students in business, teachers, business professionals, and decision makers in public and private sectors. Generally, only resources that are freely available on the Internet will be considered. It should be noted, however, that valuable business information on the Sub-Saharan African countries is also available on a number of fee-based commercial online databases, including *Dialog* [http://www.dialog.com], *Dow Jones Interactive* [http://www.dowjones.com], *EBSCO*, *Emerging Markets*, and *LexusNexus* [http://www.lexus-nexus.com]. Additionally, one should not forget the growing number of African business publications such as *African Business*, *African Financing Review*, and *African Review of Business and Technology* available in traditional print formats.

IDENTIFICATION, EVALUATION, AND SELECTION PROCESS

The *Index* is a project currently under development as part of the Business and Economic Resources Online (BEOnline) program undertaken by the Bibliographic Enrichment Advisory Team (BEAT) of the Cataloging Directorate of the Library of Congress. Established in 1996 as a pilot project, BEOnline+ is intended to serve as 'both a model and a catalyst for developing approaches to identifying and providing bibliographic control and access to electronic resources.'[8] Utilizing BeOnline+ and OCLC's Cooperative Online Resource Catalog (CORC) project applications, the electronic information sources that will be evaluated and selected for the *Index* will be provided with full MARC cataloging records.[9] The minimal identification and retrieval data will include the title of the Internet resource and its URL address. Access to the Internet-based publications will be available on the Library of Congress' African Section 'Country Website' (available on the World Wide Web at http://www.loc.gov/rr/business/african/).

Revisions of the *Index* are planned on a continuing basis, as changes in the availability, coverage, and quality of various Internet-based information resources take place.

The Internet sources selected for the *Index* were chosen to give representational examples of the wide range of electronically stored materials currently available for researching African business topics. Depending on the type of information one needs, there are a number of useful subject directories for searching Internet sites. The following examples provide a good starting point for actively identifying relevant African business information sources available on the Internet:

WEB RESOURCES FOR INTERNATIONAL ECONOMICS AND BUSINESS

Africa Online
http://www.africaonline.com

Africa South of the Sahara–Selected Internet Resources
http://www.sul.stanford.edu/depts/ssrg/africa

African Studies Internet Resources
http://www.cc.columbia.edu/cu/libraries/indiv/area/Africa/

International Business Resources on the WWW
http://ciber.bus.msu.edu/busres.htm

SELECTION METHODOLOGY AND GUIDELINES

One of the principal challenges facing anyone using electronic resources for serious information or research purposes is the evaluation of quality. This *Index* is intended as a working tool to help manage this challenge. The selected Internet resources for this project have been evaluated and selected in accordance with *BEOnline+ Selection Criteria* and current Library of Congress selection policies as outlined in *LC Collections Policy Statements (CPS)* and guidelines for print collections of business and economic materials.[10] In addition, the criterion for electronic information established by the American Library Association's Reference and User Services Association Collection Development and Evaluation Section's (ALA RUSA CODES) Collection Policy Committee was used to evaluate the Internet-based resources. Specific selection criteria considered when evaluating Internet resources included the following:

- Is content relevant and of substantial intellectual quality to meet information needs of intended audience?
- Is content useful for research and instruction?
- What is the reputation, expertise, and credentials of the author(s)/organization who produced the source materials?
- How current is the information and what is the frequency of updating?
- Is access to the site free? Is site user friendly with an effective interface?

AFRICAN REGIONAL OR COUNTRY-SPECIFIC DATA SOURCES

This section includes general reference resources that may be of assistance in providing country/region business and economic profiles, details of laws, regulations, and procedures governing business transactions, as well as travel information.

Electronic Resources

Africa Business Network
http://www.ifc.org/abn/index.htm

Includes country and investment information.

The Economist Intelligence Unit *Country Reports* and *Country Profiles*

Quarterly and annual reports summarize business, economic, and political developments and provide statistical updates.

Ernst & Young Business Information

Provides investment profiles for each African country, covering taxation issues, investment incentives, types of business establishments, exchange control regulations, etc.

Lex Africa Business Guides

Business guides feature investment information, forms of business organizations, taxation issues, exchange regulations, etc.

Mbendi Information Services–Countries of Africa
http://mbendi.co.za/index.htm

Provides information on business opportunities in the oil, chemical, mining, and other industries in the African countries, companies and organizations active in various industry sectors, country profiles, the leading business and government personalities, details of conferences and exhibitions, and a directory of products and services.

U. S. Statement Department. Background Notes
http://www.state.gov/www.backgrounds_notes

"Background Notes" provide information on U.S. relations with the country, history, and travel advisories.

U.S. State Department Travel Warnings and Consular Information Sheets
http://www.travel.state.gov

Travel warnings are issued when the State Department decides, based on all relevant information, to recommend that Americans avoid travel to a certain country. Consular Information Sheets include such information as location of the U.S. Embassy or Consulate, unusual immigration practices, health conditions, minor political disturbances, unusual currency and entry regulations, crime and security information, and drug penalties.

World Factbook. CIA
http://www.odci.gov/cia/publications/factbook/index.html

The CIA World Factbook provides information on the government, geography, people, and economies of the African countries.

GOVERNMENT DEPARTMENTS AND EMBASSY SITES

The following list provides directory sites for locating officials and diplomatic missions, as well as African national government web sites.

Chiefs of State and Cabinet Members of Foreign Governments
http://www.odci.gov/cia/publications/chiefs/index.html

Site from the U.S. Central Intelligence Agency.

Electronic Embassy
http://www.embassy.org

Provides street address, phone, fax, and links to web pages of foreign embassies in Washington, DC.

Embassy Web
http://www.embpage.org/index

Provides links to diplomatic offices across the world.

Governments on the WWW
http://www.gksoft.com/govt/

Database of national government institutions on the World Wide Web. Links to several African government web sites.

Michigan Electronic Library–Official Sites of Foreign Governments
http://www.mel.lib.edu.us/government/Gov-international-sites.html

AFRICAN STOCK EXCHANGES

The following list of resources includes a collection of links to Africa's stock exchanges.

African Stock Exchanges Association
http://www.jse.co.za/thejse/aseasims.htm

International Finance Corporation (FC). Emerging Markets Database (EMDB)
http://www.ifc.org/EMDB/EMDB

IPAnet
http://www.ipanet.net

MBendi African Stock Exchanges
www.mbendi.co.za

Abidjan Stock Exchange
http://mbendi.co.za/exch/4/p0005.htm

Abuja Commodities Exchange
http://mbendi.co.za/exch/57/p0005.htm

Botswana Stock Exchange
http://www.business-line.com/stock/afri/botsk.htm

Dar es Salaam Stock Exchange

Ghana Stock Exchange
http://www.safex.co.za

Johannesburg Securities Exchange
http://mbendi.co.za/exch/1/p0005.htm

Johannesburg Stock Exchange
www.jse.co.za

Kampala Stock Exchange

Khartoum Stock Exchange
http://mbendi.co.za/exch/32/p0005.htm

Lusaka Stock Exchange

Malawi Stock Exchange
http://mbendi.co.za/exch/19/p0005.htm

Maputo Stock Exchange
http://mbendi.co.za/exch/29/p0005.htm

Mauritius Stock Exchange
http://mbendi.co.za/exch/15/p0005.htm

Nairobi Stock Exchange

Namibia Stock Exchange
http://www.nse.com.na/

Nigerian Stock Exchange
http://mbendi.co.za/exch/16/p0005.htm

South Africa Futures Exchange
http://www.safex.co.za/

South Africa Stock Exchange
http://www.jse.co.za/

Stock Exchange of Mauritius

Swaziland Stockbrokers Ltd.

Tanzanian Stock Exchange
http://mbendi.co.za/exch/20/p0005.htm

Zambia Stock Exchange
http://mbendi.co.za/exch/10/p0005.htm

Zimbabwe Stock Exchange
http://mbendi.co.za/exch/11/p0005.htm

Privatization Link
http://privatizationlink.ipanet.net

AFRICAN BUSINESS AND INDUSTRY DIRECTORIES

The following offers a collection of useful links to regional/country business directory sites for company profiles and contact details, and trade directories.

Africa4biz.com
http://www.africa4biz.com/index-start.shtml

"African trade centre on the Internet."

Africa Trade Directory
http://www.africa-trade-direct.com

"An online database of businesses and individuals seeking trade opportunities in Africa." Database contains company profiles and key trade contacts in African countries.

African Yellow Pages and Business Web Directory
http://www.woyaa.com/ypages

"A Web Directory of African companies."

Brabys Red Index
http://www.redindex.com/links.asp

A searchable database for companies and industries in South Africa, parts of southern Africa, and the Indian Ocean islands.

COMESA Online Trade Directories
http://www.comesa.int/database/dataindx.htm

Kenya Business Directory

Mauritius Trade Directory

Mauritius Business Information System

Namibia Electronic Business Directory

Tanzania Classified Directory

Uganda Business Directory

Zambian Export Board Directory

Zimbabwe: Zimtrade Directory

Emerging Markets Directory
http://www.emdirectory.com

"Directory provides links to selected government, business, academic, and media sites related to the emerging markets of Africa."

MBendi Afropedia

Africa Directory of Products & Services
http://www.mbendi.co.za/prod/afprod.htm

Register of African Companies
http://www.mbendi.co.za/coaf.htm

Industries of Africa
http://www.mbendi.co.za/land/af/p0005.htm

Yellow Pages–Business Directories of Africa
http://yellowpages.webquest.comafrica.html

"Online yellow pages and business directories from African countries."

AFRICAN CHAMBERS OF COMMERCE

This section consists of Internet resources that provide information on African trade and professional associations and regional chambers of commerce.

Chambers of Commerce in Africa
http://www.bullion.org.za/Welkome.html

Provides links to official web sites of chambers of commerce in selected African countries.

Chamber of Mines of South Africa

"A comprehensive cyber resource of news, data and policy information on mining, with emphasis on the activity of the South African mining industry."

Database of Chambers of Commerce in Africa
http://www.fairtradefederation.com

World Chambers Network (WCN)
http://206.127.60.162/newsite/registry/default.htm

Provides links to homepages of more than 1,000 chambers and association of chambers around the world.

National African Federated Chamber of Commerce
http://www.nafcoc.co.za

Chamber of Commerce and Industry of Angola (CCIA)
http://www.ccia.ebonet.net

Chambre de commerce et d'industrie du Benin (CCIB)
http://www.planben.intnet.bj/pne/ccib.htm

Chambre de commerce, d'industrie et d'artisanat du Burkina Faso
http://www.ccia.bf

Cameroon Chamber of Commerce, Industry and Mines
http://www.g77tin.org/ccimhp.html

Chambre Internationale de Commerce et d'Industrie de Djibouti
http://www.intnet.dj/public/cicid/index.html

Addis Ababa Chamber of Commerce
http://www.g77tin.org/addishp.html

Ghana National Chamber of Commerce
http://www.g77tin.org/gncchp.html

Kenya National Chamber of Commerce and Industry
http://www.g77tin.org/knccihp.html

Mauritius Chamber of Commerce and Industry (MCCI)
http://www.mcci.org

Namibia Chamber of Commerce and Industry
http://www.stage.iafrica.com.na/ncci

Dakar Chamber of Commerce, Industry and Agriculture
http://www.g77tin.org/cciardhp.html

Cape Chamber of Commerce and Industry
http://www.ccci.co.za

Durban Chamber of Commerce and Industry
http://www.durbanchamber.co.za

Johannesburg Chamber of Commerce and Industry
http://www.jcci.co.za

Port Elizabeth Regional Chamber of Commerce and Industry
http://www.echamber.org.za

South African Chamber of Business (SACOB)
http://www.sacob.co.za

Swaziland Chamber of Commerce and Industry
http://www.business-swaziland.com/chamber

Uganda National Chamber of Commerce and Industry
http://www.nic.ug/tradepoint/html/uncc.html

Zimbabwe National Chamber of Commerce
http:/www.zncc.co.zw

AFRICAN TRADE PROMOTION ORGANIZATIONS

Ministère du Développement Industriel et Commercial. Cameroon
http://www.camnet.cm/investir/mindic

Trade Point Libreville. Gabon
http://www.untpdc.org/incubator/gab/tplib

Ghana Export Promotion Council
http://www.exportghana.org

Trade Point Nairobi. Kenya
http://www.untpdc.org/incubator/ken/tpnai/welcome.html

Mauritius Export Development & Investment Authority (MEDIA)
http://www.ncb.intnet.mu/media.htm

Ministry of Industry, Commerce, Corporate Affairs and Financial Services
http://www.ncb.intnet.mu/mic.htm

Instituto de Promoção de Exportação (IPEX). Mozambique
http://www.ipexport.org

Centre international du commerce extérieur du Sénégal (CICES). Senegal
http://www.metissacana.sn/fidak

Business, Investment, Trade and Tourism Support Services. Senegal
http://www.tradepretoria.co.za

Department of Trade and Industry (DTI)
http://www.dti.gov.za

Trade Point Pretoria
http://www.untpdc.org/incubator/zaf/tppry/welcome.html

Western Cape Investment and Trade Promotion Agency (WESGRO)
http://www.wesgro.co.za

Confederation of Tanzania Industries
http://www.ctitz.com

Trade Point Tanzania
http://www.tptanzania.co.tz

Uganda Export Promotion Board
http://www.ugandaexportsonline.com

Uganda Manufacturers Association
http://www.uma.co.ug

Zambia Export Board of Zambia
http://www.zamnet.zm/zamnet/zambus/ebz/ebz.htm

Trade Point Lusaka
http://www.untpdc.org/incubator/africahp/zmb.htm

Confederation of Zimbabwe Industries
http://www.czi.org.zw

Zimtrade
http://www.zimtrade.co.zw

AFRICAN PRIVATIZATION AND INVESTMENT PROMOTION AGENCIES

This section provides a selective listing of links to the home web sites of African government institutions involved in investment and privatization opportunities in the African countries, listed on a country basis.

National Privatization Agencies

Cape Verde: Privatization and Regulatory Capacity Building Project

Ethiopian Privatization Agency (EPA)

Ghana: Divestiture Implementation Committee

Kenya: Parastatal Reform Programme Committee

Madagascar: Comite de Privatization
http://213.186.35.82/cfdocs/madaprivat

Malawi: Privatisation Commission

Mozambique: Ministry of Planning and Finance, Enterprise Reform Unit

Nigeria: Bureau for Public Enterprise

South Africa: Department of Public Enterprise

Tanzania: Presidential Parastatal Sector Reform Commission
http://www.psrc.tanzania.cc/

Uganda: Ministry of Finance Privatization Unit
http://www.perds.go.ug

Zambia: Official Privatization Agency
http://www.zpa.org.zm

Zimbabwe: Privatisation Agency

National Investment Promotion Agencies

This section provides a selected listing of home web sites of national institutions involved in investment and privatization opportunities in the African countries.

African Investment Advisory

Centre de Promotion des Investissements–BENIN

Cellule de Gewtion du Code des Investissements (CGCI)–CAMEROON

Centre de Promotion des Investissements en Cote d'Ivoire (CEPICI)–COTE D'IVOIRE

Comite de Pilotage de l'Industrie de la Reunion

Cote d 'Ivoire Investment Promotion Center (CEPIC)

Ethiopian Investment Authority

Agence de Promotion des Investissements Prives (APIP–GABON)

Ghana Investment Promotion Centre (GIPC)

Kenya Investment Promotion Centre (KIPC)

Lesotho National Development Corporation

Malawi Investment Promotion Agency (MIPA)
http://mipa.malawi.net/

Mauritius Industrial Development Authority (MIDA)

Mozambique Investment Promotion Centre
http://www.cpinvest.org.mz/

Nigerian Investment Promotion Commission

Seychelles International Business Authority (SIBA)

South Africa–National Trade and Investment Promotion Agency
http://www.isa.org.za/default_ns.htm

Swaziland Chamber of Commerce and Industry

Tanzania Investment Centre
http://www.cats-net.com/tic/

Uganda Investment Authority
http://www.ugandainvest.com

Zambia Investment Centre
http://www.zic.org.zm/

Zimbabwe Investment Centre
http://www.zic.co.zw

AFRICAN REGIONAL ECONOMIC ORGANIZATIONS

Central African Customs and Economic Union (UDEAC)

Common Market for Eastern and Southern Africa (COMESA)
http://www.comesa.int

Membership: Angola, Burundi, Comoros, Democratic Republic of Congo, Djibouti, Egypt, Eritrea, Ethiopia, Kenya, Madagascar, Malawi, Mauritius, Namibia, Rwanda, Seychelles, Sudan, Swaziland, Uganda, Zambia, Zimbabwe.

Communaute Economique et Monetaire en Afrique Central CEMA/UDEAC
http://www.socatel.intnet.f/accueil1.html

Membership: Cameroon, Central African Republic, Chad, Congo Brazzaville, Equatorial Guinea, Gabon.

Council of Entente

Membership: Benin, Burkina, Cote d'Ivoire, Niger, Togo.

East African Cooperation (EAC)
http://www.usatwiga.com/users/eac

Membership: Kenya, Tanzania, Uganda.

Economic Community of Central African States (ECCAS)
http://www.dfa.gov.za/for-relations/multilateral/eccas.htm

Membership: Burundi, Cameroon, Central African Republic, Chad, Congo Brazzaville, Democratic Republic of Congo, Equatorial Guinea, Gabon, Rwanda, Sao Tome and Principe.

Economic Community of West African States (ECOWAS)
http://www.cedeao.org

Membership: Benin, Burkina Faso, Cape Verde, Gambia, Ghana, Ivory Coast, Guinea, Guinea Bissau, Liberia, Mali, Mauritania, Niger, Nigeria, Senegal, Sierra Leone, Togo.

Franc Zone (FZ)

Membership: Benin, Burkina, Cameroon, Central African Republic, Chad, Comoros, Congo, Cote d'Ivoire, Equatorial Guinea, France, Gabon, Mali, Niger, Senegal, Togo.

Indian Ocean Commission (IOC)
http://www.coi-info.org (French version)
http://www. coi.intnet.mu

Membership: Comoros, Madagascar, Mauritius, Reunion, Seychelles.

Intergovernmental Authority on Development (IGAD)
http://www.igadregion.org

Membership: Djibouti, Eritrea, Ethiopia, Kenya, Somalia, Sudan, Uganda.

Organization of African Unity (OAU)
http://www.oau-oua.org/index.htm

Membership: Algeria, Angola, Benin, Botswana, Burkina Faso, Burundi, Cameroon, Cape Verde, Central African Republic, Chad, Comoros, Cote D'Ivoire, Democratic Republic of Congo, Djibouti, Egypt, Equatorial Guinea, Eritrea, Ethiopia, Gabon, Gambia, Ghana, Guinea, Guinea-Bissau, Kenya, Lesotho, Liberia, Libya, Madagascar, Malawi, Mali, Mauritania, Mauritius, Mozambique, Nigeria, Rwanda, Saharawi Arab Democratic Republic, Sao Tome and Principe, Seychelles, Senegal, Sierra Leone, Tanzania, Togo, Tunisia, Uganda, Zambia, Zimbabwe.

Southern African Customs Union (SACU)
http://www.fhs.co.za/sacu.html

Membership: Botswana, Lesotho, Namibia, South Africa, Swaziland.

Southern African Development Community (SADC)
http://www.sadcreview.com

Membership: Angola, Botswana, Democratic Republic of Congo, Lesotho, Malawi, Mauritius, Mozambique, Namibia, Seychelles, South Africa, Swaziland, Tanzania, Zambia and Zimbabwe.

Union Economique et Monetaire Ouest Africaine (UEMOA)
http://www.uemoa.int

Membership: Benin, Burkina Faso, Guinea Bissau, Ivory Coast, Mali, Niger, Senegal, and Togo.

West African Economic and Monetary Union (WAEMU)

BANKS AND FINANCIAL INSTITUTIONS

African Regional Financial Institutions

This section offers a collection of links to financial institutions promoting the economic and social development of their member countries.

ACP Group–General Secretariat of the African, Caribbean and Pacific Group of States (ACP Group)

Information about the program and the 71 African, Caribbean and Pacific countries that have signed the Lome Convention with the European Union.

African Development Bank Group (AfDB)
http://www.africandevelopmentbank.com

Created by Africans in 1963, the AfDB is an international financial institution created to promote the economic and social development of its member African countries. The AfDB includes the African Development Bank (ADB), the African Development Fund (ADF) and the Nigeria Trust Fund (NTF).

African Export-Import Bank (AFREXIMBANK)
http://www.afdb.org

"The purpose of the Bank is to facilitate, promote, and expand intra-African and extra-African trade."

Association of African Development Finance Institutions (AAFI)

Bank of Central African States (BEAC)

Banks and Financial Institutions in Eastern and Southern Africa

Provides contact information and links to general country pages.

Committee of Central Bank Governors of the Southern African Development Community

Central Banks on the World Wide Web
http://www.bna.ebonet.net

Central Banks of Africa on the Internet

Banco de Mocambique http://www.bancomoc.mz/
Banco Nactional de Angola http://www.bna.ebonet.net//bna.htm
Bank of Benin http://www.bceao.int/
Bank of Botswana http://www.bankofbotswana.bw/
Bank of Burkina Faso http://www.bceao.int/
Bank of Kenya
Bank of Mauritius
Central Bank of Swaziland
Bank of Tanzania
Bank of Zambia
South African Reserve Bank
Bank of Ghana http://www.bog.gov.gh/
Bank of Kenya http://www.centralbank.go.ke
Bank of Lesotho http://www.centralbank.org.ls/
Bank of Mali http://www.bceao.int/
Bank of Mauritius
Bank of Namibia http://www.bon.com.na/
Bank of Niger http://www.bon.com.na/
Central Bank of Swaziland http://www.centralbank.sz/
Bank of Uganda http://www.bou.or.ug/
Bank of Tanzania

Bank of Zambia http://www.boz.zm/
Bank of Zimbabwe http://www.rbz.co.zw/

Bank of Central African States
http://www.imf.org/external/np/sec/decdo/beac.htm

"In 1972 the Governments of the five countries that were members of the Central Bank of Equatorial African States and Cameroon (Banque Centrale des Etats de l'Afrique Equatoriale et du Cameroun (BCEAEC)) signed a new Convention of Monetary Cooperation with France which established the Bank of Central African States (Banque des Etats de l'Afrique Centrale (BEAC)) to succeed the BCEAEC. Its members include Cameroon, Central African Republic, Chad, Republic of the Congo, Gabon, and Equatorial Guinea. BEAC is declared a 'Multinational African institution in the management and control of which France participates in return for the guarantee she provides for its currency.'"

Central Bank of West African States
http://www.bceao.int/internet/bcweb.nsf/pages/us

"The Central Bank of West African States (BCEAO) is the common-central bank of the eight (8) member states which form the West African Monetary Union (WAMU). BCEAO headquarters is located in Dakar, Senegal."

Committee of Central Bank Governors of the Southern African Development Community Development Bank of Southern Africa
http://www.dbsa.orgz

The Bank (DBSA) was established in 1983. "In 1996 it was transformed to ensure it met the needs of the new South Africa and the Southern African Development Community (SADC) region a whole. The DBSA's key purpose is to address socio-economic imbalances and help improve the quality of life of the people of South and southern Africa."

East African Development Bank
http://www.imf.org/external/np/sec/decdo/eadb.htm

The East African Development Bank (EADB) provides financial and technical assistance for the promotion of industrial development and projects to promote regional cooperation in the member countries of Kenya, Tanzania, and Uganda.

Industrial Development Corporation of South Africa
http://www.idc.co.za

Includes information on lending programs.

South Africa Reserve Bank
http://www.resbank.co.za/

"Official site of South African Reserve Bank."

West African Development Bank
http://www.imf.org/external/np/sec/decdo/boad.htm

The West African Development Bank (BOAD) was established by an Agreement signed by the Member States of the West African Monetary Union (UMOA) on November 14, 1973. The aim of the BOAD is to promote balanced development of the States of the Union and to achieve West African economic integration.

West African Monetary Union
http://www.imf.org/external/np/sec/decdo/uemoa.htm

Other International Financial Institutions

Following is a collection of links to multilateral organizations financing economic and social development programs in the African countries.

African Management Service Company (AMSCO)

Arab Bank for Economic Development in Africa
http://www.ifm.org/external/np/sec/decdo/badea.htm

"The objective of the Bank is to foster economic, financial and technical cooperation between the African States and the Arab nations."

European Commission Directorate General for Development
http://www.europa.eu.int/com/dg08/index_en.html

"Of special note is the *European Union and South Africa*: http://www.europa.eu/int/domm/dg08/south-africa/index.htm."

European Union
http://www.europa.eu.int/index-en.htm

General Secretariat of the African, Caribbean and Pacific Group of States (ACP Group)

Intergovernmental Authority on Development

International Development Research Centre, Canada
http://www.idrc.ca/tec

Provides selected working papers and online resources from project in industrial policy, trade policy, and international trade negotiations.

International Monetary Fund
http://www.ifm.org

Full-text resources available online include IMF Survey, Finance & Development, Working Papers, Staff reports, Economics working papers, and Policy Analysis papers.

International Center for the Settlement of Investment Disputes (ICSID)

Islamic Development Bank

Lake Chad Basin Commission (LCBC)

League of Arab States

Multilateral Development Bank Operations (MDBO)

Niger Basin Authority (NBA)

Organization for Economic Cooperation and development (OECD)
http://www.dc.org

Maintains active relations with African countries, NGOs, and civil society organizations.

Organization of African Unity (OAU)
http://www.oau-oua.org/

Official web site of the OAU. Available in French and English.

Organization of the Petroleum Exporting Countries
http://www.opec.org

PTA Bank
http://www.otabank.co.ke/

United Nations
http://www.un.org

"Among the United nations agencies, the Food and Agriculture Organization (FAO), the World Health Organization (WHO), and the United Nations High Commissioner for Refugees (UNCHR) are the most active in sub-Saharan Africa. Other UN programs in the region include the United Nations Development Program (UNDP), the United Nations Children's Fund (UNICEF), the International Fund for Agricultural Development (IFAD), the United Nations Population Fund, and the Protection of the Global Environment Fund."

United Nations Development Program (UNDP)
http://www.undp.org/

Includes directory of UNDP Africa offices, and full-text reports of project documents and evaluation reports.

United Nations Economic Commission for Africa (ECA)
http://www.un.org/Depts/eca/

Home page of this UN organization featuring information on its objective, programs, related donor activities, and issues of focus.

United Nations Education, Scientific and Cultural Organization (UNESCO)
http://www.unesco.org

United Nations High Commissioner for Refugees (UNHCR)
http://www.unhcr.ch

United Nations Children's Fund (UNICEF)
http://www.unicef.org

United Nations Conference on Trade and Development (UNCTAD)

United Nations Industrial Development Organization (UNIDO)
http://www.unido.org

Maintains database of procurement opportunities in developing countries.

The World Bank Group
http://www.worldbank.org

Substantial amount of full-text documents on Sub-Saharan Africa.

International Bank for Reconstruction and Development (IBRD)

International Development Association (IDA)

International Finance Corporation (IFC)
http://www.ifc.org

Private sector division of the World Bank. Web site provides research papers, working papers, and extracts from the emerging markets database.

Africa Business Network
http://www.ifc.org/abn/index.htm

Provides resources for small and large investors in Africa.

Multilateral Investment Guarantee Agency (MIGA)
http://www.miga.org

The World Bank Group's private investment guarantee agency provides two online services IPAnet http://www.ipanet/net and Privatization Link http://privatizationlink.ipanet.net.

World Health Organization
http://www.who.int

World Trade Organization
http://www.wto.org

Contains statistics on African trade and full text official documents.

U.S. GOVERNMENT SOURCES

The following resources provide direct links to U.S. government agencies promoting trade and investment opportunities in the African region.

Africa Development Foundation
http://mbendi.co.za/exch/11/p0005.htm

Established by the U.S. Congress in 1980 as a federal agency and a public corporation, the African Development Foundation is the principal agency of the U.S. Government that supports community-based, self-help initiatives that alleviate poverty and promote sustainable development in Africa. Over the last fifteen years, ADF has funded over 1,300 activities in 34 African countries.

The Africa Growth and Opportunity Act (Official Site)
http://www.agoa.gov

Official web site providing a variety of information on the AGOA. President Clinton signed the African Growth and Opportunity Act (AGOA) into law on May 18, 2000 as Title 1 of The Trade and Development Act of 2000. The Act offers tangible incentives for African countries to continue their efforts to open their economies and build free markets.

House Subcommittee on Africa

Overseas Private Investment Corporation (OPIC)
http://www.opic.gov

The Small Business Administration
http://www.sbaonline.sba.gov

U.S. Agency for International Development
http://www.info.usaid.gov./regions/afr/

Site includes a comprehensive Africa section covering programs on private sector development.

USAID Micro and Small Enterprise Development Program (MSED)

USAID/Southern Africa Enterprise Development Fund (SAEDF)

U.S. Customs Service
http://www.customs.gov

Provides import/export regulations for international trading.

U.S. Department of Agriculture (USDA)
http://www.usda.gov

Foreign Agricultural Service (FSA)
http://www.fas.usda.gov

Site includes *agriculture situation reports* for African countries (prepared at U.S. embassies) and other marketing data.

U.S. Department of Commerce
http://www.doc.gov

International Trade Administration
http://www.ita.doc.gov

Includes country profiles on business and trade-related topics.

Export Assistance Center
www.ita.doc.gov/uscs/domfld.html

Trade Information Center
http://www.ita.doc.gov/how_to_export/itatic.html

Trade Development Industry Desks

Country Commercial Guides

U.S. Department of Commerce. Country Commercial Guides

U.S. Department of Commerce Country Reports on Economic Policy and Trade Practices
http://www.state.gov/www.issues/economic/trade_reports/index.html

U.S. Department of Commerce. International Market Insight Reports

U.S. Department of Energy
http://www.doe.gov

Provides "country analysis briefs" on energy production for selected African countries.

U.S. Department of State
http://www.info.state.gov

Bureau of African Affairs
http://www.state.gov/www/regions/africa/index.html

The Bureau of African Affairs guides the operation of the U.S. diplomatic missions established in the Sub-Saharan African countries.

U.S. State Department. Background Notes
http://www.state.gov/www.background.notes/index.html

U.S. State Department Travel Warnings
http://travel.state.gov/travel_warnings.htm

U.S. Trade Representative Reports on Africa

Official homepage includes annual report on U.S. trade and development policy for Sub-Saharan Africa submitted by the President.

U.S. Department of Transportation
http://www.dot.gov

U.S. Department of the Treasury
http://www.ustreas.gov

U.S.-Export-Import Bank (EX-IM)
http://www.exim.gov/africa

U.S. Federal Trade Commission

U.S. International Trade Administration
http://www.itaiep.doc.gov

U.S. Office of the United States Trade Representative
http://www.ustr.gov/reports/africa

U.S. Trade and Development Agency (TD)
http://www.tda.gov

U.S. Trade Information Center
http://www.ftc.gov

U.S. BUSINESS AND TRADE ASSOCIATIONS

This section lists trade and other professional associations devoted to expanding Africa's private sector and providing information on business and investment opportunities in the African countries.

Africa Growth and Opportunity Act Coalition (AGOA)
http://www.usafrica.org

Africa Trade Forum

African Business Roundtable
http://www.africast.com/roundtable.html

All-Africa Businesswomen's Association (AABA)

Business Council Europe-Africa-Mediterranean (BCEAM)

BCEAM represents more than 1,500 European Union firms engaged in economic activity in North and Sub-Saharan African countries.

Club du sahel (OECD)

Committee of French Investors in Africa (CIAN)

The largest organization of French institutional and individual investors on the African continent. CIAN annually publishes, a special report known as the "Rapport Jean-Pierre Proteau," which gives information on the activities, investments, and profits of French companies operating in Africa.

Corporate Council on Africa (CCA)
http://www.africacncl.org

American organization advocating for policies and activities that will enhance business relations between the United States and Africa.

East African Enterprise Network (EAEN)

Eastern and Southern African Business Organization (ESABO)

Ghana Association of Women Entrepreneurs (GAWE)

Global Coalition for Africa

Institut International de droit du development

International Trade Centre UNCTAD/WTO

SADC-USA
http://www.sadc-usa.net

Southern African Enterprise Network (SAEN)

U.S.-Africa Chamber of Commerce

U.S.-Africa Free Enterprise Education Foundation & Business Association
http://www.usafrica.com

A non-profit organization designed to promote trade and investment between the United States and Africa through networking, trade missions, trade shows, and conferences.

U.S.-Angola Chamber of Commerce
http://ourworld.compuserve.com/homepages.usacc

"A non-profit organization of businesses united to promote trade and investment between the United States and Angola."

U.S.-South Africa Business Council

West African Enterprise Network (WAEN)
http://www.waen.com

Established in 1993 to promote cross-border trade and investment in Africa, WAEN member countries include Benin, Burkina Faso, Chad, Cote d'Ivoire, The Gambia, Ghana, Guinea, Mali, Mauritania, Niger, Nigeria, Senegal, and Togo.

SPECIALIZED DATABASES/INFORMATION SERVICES

Africa Projects and Privatisation Database: South Africa

"Excerpts from BusinessMap Privatization Database."

African Business Information Services (AfBis)
http://www.afbis.com

"An online source of information and analysis on business and economy in Africa."

African Business Network (International Finance Corporation
http://www.ifc.org/abn/index.htm

"ABN brings in one place information on resources from IFC, its partners and others that can help increase the quantity and quality of private investment in Africa."

Ernst & Young Business Information
http://mbendi.co.za/ernsty/

Provides information on investing in 51 African countries.

IFC's Emerging Markets Data Base
http://www.ifc.org/EMDB.EMDBHOME.HTM

A leading source of information on stock markets in the developing world.

Index on Africa
http://www.afrika.no/index

Investment Promotion Network
http://www.ipanet.net

Service offered by MIGA to facilitate information exchange for international investors.

Marek Africa Information Service (AFIS)
http://www.marktkinc.com/africa.html

MBendi Afropedia

"Provides information on business opportunities in the African countries, the companies and organizations active in various industry sectors, the leading business and government personalities, a directory of products, services, and development projects, details of conferences and exhibitions, and information on the African stock exchanges."

National Trade Databank

Privatization Link
http://privatizationlink.ipanet.net

"Service offered by MIGA providing online access to business profiles of state-owned companies, and details of country investment regulations."

United Nations Industrial Development Organization: Industrial Development Abstracts Database

U.S. Department of Commerce. Trade Development Industry Desks

OHADA
http://www.cm.refer.org

Official Web Site of the Organisation for the Harmonization in Africa of Business Law.

Ohada Legis
http://www.ohadalegis.com

Site focuses on the Business Legal Environment of the Francophone African Countries members of Ohada. Bilingual French-English site.

World Bank Africa Live Database

"Database of macroeconomic and sectoral indicators for the Sub-Saharan African countries."

ELECTRONIC NEWS SOURCES–FROM OR ABOUT AFRICAN COUNTRIES

BBC World Service–Africa

CNN–Africa

AllAfrica.com

Mail and Guardian–South Africa

Reuters Business Briefing

World News Connection

GENERAL REFERENCE–PRINT RESOURCES

This section selectively lists reference works in print format that contain a wide variety of information on economic and commercial issues in Africa.

Africa: Guide to Business Finance for U.S. Firms

"Provides background information, eligibility requirements, and application procedures for over 80 finance sources for U.S. firms doing business in Africa."

Africa South of the Sahara

Reference annual providing a country-by-country survey of economic, social, and political developments in the Sub-Saharan African countries.

African Business Handbook

African Banking Directory

"Contains information on public and private financial institutions in Africa."

African Stock Exchanges Handbook

Provides an overview of Africa's capital markets, including contact information.

African Stock Markets Factbook

Provides an overview of World's stock exchanges, including those in African countries.

Big Emerging Markets Country Guide

Business America

Includes features on African commercial trends and announcements of trade fairs, business leads, and investment opportunities in Africa.

Digest of Commercial Laws of the World

"Includes analysis of commercial codes from more than 100 countries."

Directory of American Firms Operating in Foreign Countries

Published in 3 volumes, with individual country lists available for purchase.

Doing Business with Africa 2000

Guide contains country-specific historical, statistical, political, and economic data.

Emerging Markets Factbook

Exporters Encyclopedia

Annual publication features trade regulations, licensing requirements, and export guidelines on a country-by-country basis.

FedEx–Africa

Handbook of African Business

International Directory of Importers

International Trade Reporter/Export Shipping Manual

Provides shipping information, documentary requirements, label/packing requirements, and standards on a country-by-country basis.

Investing in Africa

"Focuses on the mechanics, available resources, opportunities, and risks related to pursuing foreign direct investment and portfolio investment in Africa."

Key Officers of Foreign Service Posts: Guide for Business Representatives

Handbook contains names and addresses of U.S. Department of State's overseas officers, including all Ambassadors, Commercial Officers, and U.S. AID country program directors.

Political Risk Services Country Reports

Reports on economic and political developments, business climate, and forecasts for investment and trade in the African countries.

World Directory of Importers Associations

"Compilation of information on national, regional, or international trade associations."

World Investment Directory–Africa

ELECTRONIC PERIODICALS

The following resources provide information about economic conditions and business opportunities in Africa. These publications, available in print and electronic format, contain a wide variety of data, including country briefs, trade and commercial policies, marketing information, company updates, industry profiles, trade and economic statistics, product advertisements, and tender announcements.

Africa Analysis

"A fortnightly bulletin on African financial and political trends, as well as discussions of current business conditions."

Africa Business Watch

Africa Communications

A monthly magazine focused on communications, telecommunications, and information technology issues in Africa.

Africa Confidential
http://www.africa-confidential.com

Fortnightly publication provides information on economic, commercial, and political trends in the African countries.

Africa Development Bank–Business Opportunities

Africa Economic Analysis

Africa Economic Digest (AED)

Monthly publication on African economic and commercial issues. Includes tender opportunities, trade statistics, and foreign exchange data.

Africa Energy and Mining

Africa Financing Review

Provides analysis of African financial issues.

Africa Focus–Mining and Exploration

Africa Focus–Privatisation

Africa Health

Provides sector updates and product developments.

Africa Intelligence
http://www.indigo-net.com/africa.html

"Africa intelligence draws from a database of more than 18,000 articles appearing over the past five years in the *Indian Ocean Newsletter, Africa Energy & Mining, La Lettre du Continent* and *Maghreb Confidentiel*. Subscription required."

Africa Invest

Africa Investment Monitor

Monthly publication focusing on economic, political, and commercial issues in Africa. Includes country and sector information, and statistical data.

Africa Investment Update

Monthly publication providing information on African trade and investment trends. Includes profiles of major institutions working with African countries.

Africa News Now: Business & Finance

Africa Oil and Gas

Africa Recovery
http://www.un.org/ecosocdev/geninfo/afrec

Quarterly publication issued by the United Nations focusing on economic and development trends in Africa. Includes data on special development projects and upcoming events.

Africa Research Bulletin: Economic Series

Monthly news digest extracts text taken from African newspapers, news agencies, radio broadcasts, United Nations agency publications, and selected European newspapers and journals. Publisher issues a companion series, *Africa Research Bulletin: political, social and cultural series.*

Africa Review

African Business

A monthly business magazine giving up-to-date information on African economies, business, industry, markets, commodities, finance, and commerce.

African Development Bank–Business Opportunities

Africa Farmer

African Farming and Food Processing

A monthly publication focused on African farming industries.

African Financing Review

Provides analysis of African financial issues, including reports on Africa's capital markets.

African Mining

Africa Mining Monitor

African Review of Business & Technology

A monthly publication focused on selected African industries.

African Technology Forum

Provides information on developments in science and technology in Africa, including technology transfer, training and human resources.

African Textiles

Afrique Asie (France)
http://www.afrique-asie.com

French language magazine focusing on political trends in the African region. Only selected articles are available online.

Afrique Tribune (Canada)
http://www.pagel.com/afriquetribune

Bi-monthly magazine focusing on political trends in Francophone Africa. In French.

Bulletin De L'Afrique Noire

Provides summaries of political events, economic statistics, national budgets, regional organizations, and donor activities in Francophone Africa.

Business in Africa

A monthly business magazine, giving up-to-date articles and analysis on business activity in Africa; emphasis on Southern Africa region.

Communications Africa

Computers in Africa & Telecoms Update

Provides company and industry updates, country surveys, and advertisements for computers and telecommunications equipment.

The Courier

Provides country updates and articles on African development issues. Includes summary of European community financed projects.

Development Business

Fortnightly guide to consulting, contracting, and supply opportunities around the world.

The East African

Economic and Development Bulletin

Emerging Markets Africa

Fortnightly publication providing analysis of African capital markets and financial issues.

Finance Africa

Monthly publication focused on investment and banking in Africa.

Finance and Development

Provides articles and information on major economic development issues in Africa.

Findings (USA)
http://www.worldbank.org/aftdr/findings/english/findtoc.htm

"Provides reports on ongoing operations, economic and sector work carried out by the World Bank and its member governments in the Africa region."

Hart's Africa Oil and Gas

Fortnightly news and analysis of African energy sector.

Investment Legislation Review

Quarterly publication providing information on legal developments in the Africa countries pertaining to investment.

Jeune Afrique Economie
http://www.jeuneafrique.com

French magazine on Africa. Only selected articles available.

Journal of African Business

"Focuses on doing business in and with Africa."

Journal of Sustainable Development in Africa

Locate Africa

The newsletter of the African Investment Promotion Agency Network.

Marches nouveaux sur l'Afrique

Marches Tropicaux et Mediterraneens

Marches Tropicaux et Mediterraneens, 190 Boulevard, Haussman 75008, Paris, France. French language publication featuring country and product briefings and special surveys of selected industries in Africa.

Market Intelligence

Nairobi. Economic Intelligence Ltd. The electronic version of a new monthly business and finance journal with a focus on Kenya. Includes archive of back issues.

Le Monde Diplomatique sur l'Afrique

Includes archives of articles on economic issues in the African region.

The Monitor

The Networker

Monthly newsletter of the West African Enterprise Network.

PTA Business

Business Publicity and Marketing Ltd., P.O. Box 74258, Nairobi, Kenya. Monthly publication focusing on business developments in the Preferential Trade Area member nations. Includes announcements of tender opportunities.

Privatization News

Online newsletter.

South

Monthly publication provides country and sector updates for commercial, economic, political, and social issues in African countries.

South African Business Intelligence

Southscan

Southern African Analysis & Advice

A bimonthly assessment for decision makers.

Southern Africa Economist

Features business article, tender opportunities, and advertisements.

Southern Africa Investor

A monthly publication focused on recent and projected investment projects in the Southern Africa region.

Southern Africa Political and Economic Monthly (SAPEM)
http://csf.colorado.edu/pe/sapem/sapem.html

Monthly publication focusing on political and economic activities in the southern Africa region.

Southern Africa Report

Southern Africa Report Association, P.O. Box 261579 Excom 2023, Johannesburg, South Africa. Focuses on political and economic developments in Southern Africa region.

Southern Africa Report

A bimonthly assessment for decision makers.

U.S.-Africa Chamber of Commerce News Bulletin

U.S.-Africa Chamber of Commerce, 170 Broadway, New York, NY 10038. Monthly publication providing information on business developments in Africa.

World Statesman

NOTES

1. *A Comprehensive U.S. Trade and Development Policy Toward Sub-Saharan Africa.* A Report Submitted by the President of the United States to Congress. The Fourth of Five Annual Reports. December 1993, p. 1.

2. In a new demonstration of U.S. Government commitment, the Overseas Private Investment Corporation committed nearly 1 billion dollars to African private sector projects.

3. The U.S.-Africa Economic Forum is a cabinet/minister level annual meeting focused on debt relief, development assistance, and measures to improve future U.S.-Africa trade relations.

4. Today, virtually every U.S. Government agency has active programs and initiatives aimed at enhancing U.S. economic and trade ties with Africa, including the Departments of Agriculture, Commerce, Defense, Energy, Labor, State, Transportation, and Treasury, as well as agencies such as the Office of the U.S. Trade Representative, the Environmental Protection Agency, the U.S. Export-Import Bank, and the Overseas Private Investment Corporation.

5. The establishment of the Corporate Council on Africa in 1995, with a corporate membership of over 150 major corporations and firms significantly involved in Africa, is indicative of growing U.S. interest in Africa.

6. Adnan Kassar. "Private Sector Grow is Good News Out of Africa." *Journal of Commerce*. March 23, 2000.

7. Subsequent development of this index will focus on more country-specific sites.

8. The project was renamed BEOnline+ (BEOnline Plus) in January 2000, because of the expansion of the project from its initial focus on business and economics resources to include resources in other areas of the humanities and social sciences.

9. OCLC CORC . . .

10. LC Collections Policy Statements. http://lcweb.loc.gov/acq/devpol/cpsstate.html.

PART II: COLLABORATION AND INNOVATION IN AFRICA AND THE UNITED STATES

Partnership as a New Paradigm for Reference Librarians in African Studies

Peter Limb

SUMMARY. This article examines the changing paradigms of reference librarianship as they relate to the study of Africa. It discusses important issues to do with the role of the reference librarian in assisting future scholarly research. Particular attention is given to how electronic resources are influencing the nature of Africana reference services and collection development. Given the problems faced in accessing information from Africa, emphasis is also placed on how partnerships between

Peter Limb is Assistant Professor, Africana Library, Michigan State University Library, East Lansing, MI 48824-1048 (E-mail: limb@msu.edu).

[Haworth co-indexing entry note]: "Partnership as a New Paradigm for Reference Librarians in African Studies." Limb, Peter. Co-published simultaneously in *The Reference Librarian* (The Haworth Information Press, an imprint of The Haworth Press, Inc.) No. 87/88, 2004, pp.151-162; and: *Research, Reference Service, and Resources for the Study of Africa* (ed: Deborah M. LaFond, and Gretchen Walsh) The Haworth Information Press, an imprint of The Haworth Press, Inc., 2004, pp. 151-162. Single or multiple copies of this article are available for a fee from The Haworth Document Delivery Service [1-800-HAWORTH, 9:00 a.m. - 5:00 p.m. (EST). E-mail address: docdelivery@haworthpress.com].

http://www.haworthpress.com/web/REF
© 2004 by The Haworth Press, Inc. All rights reserved.
Digital Object Identifier: 10.1300/J120v42n87_05

U.S. and African libraries and scholarly institutions can help improve information access in and about Africa. *[Article copies available for a fee from The Haworth Document Delivery Service: 1-800-HAWORTH. E-mail address: <docdelivery@haworthpress.com> Website: <http://www.HaworthPress.com> © 2004 by The Haworth Press, Inc. All rights reserved.]*

KEYWORDS. Africa, libraries, reference, electronic resources, partnerships

THE CHANGING ROLE OF THE REFERENCE LIBRARIAN

The role of the reference librarian, in African studies as in other fields of study, is changing under the influence of persistent technological developments and new learning patterns.[1] One can speak of a new paradigm of reference work, not only in terms of new tools requiring new skills but also in that the very nature of the library and the librarian is changing.[2] Information users are modifying their conceptions of libraries, requiring reference librarians to master new tasks such as teaching information skills, providing effective interfaces to burgeoning e-resources, and responding to electronic queries.[3] Librarians must efficiently interact with library clients to better understand their information requirements and develop appropriate services.[4] While predictions of the imminent triumph of the virtual library have been premature, recent trends indicate that scholars increasingly expect information, including advice traditionally associated with the reference query, to be delivered to their desktops. Because clients can now more easily access information themselves, the role of the reference librarian has shifted from revealing "hidden" data and search strategies to one of providing quality context and metadata.

These changes are evident in specific reference tasks. Electronic tools facilitate collection building, book selection and compilation of bibliographies. Reference queries increasingly arrive electronically and e-mail and scholarly electronic discussion lists offer scholars the opportunity of asking such queries of a much broader range of librarians or peers.[5] Rapid growth of Web-based collections of primary and secondary sources (such as NetLibrary and digitized dissertations) and of catalogs and searching aids requires reference librarians to be fully conversant with existing Web resources or even to compile their own online guides to such resources after evaluating their utility and quality.

Reference librarians have always been concerned with the quality of bibliographic resources and have employed such media as bibliographic instruction classes, printed guides, and book reviews to impress upon library patrons the importance of using the best sources. However, the disorganized nature of the Internet and the speed of technological change are inducing new patterns or paradigms of best practice reference that often involve working out qualitative and quantitative approaches to new sources of data as they emerge. The technical and intellectual content of new electronic resources often requires close consultation or coordination with faculty or other librarians in reference and technical services to competently assess quality. Librarians can help overcome the current misgivings by some faculty about electronic resources by explaining their use, by designing user-friendly interfaces to such sources of data, and by lobbying for higher quality e-products.[6]

These developments signal important new trends among reference librarians. The librarian increasingly needs to provide context for, or mediate between, rapidly expanding quantities and formats of information, and to have a more patron-focused approach. There is a growing emphasis on partnerships.

THE REFERENCE LIBRARIAN IN AFRICAN STUDIES

The rapid growth of electronic databases and Web-based sources of information on Africa has made the evaluation of these resources by Africana reference librarians more complex, immediate, and vital. The explosion of information sources has made the organization of timely and efficient reference guides to the literature more necessary than ever. Africana reference librarians increasingly are asked to evaluate the quality and relevance of African studies databases and select appropriate Web sites for inclusion on library or university Web pages dealing with Africa.

The effect on users of these developments is profound. Johnsen observes, "Today the graduate student enters the library with 50 references on the same subject that she has found on the Internet, and just wants help to get hold of copies." He argues that it is inadequate for Africana librarians to keep doing the same tasks if with new tools: "These changed circumstances represent a challenge to our thinking and to . . . our way of working and our priorities. . . . We have to start by looking at what our patrons need from us, that is not provided by other professions . . . [such as]. . . . inputting of information into the databases. . . . [and] quality."[7]

Africana reference librarians in the United States, drawing on their bibliographic expertise of Africa and their technological skills, have responded creatively to these challenges. They have compiled a whole new generation of online subject guides to Africa-related Web sites as well as tutorials to facilitate the use of electronic resources on African studies.[8] If at times there has been duplication of effort in these Internet-based projects, the new reference tools initiated by librarians have proven popular among Africanists and encouraged publishers belatedly to enter this emergent field of African reference information. Librarians, interestingly, have thus been able to secure a niche for themselves on library servers in a world otherwise dominated by commercial publishers.

Over the last decade, Africana reference librarians also have been active in scholarly and professional e-mail discussion networks where they have adapted to new, interactive online reference scenarios. Reference queries and their answers now can be provided by distinguished scholars, as well as librarians, and in a global context. This "internationalization" of the reference query can be daunting to some, as is the prospect of local students opting to route queries to a remote librarian or professor. However, this trend also allows librarians to measure their reference competencies against expert and international yardsticks. This is apparent with the most successful African studies e-mail discussion lists in the humanities and social sciences, the "H-Africana" family of networks. This group of seven moderated networks includes among its editorial staff eight Africana reference librarians who have been involved not only in fielding reference queries but have also acted as book review editors, online and Web editors, planners, and compilers of selective dissemination of information services such as tables of contents of journals.[9]

Little published research has yet appeared on the attitudes to, and effects of, these new Africana media and the role of reference librarians in them. However, the active role of librarians in these areas should help to raise the profile of the profession at the very time when fewer patrons find it necessary to visit the physical library. Moreover, while non-librarians nowadays have access to many of the same electronic tools, the library skills and subject knowledge of Africana librarians continue to make them well placed to take the lead in these new arenas of reference provision.

In the field of collection development, Africana librarians now can use a host of electronic tools to identify and select Western imprints on Africa in a fraction of the time it once took to consult a plethora of printed bibliographies. U.S. librarians also have developed highly successful co-operative Africana acquisition and preservation schemes, such as the Cooperative Africana Microfilm Project and the Cooperative Acquisitions Program of the Library of Congress Nairobi Office. However, the chronic problems facing publishers and libraries in Africa and the growing technology gap continue to make it difficult to acquire African imprints. Moreover, with much African information still produced in printed format, the aim of Africana librarians should be to achieve a judicious balance between traditional and electronic sources of information, between "access" and "ownership," however much this may appear to depart from recent Western library preferences for the former. Many African publications, particularly journals, simply do not find their way into large Western commercial databases, and the Africana reference librarian must therefore continue to monitor and access print materials.

It is important that librarians appreciate the substantial differences between the African library and publishing worlds and their Western counterparts and do not try to reproduce solutions to collection development problems more appropriate in an American setting. To understand these issues and their implication for reference services, it is necessary to outline these African problems.

AFRICA TODAY: THE CRISIS IN INFORMATION RESOURCES AND THE RESPONSE OF LIBRARIES

A crisis in information resources has intensified across Africa in recent years. Scholarly communication continues to face enormous problems. In many African societies, the fragility of publishing and the inability of governments, educational systems, and libraries to maintain basic services reflect the state of crisis. An African "book famine" continues unabated. In 1991, Africa, with 10 percent of world population, produced only one per cent of the global output of books, with 70 per cent of its book needs imported. In this context there is an urgent need, argues Sturges, for a new African library paradigm more relevant to community needs, for forms of information delivery appropriate for African conditions. African publishing today continues to face severe problems such as weak distribution networks, low incomes, low literacy rates, weak infrastructures of libraries and bookshops, and the difficulties of marketing publications in African languages.[10] These problems deleteriously affect African librarianship in general and collection development in particular. Journals cease or become dormant for years. Manuscripts remain unpublished. The acquisition of African dissertations remains very difficult, even in neighboring countries. Keeping track of this uneven pattern of publication is part of the Africana reference librarian's tasks.

Despite such problems, significant institutions have emerged to encourage African publishing, including the Noma Award for Publishing in Africa (established 1978), the Zimbabwe International Book Fair (1983), African Books Collective (1989) and African Publishing Network (1992). Efforts have begun to overcome the drawbacks of African publishing through digitization initiatives. Thus, projects employing Encoded Archival Description hold possibilities for overcoming the enormous difficulties facing preservation of paper archives in many African countries, notably the rigors of a tropical climate and political instability, the latter graphically witnessed in the recent Guinea-Bissau civil war, when the National Archives were decimated. More recently, the growth of the Internet has raised expectations of Africans "leapfrogging" problems to make use of technological advances.

The application of new technologies to many African countries, especially in rural areas, has been limited by structural problems such as limited telephone lines, high start-up and telecommunications costs, and irregular electricity supplies. Nevertheless, in Africa e-publishing has the potential to achieve savings in subscription costs and greatly increase the speed of delivery of information. African governments, universities, and librarians increasingly perceive the potential benefits of information and communications technologies and are developing electronic resources and skills and forging new international partnerships to optimize their use of tools such as the Internet.[11]

Considerable progress in connecting Africa to the Internet has been achieved. Statistics are imprecise but by 2000 all 54 African countries had some kind of Net access in their capital cities. The use of the Net by African libraries and scholars continues to grow. Access outside the capitals remains limited and there are strong regional imbalances. The number of African dial-up Internet subscribers was estimated in May 2001 at about 1,300,000 of which South Africa comprised 750,000 and North Africa 250,000. Web-based information services are well established in South Africa.[12]

Today there are a wide range of Internet sites and other e-services in Africa. These include, for example, online newspapers, Web- and CD-ROM-based databases, e-mail discussion lists, and home pages of university departments. Online newspapers are proving popular in Africa among those of the elite with an Internet connection. E-mail and CD-ROMs, requiring less expensive hardware, have been particularly popular in Africa. Many e-mail networks link Africa-based and Western scholars and librarians. However, in many cases, Africans remain poorly represented in international e-mail networks. For instance, the H-Africa network, which has achieved substantial interaction with Africa, remains essentially Western in its subscriber base.[13] Africa is also poorly represented in the developing field of e-books and e-dissertations, though Rhodes University has joined the Networked Digital Library of Theses and Dissertations.

Despite these obstacles, investors and governments are encouraging greater connectivity. This trend will be facilitated by international partnerships but these need to be mutually beneficial if Africans are to benefit from sustainable long-term development of e-information resources. Reference librarians in both Africa and the U.S. have an important role to play in mediating these changes.

THE IMPORTANCE OF PARTNERSHIPS

The random and exploding nature of the Internet and the increasing internationalization of publishing has made librarians more conscious of the usefulness of networking as a means of making information more accessible to library patrons.[14] This trend is seen in co-operative initiatives, such as those for systems of quality information distribution in which each partner offers specific expert coverage (for instance by reference librarians) and in efforts by librarians and scholars to challenge the hegemony of publishers through partnerships such as the Scholarly Publishing and Research Coalition (SPARC). Co-operative trends are also evident in efforts to better organize Web resources, such as the Co-operative Online Resource Catalog (CORC), which enlists the electronic input of catalogers, reference librarians, and faculty to catalog Web sites, helping to break down divides between reference and technical services.

THE NEED FOR MUTUALLY BENEFICIAL PARTNERSHIPS WITH AFRICA AND THE ROLE OF AFRICANA LIBRARIANS

Partnerships will be crucial in the expansion of the Internet and other forms of new information technology in Africa. Among the major initiatives at government level in this regard are the UN System-Wide Initiative on Africa, USAID/Leland Initiative, the World Bank's African Virtual University, and UNDP's Internet Initiative for Africa. Cogburn and Adeya recently analysed the challenges of globalization and the information economy for Africa. They concluded that countries that fail to pursue the information revolution would fall further behind and argue it is thus imperative for Africans to form strategic partnerships.[15]

Effective partnerships are likely to be crucial for funding future developments in Africana information resources in both Africa and the West. In the face of continuing sharp rises in the cost of commercially provided information, librarians and scholarly associations involved in the study of Africa are seeking to create viable alternatives and develop co-operative projects to improve the quality, quantity, and usage of documentation on Africa. These projects include joint publishing ventures, exchanges, and co-publication agreements between African and Western universities, scholarly societies, publishers, and libraries. Reciprocal exchanges between American and African universities such as the African Internet Connectivity Project have increased hands-on learning and collaborative teaching for both reference librarians and faculty.[16] In the new globalized environment, institutions of learning increasingly will want to promote awareness of their collections on the Web. This in turn will provide new resources for reference librarians to meet the queries of their clients.

However alluring this emerging scenario might appear, the situation on the ground in Africa is more complex. It is important that co-operative e-ventures are undertaken in consultation with experienced advisors and in tandem with *ongoing* technical assistance so that gains are not merely transitory. The mere shipment of computer hardware to Africa without investing in ongoing training for its maintenance has been typical of past foreign aid. Digitization should not be seen as a mere panacea, particularly given the current continued reliance of many African publishers on the print format. Still, aspects of the digital revolution seem appropriate in some African settings: oral traditions and performance occupy an important place in African societies and may offer exciting possibilities in the field of audio and video digitization to enrich African studies. Africana reference librarians have the expertise to advise Western donors or partners on all such matters.

Africana reference librarians have a long tradition of forging co-operative projects both among themselves and with African partners in such areas as collection development and archives and newspaper preservation. They have been prominent in several recent projects aimed at improving access to scholarly resources in and from Africa and helping overcome the "digital divide." The following examples represent a small, if significant, sample of their current projects.

Africana librarians at Michigan State University (MSU) and Columbia University are involved in the Multi-Lingual Digital Library for West African Sources, a project to repatriate in a digital format documents and archives originally taken from West Africa to the U.S. MSU librarians also are playing a leading role in the African e-Journals Project to develop a sustainable online delivery system for African journals in the social sciences and humanities. These two projects involve a wide range of partnerships between, on the one hand, American institutions such as the MSU African Studies Center, MSU Press, MATRIX/H-Net, MSU Libraries and American scholarly bodies and, on the other hand, African scholarly bodies and publishers such as the Institut Fondemental d'Afrique Noire, the West African Research Center and CODESRIA in Senegal. To take a South African example, librarians from the National Library of South Africa, the University of the Witwatersrand, the University of Natal, and the University of Durban-Westville joined with South African archivists and faculty and American advisors from Cornell University in the Digital Imaging South Africa (DISA) project to provide electronic access to material of high socio-political interest.

The role of librarians in these projects has included the provision of advice on the quality and regularity of African publications, on African connectivity, and on other issues to do with scholarly communications and the whole context of information resources in Africa. In these and other projects, librarians are helping to develop viable new models for international cooperation and strategies for making African research materials accessible to scholars worldwide. They are taking part not only in the evaluation, but also the creation, of scholarly resources, as genuine partners and not passive custodians of information. The final products will enhance information resources in their fields, and provide reference librarians with further easily navigable tools for their work.

These projects have the potential to link up with other information and publishing ventures in other parts of the world and in other disciplines, such as African Journals Online of the International Network for the Availability of Scientific Publications, based in Oxford. Such wider international collaboration may be necessary to effectively mitigate the information crisis in Africa. However, long-term solutions to this deep-seated crisis will also require the development of Africa-based resources and competencies.[17] Such development, if it is to succeed, will have to be based, not on short-term charity, but on mutually beneficial partnerships. In this regard, both Africana and African librarians can play an important role. U.S. Africana librarians can act as mentors to librarians in Africa to impart the lessons learned by reference librarians of digitization in the West. Reference librarians in Africa can help educate their Northern library colleagues on the specific nature of the reference interview in African settings and on the particular combination of information resources that emerges in African libraries in the next few decades.

There also are ethical and political dimensions to these trends. Economic and cultural domination of Africa by the West is likely to intensify with the spread of the Internet, reinforcing the need for genuinely mutually beneficial partnerships. Africans are developing skills in employing electronic resources as tools in the educational and political spheres and are likely to forge new partnerships to secure a measure of control over their own lives. Africana librarians, with their traditional concern for the free spread of information and their experience of addressing ethical dilemmas to do with unequal information resources, are well able to mediate in this contest.

CONCLUSION

Africana reference librarians have an increasingly important role to play in twenty-first century scholarly endeavors on Africa. This takes three forms. They must help explain to patrons the new services and opportunities that will flow from constantly changing developments in electronic resources on Africa. They should help to design and implement quality interfaces to these resources. Finally, they can be part of crucial new partnerships that will benefit both African and Western libraries and scholars. Future reference strategies must incorporate these changing paradigms.

NOTES

1. Gary M. Pitkin. (Editor) *The Impact of Emerging Technologies on Reference Service and Bibliographic Instruction.* (Westport, CT: Greenwood Press, 1995); Samuel T. Huang (editor) *Modern Library Technology and Reference Services.* (New York: The Haworth Press, Inc. 1993); Anne Grodzins Lipow (editor). *Rethinking Reference in Academic Libraries.* (Berkeley, CA: Library Solutions, 1993).

2. John V. Richardson, *Knowledge-Based Systems for General Reference Work: Applications, Problems, and Progress.* (San Diego, CA: Academic Press, 1995); Darlene Weingand, "Competence and the New Paradigm: Continuing Education of the Reference Staff," *The Reference Librarian,* 43 (1994): 173-182.

3. Hannelore B. Rader, "Information Literacy in the Reference Environment: Preparing for the Future," *The Reference Librarian,* 71 (2000): 25-33.

4. Lorene Sisson and Donna Pontau, "The Changing Instructional Paradigm and Emerging Technologies: New Opportunities for Reference Librarians and Educators," *The Reference Librarian* 49/50 (1995) pp. 205-216.

5. Marc Meola and Sam Stormont, "Real-Time Reference Service for the Remote User: From the Telephone and Electronic Mail to Internet Chat, Instant Messaging, and Collaborative Software," *The Reference Librarian* 67/68 (1999): 29-40.

6. A. Kasowitz, B. Bennett, and R.D. Lankes, "Quality Standards for Digital Reference Consortia," *Reference & User Services Quarterly,* 39 (2000): 355-63; D. Greenstein. "Creating Digital Library Services: Key Challenges," *CLIR Issues* 14 (2000). See also the current study to test and refine quality standards to describe digital reference services: http://quartz.syr.edu/quality/.

7. T. Johnsen, "Africana Librarians on the Information Highway: Do We Need to Reconsider Our Directions?" in Nancy J. Schmidt (editor), *Africana Librarianship in the 21st Century: Treasuring the Past and Building the Future: Proceedings of the 40th Anniversary Conference of the Africana Librarians Council.* (Bloomington, IN: African Studies Program, Indiana University, 1998): 66-68.

8. See, inter alia, Karen Fung, "Africa South of the Sahara: Selected Internet Resources" http://www-sul.stanford.edu/depts/ssrg/africa/; Joe Caruso, "African Studies Internet Resources" http://www.columbia.edu/cu/libraries/indiv/area/Africa/; Gretchen Walsh, "Web Resources for the Study of Africa," http://www.bu.edu/library/training/aslclass.html.

9. P. Limb, "H-Africa and the Wider H-Net Family of African Studies: Problems and Prospects of the Electronic Future" paper to "The Electronic Future: Africa on the Net" SCOLMA Conference, University of London, June 2000. See http://www2.h-net.msu.edu/~africa/.

10. E. Rathgeber, "African Book Publishing: Lessons from the 1980s," in P. Altbach (ed.), *Publishing and Development in the Third World* (London: Zell, 1992): 77-100; Paul Sturges, and Richard Neill. *The Quiet Struggle: Information and Libraries for the People of Africa.* 2nd ed. (London: Mansell, 1998); P. Altbach and Damtew Teferra (editors), *Publishing in African Languages: Challenges and Prospects* (Chestnut Hill, Ma.: Bellagio, 1999).

11. "Africa in the Age of Information Technology," *Africa Recovery* 13, 4 (1999): 13-27; G. Nulens and L. Van Audenhove, "An Information Society in Africa?: An Analysis of the Information Society Policy of the World Bank, ITU and ECA," *Gazette: International Journal for Communication Studies* 61 (1999). For one instance of how African librarians are creatively employing e-resources see: A. Mutshewa and K.N. Rao, "Enhancing Access through Electronic Resources: The University of Botswana Experience," *Library Hi-Tech* 18 (2000).

12. *Africa on the Internet* (New York: APIC, 2000) http://www.africapolicy.org/inet.htm; Mike Jensen, "African Internet Status May 2001," http://www3.sn.apc.org/

africa/afstat.htm; Z. Nyiira, "Information and Communication Technologies: Experience with Rural Community Telecentres," paper to INET 2000, http://www.bamako2000.org; P. Limb, "New Scenarios on Africa, African Studies, and the Internet" (*Mots pluriels*, forthcoming, 2001). Even in South Africa the picture is very uneven: see Yusuf Sayed, *The Segregated Information Highway: Information Literacy in Higher Education.* (Cape Town: University of Cape Town Press, 1998).

13. Limb, "H-Africa and the Wider H-Net Family of African Studies."

14. M. Gardner, J. DeVries and C. Kaag, "How Many Trees in a Forest: Creating Digital Reference Services in Agriculture" in A. Kasowitz and J. Stahl (editors) *Facets of Digital Reference: The Virtual Reference Desk, 2nd Annual Digital Reference Conference, Oct 16-17 2000* http://www.vrd.org/conferences/VRD2000/proceedings/.

15. D. Cogburn and N. Adeya, "Globalization and the Information Economy: Challenges and Opportunities for Africa," paper to African Development Forum, 1999 http://www.un.org/Depts/eca/adf/infoeconomy.htm#exploring.

16. See: http://www.matrix.msu.edu/connect/.

17. http://www.inasp.org.uk/ajol/index.html; K. Nwalo, "Managing Information for Development in the 21st Century: Prospects for African Libraries, Challenges to the World," paper to 66th IFLA Council, Jerusalem, August 2000. On problems of library consortia in South Africa see C. Darch and P. Underwood, "Dirt Road or Yellow Brick Superhighway? Information and Communication Technology in Academic Libraries of South Africa," *Library Hi Tech*, 17 (1999): 285-297.

Reading African Women's Writing: The Role of Librarians in Expanding the Canon

Miriam Conteh-Morgan

SUMMARY. This paper will briefly review the canon debate in African literature, situating it within a wider context of debates on other non-Western, non-central or emerging disciplines. It will then examine ways in which reference services can respond to the challenge of canon expansion, and how librarians can impact the study of African women writers in universities and colleges. I will approach these topics from two perspectives. The first involves reference librarians in their traditional role as information mediators. Using the works of female writers as examples in instruction sessions and reference guides are ways in which traditional methods can be given a new twist. In so doing, reference librarians will be combining intercultural literacy with information literacy. A bibliography of selected works will also be given that will help general reference librarians strengthen their collections and educate themselves on the subject.

The second will be on ways in which librarians can add a layer to traditional mediating by becoming academic activists. In other words, instead of passively waiting for courses to be created and then supporting

Miriam Conteh-Morgan is Assistant Professor, Bibliographer for Linguistics, African Studies and French, Information Services Department, The Ohio State University Libraries, 1858 Neil Avenue Mall, Columbus, OH 43210 (E-mail: conteh-morgan.2@osu.edu).

[Haworth co-indexing entry note]: "Reading African Women's Writing: The Role of Librarians in Expanding the Canon." Conteh-Morgan, Miriam. Co-published simultaneously in *The Reference Librarian* (The Haworth Information Press, an imprint of The Haworth Press, Inc.) No. 87/88, 2004, pp. 163-178; and: *Research, Reference Service, and Resources for the Study of Africa* (ed: Deborah M. LaFond, and Gretchen Walsh) The Haworth Information Press, an imprint of The Haworth Press, Inc., 2004, pp. 163-178. Single or multiple copies of this article are available for a fee from The Haworth Document Delivery Service [1-800-HAWORTH, 9:00 a.m. - 5:00 p.m. (EST). E-mail address: docdelivery@haworthpress.com].

http://www.haworthpress.com/web/REF
© 2004 by The Haworth Press, Inc. All rights reserved.
Digital Object Identifier: 10.1300/J120v42n87_06

them, librarians can market to faculty ideas for possible uses of the Africana collection and thus provide impetus for new course development. Suggested initiatives include developing theme-related guides or readers' advisory based on African women's texts, and distributing them to other Area Studies faculty–an obvious way to encourage comparative, interdisciplinary research and teaching. Librarians can also hold workshops to demonstrate how works such as Aidoo's *Changes* or Dangaremgba's *Nervous Conditions* that examine the many faces of modern Africa can be discussed in social history, politics or education courses; or Alifa Rifaat's works dealing with women in Islamic communities in a religion or comparative law course. Additionally, libraries need to go beyond in-house, library-only lectures to organizing, for example, campus-wide author lecture series.

To effectively implement these initiatives, reference librarians should collaborate more closely with Africana and Area Studies bibliographers. As librarians in the 21st century, we should be more proactive in our academic communities. We can generate impetus for breaking the literary canon and broadening literary research, foster greater understanding of African culture, while still playing our time-honored roles of guide, mediator, culture-keeper, and agents of change. *[Article copies available for a fee from The Haworth Document Delivery Service: 1-800-HAWORTH. E-mail address: <docdelivery@haworthpress.com> Website: <http://www.HaworthPress.com> © 2004 by The Haworth Press, Inc. All rights reserved.]*

KEYWORDS. Africa, women writers, literature, canon, teaching

INTRODUCTION

Library literature's attention to African Studies in general has focused almost exclusively on collection development and cataloging issues (for example, Malanchuk, 1991; Aderibigbe and Udoh, 1990). The few works that specifically discuss African literature also approach it from the acquisitions and cataloguing angle (Amaeshi, 1985; Wolcke-Renk, 1984). To date, only one article in the electronic database Library Literature deals with African women's writing, and that, too, has a collection development bias (Richey, 1995). Similarly, works suggesting ways in which librarians can expand literary canons tend to approach the topic from a collection development standpoint (Doherty 1998; Krazert and Richey, 1998; Quinn, 1995), and only a few deal specifically with literary reference (Benefiel, Miller and Ramirez, 1997; Adams and Benefiel, 2000).

Going beyond collection development, and thinking about reference and outreach services that could help open up the canon is what this article will discuss. Indeed, it has been acknowledged that librarians "can . . . force the canon to evolve and become more inclusive" (Doherty, 1998, p. 405). I will examine, from two perspectives, ways in which reference librarians can help create an enabling environment for the study of African women writers in U.S. universities and colleges, thus helping to expand the African literary canon. The first discusses how reference librarians can use some traditional methods in their role as information mediators to make African women's writing more visible. The other perspective examines ways in which librarians can add a layer to traditional mediating by taking a more proactive approach. In other words, instead of passively waiting for courses to be created and then supporting them, librarians can market to their campus community new approaches and ideas for possible uses of African women writers' works that could serve as an impetus for course development or enhancement. This philosophy is undergirded by the belief that "librarians know that their libraries hold far more useful material than their audiences–or their potential audiences–generally recognize" (Cullen, 1988, p. 76). It is hoped that these strategies would stimulate the opening of the literary canons, African and world.

While the suggestions given can be applied to other areas or disciplines, examples and strategies will focus on the use the works of African women writers within the contexts of library outreach, and interdisciplinary and intercultural teaching and research.

BACKGROUND

The study of Africa was introduced into the curriculum of institutions of higher learning in the United States as a result of parallel and interconnected developments of the 1960s: the Black Consciousness movement in the U.S., the Cold War, and the decolonization movements in Africa which created the need for the systematic study of other regions of the world. One can say that African literature came of age when, two decades later, in 1986, Nigeria's Wole Soyinka won the Nobel Literature Prize, and was quickly followed by Egypt's Naguib Mafouz and South Africa's Nadine Gordimer. However, it is a literature still relatively unknown to many non-Africans and little explored on many U.S. campuses primarily because the study of African writers has remained largely within Black/Africana Studies programs, and has not made really significant inroads into the central curriculum of many institutions. Arguably, writers like Wole Soyinka, Chinua Achebe, Ngugi wa Thiongo, the "presiding triumvirate" of Anglophone African literature (Lindfors, 1995, p. 59), and the Senegalese (francophone) Leopold Senghor are better known outside of Africana Studies departments as they are read in literature courses in English, Comparative Studies, or French departments, and have more critical works devoted to their writing.

Female writers have not been similarly privileged in curricula or other canon-conferring sources as anthologies. When Lindfors applied the Famous Authors' Reputation Test he devised to examine the frequency with which Anglophone writers were discussed in African literature journals and books published between 1936 and 1986, of the thirty-seven authors identified, six are female; none, however, appears in the first fifteen spots. The same test was applied to two African literature journals, *Research in African Literatures* and *African Literature Today*, and to conference presentations of the African Literature Association (ALA) and African Studies Association (ASA) for the period 1975 to 1997, to determine which women writers, Anglophone and francophone, were the subject of critical analyses (Conteh-Morgan, 1999). It was revealed that women writers have not had much representation in these venues either: only fifty out of the combined eight hundred conference papers identified were on women writers, and not all of them are African. Another similarity between both studies is that Bessie Head came out on top of the list of women writers.

African women writers do not fare much better in the commonly used research databases, subject searches on specific authors conducted in the *MLA International Bibliography* (Jan. 29, 2003) show. The authors searched were: Nadine Gordimer, Bessie Head, Mariama Ba, Buchi Emecheta, Tsitsi Dangarembga, Assia Djebar, and Ama Ata Aidoo, all of whom appear on the Lindfors list and/or Africa's 100 Best Books of the 20th century. The top three hits are Gordimer (313), Head (168), and Djebar (121). They are followed, in descending order, by Emecheta, Aidoo, Ba, and Dangarembga. In *Literature Online*, 51 of the 229 African authors included in the database are female (Jan. 18, 2003).

Ama Ata Aidoo, the 1992 Commonwealth Prize winner for her book *Changes*, speaks of the collective pain of women writers: "It is especially pathetic to keep on writing without having any consistent, active, critical intelligence that is interested in you as an artist" (Aidoo, 1988). This observation is all the more glaring when one compares the representation of two Nobel Prize winners in the MLA: Gordimer's 313 hits as against Soyinka's 588, despite the fact that the former is considered part of two literary traditions, African and British.

With women's voices seemingly lost amid the "humming and bustling" of their male counterparts (James, 1990), more of their works needs to break through the hegemonic control of the canon-conferring establishment; in short, the African literary canon needs to be opened up. Librarians can be useful in bringing more visibility to African women's writing on their campuses by helping "to raise the threshold of access and affirmation" (Allan, p. 55).

DEFINING THE CANON

It will be worthwhile to consider at this point some definitions of the term "literary canon" and briefly revisit the canon debate. There are a multitude of definitions, but they all share a few basic characteristics. A literary canon, as defined by those with a "classical" point of view, consists of a body of works recognized for their literary quality, timelessness and universality (Heinzkill, 1990). Gates (1990) defines the canon as works by "'crucially central' authors [who are] indispensable to an understanding of the shape, and shaping, of the tradition" (p. 102). Implicit in both views is the notion of a common interpretation of what constitutes a canonical work. Indeed, consensus on what literary quality is and the tradition that defines it can only be grounded in the ideals of a community of "experts" and readers; ideals shared basically because of the common heritage or consciousness of the group.

However, these definitions raise a number of questions. The notion of timelessness suggests that hallowed works remain that way forever, and are not open to new interpretations or influences that could "dethrone" them. But it is also known that canons evolve, particularly because "canon formation and the rise and fall of artistic and ideological trends are interrelated" (Szegedy-Maszak, p. 20). The definitions also suggest that a multiplicity of traditions exists, with canons based on these different traditions. As such, this not only undermines the issue of universality, but also raises the other question of whether these multiple canons will independently continue to orbit in their own proscribed spaces (or traditions), or merge at some point. Canon purists would like to believe the former, but Heinzkill (1990), with particular reference to English literary studies, thinks that there will be a merging of canons from different cultures that all share a common language tradition, English–put differently, a super canon created out of the plurality of canons of literatures in English. Another school of thought holds the view that multiple canons will recognize each other's status as equal but remain separate. If one subscribes to the former position, then many African writers will become part of the canon of literature in English, French, and Portuguese; otherwise, they will remain a part of their continental or national canons.

NEW CANONS, NEW IMPERATIVES

Implications for the Faculty

Whether or not one subscribes to the theory of single or multiple canons, reality points to significant changes in the academic world that have had an impact on the canon debate. The re-reading of texts and the application of non-literary theories to literary texts has led to novel interpretations of literary works. For example, there has been a shift toward incorporating perspectives from cultural studies and history to focus on the contexts in which texts are produced and received. Additionally, insights gained from other literary traditions, and readings from the perspective of the "subaltern" have led to fresh examinations of the classics of the western tradition, and ultimately to a questioning of their stranglehold on emerging canons. Theories of *post-isms*–postmodernism, and postcolonialsm to name two–have also provided liberating approaches to critical analyses. As such, voice and space have been given to the hitherto unheard and unseen.

As has been generally acknowledged, this academic climate has had a salutary effect on, for example, gender studies and area studies. In areas where both these disciplines intersect, for example, "the new trend toward global women's studies has moved Africa to a more central position" (Berger, 1997, p. 10). But more importantly, these changes of direction mean that boundaries of disciplines are no longer fossilized or clearly demarcated, and that faculty need to be reaching out to colleagues in other departments and disciplines. According to David Chioni Moore (2001), "Postcolonial critique has also illuminated parallels between areas heretofore seen as noncomparable, such as Senegal and India, and it has energized fields such as Irish Studies" (p. 112). These centrifugal approaches have had enormous effects on the study of Africa. Berger believes "the prospect of new collaboration across regional and disciplinary boundaries promises to enhance rather than threaten African Studies" (p. 12), for it will bring "both area-based and disciplinary knowledge to bear on particular issues" (p. 5). In short, the "I word" (Ryan, quoted in Searing, 1996), "interdisciplinarity," is what is now driving research, publication, and teaching.

There is indeed a new dawn for African Studies in general, the right climate for the works of African women in particular to receive the wider recognition they deserve. Christopher Miller (1993) has it right when he asserts that there is currently "a positive intellectual atmosphere for the teaching of African literature, an atmosphere conducive to multicultural inquiry and intercultural literacy" (p. 219).

The Role of the Library

For many teaching faculty, however, there is a gap between wanting to take advantage of the favorable atmosphere and actually incorporating new initiatives into the curriculum. Hunter (2000) points to another group of professionals on campuses that can bridge this divide. As it is widely acknowledged, research, especially in the major literary databases, presupposes some knowledge of authors' names, as thematic searches are not always very fruitful. On the need for intercultural and interdisciplinary work, Hunter acknowledges that:

> [faculty] are individually and collectively ill equipped by training to do this work. In our own "cultural" investigations, not to mention those we lead or provoke our students to do, we do not know our way around. We are going to be dependent . . . on those whose knowledge of the bibliographies, texts, and materials of other disciplines and other subject areas is larger, broader, and especially deeper than ours . . . The cries you hear from faculty these days . . . will inevitably be directed mostly to [librarians]. (p. 296)

Cries for help and the knowledge that faculty expect librarians to provide research-related answers is not new. But in this brave new world he describes, librarians have an even more pivotal role to play to bring together, in a coherent and cohesive whole, the seemingly discrete strands of the multi-canon, intercultural, and interdisciplinary mosaic. As a result, "A librarian not only must have specialized knowledge of [a] field as a whole but also must be a generalist at ease with sources in a number of more-or-less related fields" (Adams and Benefiel, 2000, p. 258).

Librarians themselves have long been aware of the library's unique position as the site on campus where all of these strands come together, and their leadership role in using resources that facilitate the intercultural and interdisciplinary connections. Having historically responded to and supported the academy's enshrinement of the Great Books, librarians may now need to participate in enlarging the canons. By being actively involved in the curricular reforms on campus and becoming "co-creators of the curriculum" (Pelster and Baker), they can give more visibility to the works in their collections hitherto unfamiliar to the majority, not least, those of African women writers.

TRADITIONAL METHODS AND INNOVATIVE STRATEGIES

Reference Service

Although the various activities that are at the heart of librarianship will remain unchanged for the foreseeable future, the way those activities are carried out will evolve to match the new environments in which information is produced, sought, and used. As a result, in the words of Shiri, the mother-narrator in Maraire's *Zenzele*, "we [librarians] are all bridges," between old needs and new forms of delivery, and between new needs and uses. Or as Ramatoulaye in Mariama Ba's *So Long a Letter* puts it, we have to necessarily become "messengers of a new design" (p. 25).

In being able to mediate between actual or envisaged information needs on the one hand, and the resources to meet those needs on the other, reference librarians have always sought innovative ways of delivering and adding value to their services. It will be no different when that need or resource happens to be related to African women's writing. Generalists can bring those same skills to bear on subject specialties like African literature and their patrons will continue to expect the same level of expertise and service. They would need to learn more about the subject from, for example, the texts listed in Richey's article, and more recent publications such as Limb and Volet's *Bibliography of African Literatures*, Parekh and Jagne's *Postcolonial African Writers*, and the growing number of dictionaries and encyclopedias put out by renowned publishers of reference resources. Librarians can also mine the Web for university-sponsored and enthusiasts' web sites (see Appendix) that can be bookmarked on reference desk computers.

Instruction

The move away from tool-based instruction to emphasis on critical skills and concepts that cut across individual tools is grounded in the philosophy of empowerment for users. Armed with information literacy skills, any user can search for information to meet their academic, personal, or professional needs.

One other way in which reference and instruction librarians can make African women writers more widely known is by incorporating examples from their works in instruction sessions. Typically, when literary examples are used in regular instruction classes, they tend to be from the established canons and not the emerging ones. So, for example, in teaching patrons how to search in various databases such as *MLA International Bibliography*, *Academic Search Premier*, and *Humanities Abstracts*, librarians may use the author Bessie Head to show users how to critically evaluate results (compare number and relevance of results), and determine which is the best source for their specific information need. Even if students had not been familiar with the author before their instruction session, the results of the various searches can help them appreciate the place of the writer in the African literary tradition.

Using the works of African women writers to teach various search concepts goes beyond teaching information literacy. It can also help foster intercultural literacy by exposing students to other literary traditions not familiar to them. Intercultural literacy would help them better understand that the human condition can be displayed in many different, cultural idioms; an understanding that could in turn prompt "research into the processes by which cultures are formed and . . . [encourage] analysis of how cultures constitute themselves by reference to each other" (Miller, 1993, p. 217). As one who has taught African Literature as a general education requirement, it became abundantly clear to me that many American students had never imagined that there existed a body of literary works written by Africans until a non-western requirement came along. For those who may not have taken such a course, library instruction could perhaps plant the seed of inquiry.

Research Guides

Creating pathways to information, or tips on searching for various types of information are staples of reference librarianship. These become particularly necessary for accessing fiction whose assigned subject terms may not always reveal the themes explored in the works. An unskilled searcher looking for works that deal with the theme of education or lack of its opportunities in Africa may not be able to directly retrieve a novel or play in many of the databases currently available. This is where the mediator-librarian comes in. By collaborating with African

Studies librarians, reference librarians can create thematic guides that would group, for example, Nawal El Sadaawi's *Woman at Point Zero*, Tsisti Dangaremgba's *Nervous Conditions*, Ama Ata Aidoo's *Changes*, or Simi Bedford's *Yoruba Girl Dancing*. Each addresses the theme of women's educational opportunities from different yet sometimes overlapping perspectives. These works, or parts of them, could be read in a comparative education course, or in social history or sociology courses as they each present scenarios along the continuum of social change.

Having online counterparts to the print guides is one way of assuring wider knowledge of the existence of these books, and creating a potential information need. Guides, as it is widely recognized, help us "publicize and explain our collections and educate patrons" (Pankake, p. 329). But publicizing, explaining, and educating should not be limited to just faculty or students. Subject specialist librarians can also be educated and later enlisted in the bid to expand the canon and foster interdisciplinary collaboration. These guides can be made available to other librarians on campus who can then discuss new possibilities with their faculty. For example, the short stories of the Egyptian writer Alifa Rifaat that deal with the place of women in Islamic societies, or Efua Sutherland's *The Marriage of Anansewa* that deals with marriage agreements can be used as case studies in law classes focusing respectively on Islamic law and social contracts. Or Assia Djebar's *Fantasia* which is set during Algeria's war of independence in a political science course on decolonization, or Buchi Emecheta's *The Joys of Motherhood* in urban migration classes. *Zenzele* is an excellent choice for classes dealing with modern African families. It would also be interesting to have Werewere Liking's plays studied in theatre courses on the avant-garde. Additionally, other area or ethnic studies faculty may also find these guides useful for drawing inter-region parallels and contrasts. For example, *Nervous Conditions* and el-Sadawi's *Walking Through Fire* lend themselves to interesting comparative analyses with Esmeralda Santiago's *When I Was Puerto Rican* or *Almost a Woman*, or Amy Tan's *The Joy Luck Club*.

Displays

Traditionally, libraries have displayed their new acquisitions, or built displays around timely events and cultural themes. The list of Africa's 100 best books could be one way of bringing the public's notice to the literature from the continent. However, display boards and areas are only seen by those who physically walk into the library, and as many librarians know, only a tiny fraction of a campus' population visits the library. Consequently, the essence of the display is lost on a large proportion of the institution's community.

One strategy for reaching a wider audience is by "taking it to the streets." There is nothing to prohibit libraries from taking their displays to other parts of campus. To spark an interest in students, book jackets of the works of African women, or copies of relevant video covers can be exhibited in their Union buildings, and traditional and themed dorms to stimulate intercultural literacy and an engagement with African/international issues. Within the limits of campus posting laws, no place–elevator, bus stop, eating places–should be beyond the reach of the librarian who truly wants to market a collection (the example of the Poetry Society of America's display of poems in mass transit systems to celebrate National Poetry Month every April is worthy of emulating). It is worth remembering that the unfamiliar has a way of stimulating curiosity and ultimately, learning.

Faculty Clubs, with their tradition of inspired debates could be another venue for extra-library displays aimed at catching the faculty's attention. Other possibilities worth exploring are department buildings. These tend to house faculty in related disciplines, so displaying "nonrelated" materials could yield interesting results. For example, by displaying book covers in non-Humanities buildings such as those housing Law, Political Science, or Agriculture departments, faculty could read the descriptions and make pertinent interdisciplinary connections. This in turn could lead to visits to the library to learn more, and possibly result in some kind of faculty-librarian collaboration. As Searing (1996) asserts, "Services alerting interdisciplinary scholars to a range of new information *outside* [sic] their core fields are more valuable than typical SDI services based on narrow interest profiles" (p. 322). Creating counterpart virtual displays and making them prominent on the library home page is another effective way of reaching many more patrons.

Author Presentations

Many speakers invited by libraries tend to be either information service providers or other librarians. In other words, speakers are chosen mostly because their message relates directly to the activities of the host library or to the library world at large. This rather insular view gives the impression that librarians, whose work takes them through a wide variety of knowledge areas, are narrowly focused on library-only issues, and are excluding the producers of that very knowledge they want their patrons to use. This anomaly can be remedied if libraries invite authors to speak to librarians. Authors discussing their works in libraries will inspire more meaningful connections between texts and librarians' use of those texts to answer reference questions. If librarians understand the various contexts in which writers create their works, they can incorporate that understanding in their baseline competencies, and impart that knowledge to patrons via reference services; this can only make for enhanced, value-added service and greater patron satisfaction.

With respect to African women writers, the majority live outside the U.S., but occasionally attend professional meetings here. To give an example, Nadine Gordimer addressed the African Literature Association (ALA) 2001 conference in Richmond, Virginia. Conferences such as this, or the African Studies Association of North America (ASA), offer opportunities for initiating contacts with them, learning about their itineraries, and perhaps inviting them to speak on campuses. Indeed, it would be much cheaper to invite them to speak on campuses while they are in the United States, and more so if the cost of bringing them to a campus can be shared with other interested departments. By hosting authors, libraries will contribute to the campus cultural calendar, and reiterate their centrality to the wider community (a fact often overlooked by many patrons).

Faculty-Librarian Presentations

Librarians can also offer workshops to faculty or hold brown bag sessions, either in the library, through Faculty Development, or other campus offices. One can envisage a session titled "African women's writing in an interdisciplinary context" based on the research guides discussed earlier in this paper. Librarians can also collaborate with teaching faculty to give joint presentations. In 2000, for example, Ohio State University's library director and a professor in East Asian Studies participated in an interdisciplinary forum titled "Old Culture/New Media." Sponsored by the College of Humanities' Institute for Collaborative Research and Public Humanities, the series, *Parallel Lines*, brings together "faculty engaged with similar issues . . . to make presentations in an occasional brownbag lunch series" (http://www.cohums.ohio-state.edu/HI/research.html, Jan. 29, 2003). The discussions are traditionally drawn from different disciplinary perspectives, and such an avenue is clearly one possible way of making African women writers more widely known and their works more accessible.

CONCLUSION

How else can librarians participate in new curricular reforms and show academic leaders across campus that they can do more than passively support new initiatives? The examples and suggestions discussed above should all form part of the communication that needs to go beyond the library's four walls. Twenty-first century librarians must position themselves more centrally in research and curricular activities on campus. By marketing their collections and expertise, and "[b]y presenting library services in a way that complements and reinforces the educational themes that campus leaders themselves are discussing and espousing, librarians can bring the library into a more central and vital position in the curriculum" (Pelster and Baker, 1992, p. 83). They must actively seek out new markets for and uses of their collections, move the boundaries that have allowed parts of library collections to be narrowly defined and used, and make the works of writers from emerging traditions more widely visible and read. Until research tools become more representative and searchers more proficient, librarians will serve as awareness agents on their individual campuses.

REFERENCES

Adams, Michael and C. Benefiel. 2000. Literary reference into the new century. In: *Literature in English: A Guide for Librarians in the Digital Age.*

Allan, Tuzyline. 2001. We Will Be Heard! *Black Issues Book Review* (March-April): 53-55.

Aderibigbe, M. R. and D. J. E. Udoh. 1990. LC subclass PL8000-8844: A case for revision. *Cataloging & Classification Quarterly* 10, 3: 77-90.

Aidoo, Ama Ata. 1988. To be an African woman writer–an overview and detail. In *Criticism and ideology: Second African writers' conference*, edited by Kirsten Holst Petersen. Uppsala: Scandinavian Institute of African Studies.

Amaeshi, Basil. 1985. African literature as a main new class. *International Library Review* 17: 39-50.

Benefiel, Candace, Jeannie Miller and Diana Ramirez. 1997. Baseline competencies for the academic reference desk. *Reference Services Review* 25, 1: 83-93.

Berger, Iris. 1997. Contested boundaries: African Studies approaching the millennium. *African Studies Review* 40, 2: 1-14.

Conteh-Morgan, Miriam. 1999. *The female voice in African literature: An assessment of its impact.* Unpublished Master's thesis, Kent State University.

Cullen, Charles T. 1988. Libraries and humanities: The case for scholarly activism. In *Libraries and the search for academic excellence*, edited by Patricia Senn Breivik and Robert Wedgeworth. Metuchen, New Jersey: Scarecrow Press.

Doherty, John J. 1998. The academic librarian and the hegemony of the canon. *Journal of Academic Librarianship* 24, 5: 403-406.

Gates, Henry Louis. 1990. The master's pieces: On canon formation and the African-American tradition. *The South Atlantic Quarterly* 89,1:89-110.

Heinzkill, Richard. 1990. The literary canon and collection building. *Collection Management* 13, 1-2: 51-65.

Hunter, J. Paul. 2000. The return to history in English studies. In *Literature in English: a guide for librarians in the digital age*, edited by Betty H. Day and William A. Wortman. Chicago: Association of College and Research Libraries.

James, Adeola (ed.). 1990. *In their Own Voices: African women writers talk.* London: James Curry.

Krazert, Mona and Deborah Richey. 1998. Native American Literature: Expanding the canon. *Collection Building* 17, 1: 4-15.

Limb, Peter and Jean-Marie Volet. 1996. *Bibliography of African literatures.* Lanham, MD: Scarecrow Press.

Lindfors, Bernth. 1995. *Long drums and canons.* Trenton, New Jersey: Africa World Press.

Malanchuk, Peter. 1990. African acquisitions: Strategies to locate and acquire current and retrospective Africana. *Library Acquisitions* 15, 4: 453-461.

Miller, Christopher. 1993. Literary Studies and African Literature: The Challenge of Intercultural Literacy. In *Africa and the disciplines: The contributions of research in Africa to the social sciences and humanities*, edited by Robert H. Bates, V.Y. Mudimbe, and Jean O'Barr. Chicago: University of Chicago Press.

Moore, David Chioni. 2001. Is the post- in postcolonial the post- in post-Soviet? Toward a global postcolonial change? PMLA 16, 1: 111-128.

Pankake, Marcia. 2000. Faculty liaison: Librarians and faculty as colleagues. In *Literature in English: a guide for librarians in the digital age*, edited by Betty H. Day and William A. Wortman. Chicago: Association of College and Research Libraries.

Parekh Pushpa and Siga Fatima Jagne. 1998. *Postcolonial African writers: A bio-bibliographical critical sourcebook.* Westport, Conn.: Greenwood Press.

Pelster, Natalie and Betsy Baker. 1992. Curriculum reform: Catalyst for building strong faculty/librarian partnerships. In *Academic libraries: Achieving excellence in higher education*, edited by Thomas Kirk. Chicago: Association of College and Research Libraries.

Quinn, Brian. 1995. Some implications of the canon debate for collection development. *Collection Building* 14, 1: 1-10.

Richey, Debora. 1995. Black African women writers: A selective guide. *Collection Building* 14, 1: 23-31.

Searing, Susan. 1996. Meeting the information needs of interdisciplinary scholars: Issues for administrators of large university libraries. *Library Trends* 45, 2: 315-342.

Szegedy-Maszak, Mihaly. 2001. *Literary canons: national and international* (Studies in Modern Philology 16). Budapest: Akadémiai Kiadó.

Wolke-Renk, Irmtrauad. 1984. Acquisition of African literature–Problem and challenge for book dealer and librarian. *IFLA Journal* 10, 4: 377-84.

APPENDIX. Selected Web Sites on African Women Writers

African Women's Bibliographic Database
http://www.africabib.org/women.html (Jan. 30, 2003)

Davis Bullwinkle's large AfricaBib database on Africa includes this database that lists over 25,000 citations to articles, conference papers, and books on women's literature. It is searchable by region/country, or subject. Display options include by title, author, or date.

African Women Writers
http://www.britishcouncil.org/virtual/africanwomen/ (Jan. 30, 2003)

This virtual publishing exhibition, mounted by the British Council for the Frankfurt International Book Fair 2000, "celebrates the quality and diversity" of women writers from Africa. While the site only provides a synopsis of the authors' works, it is useful for its list of well-known and not so popular authors.

African Writers: Voices of Change
http://web.uflib.ufl.edu/cm/africana/writers.htm (Jan. 30, 2003)

Hosted by the University of Florida, the project includes pages on women writers. Information provided include bio-bibliographies, a bibliography of critical works, and links to similar web sites.

Anglophone & Lusophone African Women's Writing
http://www.ex.ac.uk/~ajsimoes/aflit/default.htm (Jan. 30, 2003)

This site gives "detailed bibliographies, biographies of selected figures" (author's description) and points to links related to African women's writing.

A Celebration of Women Writers
http://digital.library.upenn.edu/women/ (Jan. 30, 2003)

This is one of the better-known web projects on women writers from around the world. It brings together other web sites devoted to a writer, and allows for searching by author's name, or country of origin, time period, or ethnicity. There is, however, no separate category for African writers; some are found under the category "African-American."

Contemporary Postcolonial and Postimperial Literature in English: Postcolonial and Postimperial Authors
http://www.scholars.nus.edu.sg/post/ (Jan. 30, 2003)

Part of a larger site on the culture, politics, and literary periods of former colonies, the site has a short list of African writers that includes some women. It provides biographical information on authors, a list of their published works, and student papers about the works.

Gender in African and Other Postcolonial Literatures
http://faculty.pittstate.edu/~knichols/carib.html (Jan. 30, 2003)

This directory is part of Professor Kathleen Nichols' (Pittsburgh State University, KS) postcolonial literature web project. The section on African women has links to a few authors only, but it also gives useful links on the political and cultural context of African literature.

Reading Women Writers and African Literatures
http://www.arts.uwa.edu.au/AFLIT/FEMEChomeEN.html#english (Jan. 30, 2003)

Primarily devoted to francophone women writers, this bilingual site (in French and English) provides a useful bibliography of critical works. The works of francophone writers available in translation are also listed. Also has links to Lusophone and Anglophone women writers.

Designing an Anglophone University Undergraduate Library Collection for a Francophone West African Environment

Akilah Shukura Nosakhere

SUMMARY. In 1997, the Office of West Africa Programs at Georgia State University in Atlanta, Georgia, USA, and the Ministry of Education of Cote d'Ivoire embarked on a venture called *Project Link* to develop an English-speaking international university in Grand Bassam, Cote d'Ivoire. The mission of the proposed *International University for Development in West Africa* in Cote d'Ivoire is to offer educational opportunities based on the American Higher Education Model presented in English to Ivorians and other West African students within the West Africa region. The proposed undergraduate university curriculum is designed to offer life-long educational opportunities that appeal to the whole West African region as well as to the prospective students living in and near Grand Bassam, Abidjan, and Yammousoukro. In January 2002, the Agency for Education and Development of Abidjan, one of the sponsors of the international university, invited a group of six specialists from Georgia State University (GSU) to visit the proposed site and work

---

Akilah Shukura Nosakhere is Special Collections Librarian, Special Collections Reading Room, Atlanta University Center Robert W. Woodruff Library, 111 James P. Bawley Drive, Atlanta, GA 30314 (E-mail: Akilah@auctr.edu).

[Haworth co-indexing entry note]: "Designing an Anglophone University Undergraduate Library Collection for a Francophone West African Environment." Nosakhere, Akilah Shukura. Co-published simultaneously in *The Reference Librarian* (The Haworth Information Press, an imprint of The Haworth Press, Inc.) No. 87/88, 2004, pp. 179-187; and: *Research, Reference Service, and Resources for the Study of Africa* (ed: Deborah M. LaFond, and Gretchen Walsh) The Haworth Information Press, an imprint of The Haworth Press, Inc., 2004, pp. 179-187. Single or multiple copies of this article are available for a fee from The Haworth Document Delivery Service [1-800-HAWORTH, 9:00 a.m. - 5:00 p.m. (EST). E-mail address: docdelivery@haworthpress.com].

http://www.haworthpress.com/web/REF
© 2004 by The Haworth Press, Inc. All rights reserved.
Digital Object Identifier: 10.1300/J120v42n87_07

with an Ivorian team of technology and curriculum experts to produce a work plan for the renovation of an existing campus in the scenic coastal town of Grand Bassam about 50 miles east of Abidjan. In addition to recommending physical and technical upgrades to the campus site, the American and Ivorian specialists were to advise AED on the administrative organization of the proposed institution, develop a curriculum model and suggest resources for the university library. This paper will highlight the role of the GSU Collection Development Specialist during the 10-day site visit in January 2002 and provide an update since the 2002 site visit. *[Article copies available for a fee from The Haworth Document Delivery Service: 1-800-HAWORTH. E-mail address: <docdelivery@haworthpress.com> Website: <http://www.HaworthPress.com> © 2004 by The Haworth Press, Inc. All rights reserved.]*

KEYWORDS. Africa, library, collection development, African libraries, project link

In 1998, Georgia State University received a three-year grant from USIA totaling over $100,000 to partner with the University of Cocody in Cote d'Ivoire to begin an exchange of faculty, curriculum, and educational models. Faculty from Georgia State's J. Mack Robinson College of Business, the Andrew Young School of Policy Studies, and the College of Education began collaboration to develop a framework for a public policy center, a program of management development for private sector managers leading to an American style MBA program to be offered at a university based in West Africa.

The idea of an International University for Development in West Africa soon evolved and for the past five years students, faculty, and administrators at the two universities, along with the Ivorian Ministry of Higher Education and Scientific Research have been working to make Project Link a reality.

Officially, I became involved with Georgia State University's Project Link in March 1999 when Dr. Doris Derby, Director of the Office of African American Student Services and Programs (OAASSAP), approached me about joining an ad hoc committee organizing to send interested African American students to the University of Cocody in Abidjan to study for the 1999 summer term.

The goal of this committee was to launch a short-term study/travel program allowing GSU students to attend summer classes at the University of Cocody in Cote d'Ivoire. As a member of the VISACUD committee it was my responsibility to coordinate the creation of an orientation handbook on Cote d'Ivoire for program participants and contribute to the selection of articles on African American culture and history to serve as "ice-breakers" in English language instruction modules planned for Ivorian students studying English in the Business School at the University of Cocody.

Volunteers in Service and Cross-Cultural Dialogue (VISACUD) became the name of the student exchange program developed by Dr. Derby's committee. VISACUD represented the emerging relationship between Georgia State University and the country of Cote d'Ivoire. Eight students were selected to participate in the new study abroad program. Each of them submitted research proposals and received course credit for completed projects related to their experience in Cote d'Ivoire.

While in Abidjan the students were housed with Ivorian families and attended many cultural activities as well as classes and seminars at the University of Cocody. For many of the participants this was their first time abroad so there was plenty of excitement and anticipation. VISACUD proved to be a successful 4-week experience where African American students traveled to Abidjan Cote d'Ivoire to experience life and study in West Africa.

Unfortunately, the coup of December 25, 1999, where the government led by President Henri Konan Bedie was overthrown, and the remaining unstable political climate has since prevented OAASSAP from organizing other study-abroad opportunities in Cote d'Ivoire. However, efforts to establish the International University continued under the leadership of the GSU Office of West Africa Programs led by Assistant Vice President for Public Affairs, Dr. Stephen Langston.

In September 2001, Charlene Hurt, the University Librarian at Georgia State, encouraged me to join Dr. Stephen Langston, leader of Project Link and Vice President of Public Affairs, in planning for an Africa-based university in Grand Bassam, Cote d'Ivoire. Aware of my professional interest in academic library development in Africa and my past service with VISACUD she realized that this was a great opportunity for the University and me. Even though my hands were already full serving as head of the Library's Department of Collection Development, she enabled me to work with Dr. Langston and the team of other GSU academic professionals to develop the shared vision of the International University of Development in West Africa.

As a collection development specialist, my task was to produce a library collection development policy and provide a table of recommended print and electronic resources for the library of the proposed university. I began by outlining the needs of the library based on the concept statement for the International University and other documents provided by Dr. Langston.

The proposed International University of Development in West Africa would initially offer an undergraduate academic program with great emphasis on English language acquisition to ensure that all students have the language skills necessary to succeed in their studies. The curriculum would also focus on the global perspectives of business and economics, computer information systems, human resource development, conflict resolution, education, and health policy studies. In addition to supporting these primary areas, the library would support general study in the areas of mathematics, natural and social sciences, including traditional and popular Ivorian culture, local and world history, African Studies, and African Diaspora Studies.

A site visit was scheduled from January 10-28, 2002 and the GSU team was expected to have preliminary proposals ready for review by the coordinating organization, the Agency for Education and Development (AED) in Abidjan, by the first week of January. With this deadline in mind, I spent nearly every weekend and the holiday break writing and refining the collection development policy.

I collected database cost information from vendors to provide a realistic estimate of library startup costs for this ambitious project. I also reviewed publisher catalogs and the online library catalogs of GSU Pullen Library and other university libraries to assemble samples of resources appropriate for the proposed collection.

The preliminary proposal contained recommended library resources and projections of associated cost over a five-year period. Samples of library resources in various formats with pricing and inflation growth projections were summarized in the preliminary report. Institutional membership fees in academic and library associations, such as the Association of African Universities, African Virtual University, Association for the Development of Education in Africa, the Soros Institute, the West Africa Library Association, and the International Federation of Library Association are also included in the proposal. These and other organizations could serve as possible institutional partners for the new university and assist in additional library development.

Start-up cost for resources and institutional memberships alone was estimated in the preliminary proposal at $86,000. Of course, this figure did not include library automation software, computer hardware, workstations, and library furniture that would be necessary for library start-up. Equipment costs were included in the Facilities and Technology sections submitted by my GSU colleagues, John Harris, academic facilities management professional, Mark Roberson, information technology expert, and Dr. Carla Relaford, a specialist in distance education. After meeting with Ivorian librarians at the International School of Abidjan (K-12), I included in the final figures a quote for the purchase of SIRS Mandarin library automation software. The use of the same automation system provides opportunities for these two institutions to share resources and seek other consortia ventures in the future.

The ten days we spent in Abidjan were exciting and exhausting at the same time. On our first day we made all of the necessary visits to government and city officials. A luncheon in our honor was held at the home of former Prime Minister Kablan Duncan, an avid supporter of the International University project. There we were introduced to the traditional leaders of Grand Bassam, the Mayor, the Chief of Police, and local business people and treated to a lively reception of traditional dance and entertainment. Each evening we could gather and discuss the day's events, revise and refine the ever-evolving work plan we came to produce.

Each day we would convene with our Ivorian counterparts at Grand Bassam or with local educators or entrepreneurs in Abidjan to clarify details and move closer to the production of the final work plan, which was presented at a televised news conference on our final day in Cote d'Ivoire.

After five years of collaboration and planning with the Ivorian Ministry of Higher Education and Scientific Research, the Agency for Education and Development, and others, Georgia State University has not given up on establishing a university in West Africa. On September 19, 2002 when the latest coup attempt occurred, Dr. Langston and Sam Koffi of the GSU Office of West Africa Programs were in Abidjan continuing to push for the realization of this vision. Both are now safely back in the United Sates.

In early September 2002, Dr. Kofi Q. Dadzie, Associate Professor of Marketing at the J. Mack Robinson School of Business at Georgia State University, reported that a marketing plan for the International University project is underway. Unfortunately, all plans are now tabled due to the latest political violence in Cote d'Ivoire.

In the future, efforts to secure financial supporters throughout the United States and abroad for this project will be resurrected and one day the international university will become a reality in Cote d'Ivoire. On that day, we will congratulate the government of Cote d'Ivoire, the Agency for Education and Development, Georgia State University, and the Office of West Africa Programs for establishing a solid foundation for providing a 'Western-style education with African values.'

APPENDIX A

Collection Development Policy
International University
Grand Bassam, Cote d'Ivoire West Africa

Purpose of the Collection: The Library is to serve an undergraduate academic curriculum largely defined by American higher education practices to support the present and anticipated curricular needs of students and faculty. The Library will reflect the international perspective of all subject disciplines while collecting extensively in English language materials in support of the mission of the institution. The Library will also support the development of life-long independent learners by collecting at the general academic through the American master's degree level.

General Collection Guidelines:

a. **Languages:** English will be the primary language of the collection to support instruction in the English language. However, materials in French and major indigenous languages will also be collected as available and appropriate.
b. **Chronological Guidelines:** Most acquisitions will focus on contemporary world society while selectively adding comprehensive historical and analytical treatments of subjects in retrospect from the latter half of the 20th century.
c. **Geographical Guidelines:** The Library will collect materials on the history and culture of continental African people, particularly Ivorians, in regional and international economics, cultural and health research, issues and practices from early times to present. The collection will also include materials related to contemporary American Higher Education and American Business theory and practice.
d. **Treatment of Subject:**

The collection will consist largely of electronic resources purchased annually to provide access to students and faculty of the International University. Digital resources delivered via the Internet will serve a major curricular need, however, other resources, e.g., CD-ROM, DVD, and videotape will also be collected. The general reference collection for undergraduate students will include a number of print resources in a variety of subject disciplines.

The collection will also include blanket orders with select publishers to receive most major series and research monographs in targeted subject areas. A collection of current print journals and news resources in business and Africana Studies will also be maintained.

Business Resources: Essential business reference resources including directories of companies, company and industry descriptions, comparisons, and rankings will be collected in print. Resources on the culture of business, business etiquette, and business leaders from throughout the world will be collected selectively.

Education Resources: Materials providing socio-economic and education statistics, testing and measurements, and research methodology will be collected extensively. Particular emphasis will be placed on the collection of resources about African educational theory and practices whenever available and appropriate. Reference titles on major topics in the study of education in the United States including educational theory and practice, educational psychology, pedagogy, learning disabilities, and curriculum studies, for example, will be collected selectively.

Medicine and Health Care Resources: The majority of all medical and health care will be available digitally in full-text and image formats via the Internet whenever possible. Basic health and medical print resources uniquely related to African health issues, research and practices will be collected selectively.

General Undergraduate Resources: The general collection will be made up of resources at the undergraduate college reading level and require no prior knowledge of the subject material. Most basic reference titles in a number of disciplines (science, literature, composition, history, mathematics, popular and traditional culture, and religion) will be collected broadly. English language instructional resources will also be collected to supplement English language instruction.

e. **Types of Material:** The electronic resources will be accessible through a network provided by the International University and will include both subscription and free Internet-based resources. It is envisioned that the reference collection will contain about 500-1,000 titles primarily in English and in digital and print formats. A browsing periodical collection of about 25 print titles will supplement the e-journal collection. The print collection will provide access to pertinent Africana Studies materials not yet available in digital or CD-ROM formats. The types of print resources collected will include monographs, handbooks, directories, dictionaries, yearbooks, desk references, specialized encyclopedias, almanacs, and selected international documents. Historical and analytical treatments of all aspects of the African experience will be added selectively. Materials will be collected based on content, however, CD-ROM format is preferred and will be collected whenever available.

f. **Date of Publication:** Recent materials from the late 20th century forward will be emphasized. However, selective retrospective collection of classic African Studies materials in English, French and indigenous languages will be collected as available and appropriate. The majority of reference titles will be updated annually to ensure currency. Periodical back issues in print will be retained selectively and will be dependent upon demand, the availability of electronic access to archival collections, and the availability of storage space.

APPENDIX (continued)

Observations and Qualifications by Subject Subdivision and Collecting Level: the *Pacific Northwest Conspectus* model (USA) has established levels to describe the depth of a collection. *A level of 3C is appropriate for this library project and provides for the development of a collection at the Advanced Study Level.

Subject Subdivision	Collecting Level
English Language Instruction:	3c
Grammar	
Composition	
Conversational English	
American Literature	
Computer and Research Skills Development:	3c
Time Management	
Information Literacy	
Computer Literacy	
Keyboarding	
Computer Operation	
Software Manipulation	
Business Administration:	3c
Organizational Behavior	
Corporation Finance	
Marketing Management	
Decision Strategy	
Managerial Accounting	
Electronic Commerce	
Information Technology	
International Business Environment:	3c
Marketing	
Banking and Economics	
Risk and Finance	
Taxation	
Technology and Global Competition:	3c
Global Marketplace Policy and Strategies:	3c
Global Portfolio Management:	3c

Subject Subdivision	Collecting Level
Multi-National Banking and Finance:	3c
Multicultural and Cross-National Environments	
World Civilizations and Culture:	3c
Geography and Environment	
African Studies–Cote D'Ivoire (Ivory Coast):	3c
Academic level English language monographs concerning all aspects of Ivorian society will be collected.	
African Studies–West Africa Region:	3c
History and Arts	
Technology	
Economy	
Political Thought	
Peoples and Cultures	
Languages and Literature	
Performing Arts & Cinema	
Traditional and Popular Culture	
African Studies–East, South, North Regions and the African Diasporas (Europe, United States, Caribbean, Asia, etc.)	3c
Conflict Resolution and Negotiation:	3c
Conflict Resolution Skill Training	
Arbitration and Mediation	
Building Peace	
Violence Prevention	
Truth and Reconciliation	
Human Rights	
Problem Solving Skill Development	
Safe Schools and Civil Communities	
Aid and Conflict	
Media and Conflict	

***Advanced Study Level 3C**

"Adequate for honors undergraduate instruction or sustained independent study; adequate to maintain knowledge of a subject required for limited or general purposes but not strong enough for original research in a subject. Includes the most important primary and secondary literature, a selection of basic representative journals/periodicals, and fundamental reference and bibliographic tools pertaining to the subject."

Source: *Pacific Northwest Conspectus Collecting Levels.* A handout.

Frog Voices, Whispers, and Silences: Problems and Issues in Collecting for an African Studies Library in Africa

Colin Darch

SUMMARY. This article is an attempt to respond to two questions about discrete special African studies collections in African university libraries. First, do we need to have such collections at all? Second, if we do, how can we write collection development policies that make sense, given the present turmoil in African studies and indeed in the social sciences in general? Librarians have a responsibility to recognise that their practice cannot be value-free, and that their collections are biased by the choices made by writers, by publishers, and by themselves. Their duty, especially in Africa, may simply be to ensure that African voices are not drowned out in their collections. *[Article copies available for a fee from The Haworth Document Delivery Service: 1-800-HAWORTH. E-mail address: <docdelivery@haworthpress.com> Website: <http://www.HaworthPress.com> © 2004 by The Haworth Press, Inc. All rights reserved.]*

KEYWORDS. Academic libraries, African studies, Africana librarianship, collection development policies

---

Colin Darch is Senior Information Specialist, University Library, University of Cape Town, Private Bag Rondebosch 7700, South Africa (E-mail: picc@ched.uct.ac.za; web site: http://members.tripod.com/~Colin_Darch/).

[Haworth co-indexing entry note]: "Frog Voices, Whispers, and Silences: Problems and Issues in Collecting for an African Studies Library in Africa." Darch, Colin. Co-published simultaneously in *The Reference Librarian* (The Haworth Information Press, an imprint of The Haworth Press, Inc.) No. 87/88, 2004, pp. 187-207; and: *Research, Reference Service, and Resources for the Study of Africa* (ed: Deborah M. LaFond, and Gretchen Walsh) The Haworth Information Press, an imprint of The Haworth Press, Inc., 2004, pp. 187-207. Single or multiple copies of this article are available for a fee from The Haworth Document Delivery Service [1-800-HAWORTH, 9:00 a.m. - 5:00 p.m. (EST). E-mail address: docdelivery@haworthpress.com].

http://www.haworthpress.com/web/REF
© 2004 by The Haworth Press, Inc. All rights reserved.
Digital Object Identifier: 10.1300/J120v42n87_08

INTRODUCTION

Why put African materials in special collections? If there is an answer to this question other than the purely pragmatic, we must disentangle two problems–how the various 'area studies' constitute themselves as an array of academic disciplines, and the subordinate question of what kind of special library support, if any, such disciplines may require.

Let us take the second question first. At a superficial glance, special library collections devoted to Africa make some kind of organisational sense, at least in academic institutions in Europe and the Americas.[1] This may be partly, but not exclusively, because it is relatively easy for librarians to identify materials about Africa and to place them in a dedicated collection. But is there anything about African studies, or about its literature, that *requires* exceptional, separate, or discrete library treatment, as opposed to the usual specialist bibliographic and reference knowledge? Are African studies like law, or music, or fine arts–disciplines typically supported by a literature that is so physically or bibliographically 'different' that practice requires separation? The quick answer is no, but if 'African studies' are in the curriculum in some shape or form, or are a research focus, then it may be a reasonable choice to concentrate library expertise, as well as the material in many instances, to serve the needs and for the organisational convenience of specialist students and researchers.[2]

There is still a difficulty, and it arises from the question about how area studies are constituted. In the United States, at least, there seem to be elevated reasons for studying Africa:

> [k]nowledge of the other; knowledge of the self: the journey to Africa supports both projects. But most urgently it pushes students to consider the relationship between the two: between self and other, West and non-West, "developed" and "underdeveloped." African studies is a way of studying Africans; but it is also, even more significantly, a way of studying the processes of globalisation.[3]

This may be a fair–or at least clear–enough post-colonial argument for African *studies*, at least for North Americans. But why do *African* academic institutions need to have special academic centres and special collections devoted to Africa in the libraries? For us in Africa, this particular distinction between 'self' and 'other' clouds the issue, and we are firmly and unhappily on the receiving end of the processes of globalisation. In fact, we may even ask what we mean by 'African studies' in Africa, when presumably African universities teach the social sciences by building on local knowledge, by using local and national experience, and by recognising that African experience is a point of departure rather than a point of reference. What do we mean by an African studies collection in the library when presumably the collection development policy of the whole university library service is also committed to using national experience as a point of departure for the local production of knowledge? Why, if the whole collection is infused, as it should be, with accounts of different aspects of our own African reality, is there usually some physically closed off section of the library building devoted especially to a record of African experience, written as it happens mainly by outsiders?

These are, of course, ironical questions as well as big ones. University teaching and university libraries in Africa do not often take local and national experience as a starting point; collections consist overwhelmingly of books and periodicals brought from Europe and North America; we in Africa all too often reflect other people's views of ourselves.[4] Further questions about special African collections in African university libraries arise: do we need to have such collections at all? Can we write collection development policies that make sense, given the present turmoil in African studies and indeed in the social sciences in general?

Some hidden assumptions lurk behind library practice *in* Africa with regard to material *on* Africa.[5] There is a largely uncritical attitude towards post-colonial insights into the character of the corpus of academic analysis on Africa–especially the idea of Northernness as 'self' and Africanness as 'other.' This may be a reflex of the nearly universal use of European languages in the African academy, as well as of the troubled history and present characteristics of African area studies as a discipline. Equally important is a grave crisis of sustainability of libraries on the continent, as African librarians attempt to reproduce a model developed in hugely different–and richer–social, economic, and political conditions.[6] It is far from obvious, even if we accept the need for special library collections on Africa in Africa, that they should simply and inadequately reflect, in conditions of immense poverty and indebtedness, the characteristics of what are indubitably the great North American and European specialist libraries.

WHAT ARE AFRICAN STUDIES?[7]

For librarians, as for other academics, 'African studies' do not constitute an easily demarcated discipline, despite what appears to be the term's obvious commonsensical signification. The idea of 'Africa' as an object of study is fraught with difficulty, as many modern scholars have forcefully pointed out: 'Africa is not a given, we make it as we make our own history.'[8] Not only is it not given, its meaning has changed and continues to change over time, and it is arguably more contested academically and politically in our present epoch than it has ever been before. William Martin has written of 'uncertainty and challenges from multiple perspectives' with regard to African studies and of 'growing chaos within the social sciences' in general.[9] Librarians in the field are aware of all this, of course, but perhaps do not always see these struggles as having a lot to do directly with their own practice. However, as soon as we attempt to write a coherent collection development policy, it is obvious that these problems are more than administrative issues. Should an Africa-focused collection in Africa include diaspora studies, or collect works on the black experience in the United States, the Caribbean and Brazil?

For librarians, insights from one kind of area studies do not necessarily transfer easily to other areas. Expressions such as 'European,' 'African,' 'South Asian' or 'American' do not signify in equivalent ways. 'European studies' is not the logical or epistemological equivalent of 'African studies,' and cannot be so. In Africa the terms 'European' and 'African' are commonly used as racial definitions, code words for white or black, as when Afrikaans-speakers are termed 'white Africans.' But most collections would stop short of basing policy on such racial distinctions, for compelling reasons.

Considering this, why do we divide the world up into continents in order to study it? Inglehart and Carballo have pointed out that '[area] studies centers [. . .] are based on the assumption that Latin America (like Africa, the Middle East, etc.) are more than arbitrary geographical expressions: they define coherent cultural regions, having people with distinctive values and worldviews that make them think differently and behave differently from people of other cultures.'[10] But if this is so, why should Portuguese-speaking Brazil fall under 'Latin American studies' alongside Spanish-speaking Chile, for example, but not alongside Lusophone and African Angola, its 'eastern frontier' to which it is linked by culture, history, and oceanic trade? The answer of course is that most existing regional definitions are 'the product of processes of

Western imperial "discovery" and conquest.'[11] The nature of the terminology frequently gives the game away–the 'Middle' or the 'Far' East are only that way if you are in some sense standing in Europe (the 'West'). These definitions often lead to reductionist usage and reinforce undifferentiated characterisations–of Africa as the dark and savage place of nineteenth century geographical literature and CNN news reports.

There are alternative ways to establish 'areas' that may give nightmares to cataloguers but that also promise rich insight. Landmasses are not the only game in town. We already know about the Pacific Rim, and Paul Gilroy has constituted the Black Atlantic[12]; but these are still based on some idea of physical proximity. There are many other kinds of culturally definable areas possible.

The fuzziness of ostensibly uncomplicated geographical categories emerges if we examine an apparently straightforward expression such as 'southern Africa.' Where and what is southern Africa? During the years of apartheid, South African writers commonly used the term quite narrowly to mean South Africa, Botswana, Swaziland, and Lesotho, plus the so-called TBVC states (Transkei, Bophutatswana, Venda, and Ciskei, the nominally 'independent' bantustans). Thus, South African usage assigned content to the expression in order to legitimate the politically illegitimate.

In neighbouring countries, by contrast, the term referred, in effect, to the member states of SADCC (the Southern African Development Coordinating Conference, now a community). But that definition includes Tanzania, a country normally considered geographically part of the eastern African region, even if it has *politically* become southern African.[13] Going further, if we take the degree of integration of different states into the South African-dominated *regional economy* into account, then Angola, for example, with historically weak links to the system, is only marginally 'southern African.' At an even more detailed level, some parts of some countries are more 'southern African' than others. Mozambique south of the Sabie River, for instance, constitutes an important and integral part of the South African migrant labour network. The central and northern Mozambican regions are largely outside it. 'Intellectuals,' as Seekings argues–and I believe this includes librarians–'have for too long accepted the logic of comparison within areas whose boundaries generally originated in the former imperial powers of the west [. . .] and subsequent geopolitical rather than intellectual factors.'[14]

The difficulties are not only geographical. Do African studies include the study of African law, of African medicine, of African engineering? Which social sciences fall within the framework, which ones are excluded? For some scholars, area studies are a branch of comparative politics, admittedly of a strongly cross-disciplinary character; for others, and more polemically, the term has the purpose of locating Africa as the object of study by establishing its otherness.

To take an instrumentalised view, libraries can only collect actually existing and recorded texts, publications, regardless of how we understand those words. At first glance, a 'discipline' such as 'African studies,' founded primarily but not exclusively on a geographical definition, should have clearer boundaries and be less complicated to maintain than a conventionally constituted one such as economics or chemistry. It should be easier to decide whether a book is about Gabon or Senegal or not, for example, than whether it is about sociology, physics, or history. Unfortunately, things are not so simple. The time is long past when we could collect comprehensively in any entire discipline, and to that extent, our collections will constitute *an interpretation* of the state of the disciplines that they focus on. The judgements that we–academics and librarians–make about what to include and what to leave out will amplify some voices, silence some, and reduce others to a whisper, locally but effectively. In and of itself, the collection will present a certain view of the world.

A Place, a People, an Experience?

But still, librarians worry about what we are supposed to be collecting. Works about a continent, works about a (racially-defined) people who live on that continent, works about the experience of these people dispersed around the world by the experience of slavery? The emergence of the Afrocentric paradigm from the 1960s onwards has sharpened librarians' awareness of this issue, but has left them with a new set of difficulties. Some proponents of Afrocentrism argue that 'it is valid to posit Africa as a geographical and cultural starting base *in the study of peoples of African descent*.'[15] In such a formulation, it is the *experience of African people*, wherever they are, that is the object of study, and African studies collections may thus expand to enfold and include African-American studies and such topics as the black experience in Brazil, Cuba, the Caribbean, and throughout the entire diaspora. The geographical focus on which African studies might have lazily rested shifts and opens out as its tidy borders blur and merge into a broader and more inclusive kind of social science.

The shift from a purely geographical foundation to one that takes account of people and experience does not solve the librarians' problems, however. Who are these African people and how are they defined–by skin colour, by race, by cultural practices? In the reductionist and populist account, Afrocentrism starts and finishes as a question of skin colour, and has as much to do with the politics of race in the United States as with the production of knowledge in Africa itself.[16] Thus, the Senegalese historian and philosopher Cheikh Anta Diop, now acknowledged as a 'father of Afrocentrism,' is commonly represented as wanting to show that the Egyptian pharaohs were black, by looking for melanin in their mummified remains.[17] The deeper significance of Diop's work, however, lies in a much broader question, namely 'whether history before the arrival of the White Man could be understood as a social history, or whether the limits of our understanding were the limits of archaeology, however reconstructed.'[18] In such an account, Afrocentrism becomes an historical concept as well as a philosophical one, but in both cases, the meaning is the same–Africa stands at the centre of everything.

Why is this important for librarians in Africa? Because the very idea of 'African studies' emerged within a hegemonic and Eurocentric intellectual tradition, and was *essentially* concerned from its beginning with the study of the 'other,' whatever the specific or local *objective* impetus might have been. Thus, the funding of African studies in the United States after the Second World War took place as part of a strategic engagement with the world made necessary by Washington's desire for hegemony. But we need only contrast the subjective construction of African studies (and other post-colonial area studies) with the process of construction of European studies, or American studies in Britain, to see that it was always invested with ambiguity, and has always been contested.

The literature and thus our collections reflect this, in Africa as elsewhere. The earliest Europeans who wrote on Africa did not work within an academic tradition. Rather, as missionaries, scholars and explorers, they thought and wrote within what amounted to a system of private enterprise, needing to sell their knowledge in the marketplace.[19] Meanwhile, the earliest African authors either assimilated to a European literary tradition and wrote in English, French, or Portuguese, or else produced ethnohistorical works in their own tongues for a tiny readership of missionaries and educated compatriots.[20] This was a parallel but largely devalued tradition.

By the late 19th and early 20th centuries this freelance mode of intellectual production had begun to be gradually supplanted by research 'controlled directly by colonial governments,' as even conservative commentators have admitted.[21] Much research in colonial times was tainted since 'numerous investigations [were] intended to aid policy makers' and direct subsidies from government funds paid for them.[22] New sub-disciplines emerged to play new roles and interpret new data. From the 1930s, 'governments drew increasingly on the assistance of professional anthropologists and sociologists, as well as archaeologists and others to supplement the information previously amassed [. . .]'[23] Many scholars were actually eager to build relationships with the structures of colonial power. British anthropologists, for example, 'tried intermittently to persuade the government that [they] could indeed help in the affairs of colonial rule. By the mid-1920s the nature of the interface between scholarly and administrative interests in Africa had become clearer.'[24] Indeed, by the 1930s, it was explicit: it is sometimes argued that 'African studies' in the English-speaking world were kick-started in the United Kingdom by Lord Hailey's *African Survey*, first published in 1938 and intended as a handbook for serving British colonial administrators.[25] The institutional base emerged much later and in different circumstances in the post-war United States, when Melville Herskovits founded the first university programme in African Studies at Northwestern University in 1951.[26]

Mamdani has described the close relationship between the colonial enterprise and the academy in the following way: 'The colonial construction of knowledge about Africa was based on three key disciplines. The first was archaeology, with its construction based on unearthed artefacts. The second was anthropology, with its focus on an essentialised African, the Muntu. And the third was history, which was literally synonymous with the history of the white man on the continent.'[27]

The colonial authorities encouraged local knowledge production by settlers. In Mozambique, for example, there was the *Sociedade de Estudos de Moçambique* with its own journal, ceasing publication only at independence in 1975; in Northern Rhodesia there was the Rhodes-Livingstone Institute with its strong publishing tradition in anthropology. African studies at the University of Cape Town go back to 1918, when the School of African Life and Languages was set up.[28]

How can we describe library collections founded during this period, constituted for these purposes, and consisting of this kind of literature, as anything other than colonial libraries, unless our practice is consciously intended to transform them by empowering, in creative new ways, other voices to speak on the colonial and post-colonial experience in Africa? This question is not rhetorical, and applies as much, if not more so, to the great collections in South Africa as it does to the libraries of other parts of the continent. At the heart of these difficulties over the older colonial 'African studies' collections, we find the problem of anthropology, the discipline and practice that produced much of the early Northern academic writing on Africa. In turn, at the heart of the difficulty over anthropology lies the illusory, persistent, and evolutionist concept of the 'primitive society,' developed in Victorian times by such classicists as Henry Maine, John M. McLennan, and Lewis Henry Morgan.[29] As the colonial enterprise ended in Africa, anthropology as a discipline started to practice a little introspection, and has found itself in ideological and methodological trouble ever since.[30] By the early 1970s, a younger generation of anthropologists were beginning to deconstruct their own practice in such texts as the collections edited by Dell Hymes and Talal Asad, and the discipline has never fully recovered from the critiques that were mounted.[31] This is not the place to summarise these extensive and prolonged debates, but it is probably worth picking up a few of the points made as they bear on library practice, especially with regard to collection development in 'African studies' libraries located on our continent.

Anthropology is seen uncompromisingly by many as 'the child of imperialism,' to use Kathleen Gough's compelling phrase.[32] It represents the view of the coloniser, looking at subject peoples whose voices cannot be directly heard. An African scholar who feels hostile towards the discipline, writes Archie Mafeje, 'does not have to be a trained anthropologist. Familiarity with classical anthropology texts is sufficient.'[33] It is not very hard to see why this might be so. The anthropologist, wrote E. E. Evans-Pritchard as late as 1951, 'studies primitive societies directly.'[34] Only a couple of years later, S. F. Nadel stated that anthropologists 'attempt to extend our knowledge of man [sic] and society to "primitive" communities, "simpler peoples," or "preliterate societies."' Amadiume calls African responses to such anthropological writing '*nzagwalu* literature,' explaining the expression as an Igbo response to insults suffered.[35] She puts her finger firmly on the crucial point regarding the material when she points out that 'in [being ashamed of associating with anthropology, Africans] face a dilemma, because, unfortunately, a lot of the archival information that Africans need in order to move forward is trapped in this subject.'[36] Not only Africans: there have been attempts by modern Northern anthropologists to rework the field notes of earlier predecessors.[37]

FROG VOICES, WHISPERS, AND SILENCES

According to the anthropologist William Willis, the African-American novelist Richard Wright used the term 'frog perspectives' to describe the way in which 'facts' are often seen by the oppressed from a special point of view, which differs sharply from the perspective of the oppressor.[38] Liking the expression, I searched for the text in the library of the University of Cape Town, but found only five works by Wright in the collection, none of them the one I needed. Wright had himself become a frog voice.

Implicit in the way a traditional academic library represents its collections is the idea that a multiplicity of voices are heard, and that the collection is thus in some sense representative of what is reasonably believed and known. The problem with African studies collections in Africa is that the voices heard are overwhelmingly the voices of the colonisers, and the frog voices are silent. Emphatically, it is not the role of librarians to create new silences, but they can and have on occasion, working with academics, reintroduced silenced frog perspectives to the record. Bontinck's series on African travellers in equatorial Africa in *Zaire-Afrique* in the late 1970s and early 1980s, or Gerhard Liesegang's recovery of early black Mozambican authors in the pages of *Arquivo* in Maputo are examples of what might be more commonly attempted.[39]

But the whispers and silences in library collections will remain, as long as the production of knowledge about Africa remains marginal to the academic enterprise in Africa itself, and is subordinate to a racial hierarchy elsewhere. Students often see this clearly. In the United States they are commonly dissatisfied with the way institutions treat African and diaspora studies, seeing low funding levels and under-representation in the curriculum as an expression of racism. In May 1999, for example, students took to the streets of Washington, DC to protest what they said was a clear and deliberate pattern of under-funding and under-resourcing of the African Studies programme, one of eleven area studies programmes at Georgetown University.[40] There have been dozens of such student protests, focussing on curriculum issues or targeting specific teachers.

Such a situation is related to the particular conditions that have prevailed and that continue to prevail 'favour[ing] the production of white intellectuals (including radical white intellectuals) and block[ing] the production of black intellectuals'–or indeed of female intellectuals.[41] A stroll around the grounds of any elite South African universities may confirm this truth, and library shelves will reflect it, too. The production of knowledge and its concrete manifestation, the writing of texts, has historically been the task of predominantly male elites, supported, of course, by the labour of the mass of the excluded. Worldwide, over the last few centuries, a European and white male stratum has dominated the production of what is now a dominant global mode of knowledge, both in form and in content. But the dominant mode of knowledge has also historically presented itself as both value-free and as universal. Both of these positivist claims have come to be widely rejected. The idea that library practice is in some sense neutral or value-free persists, however, and I shall return to this later on.

The gendered, class-based and racial organisation of human societies underlies the production of a Eurocentric and dominant mode of knowledge, but once we can see this reality for what it is, it becomes entirely logical to ask, in Mudimbe's words, 'To what extent can one speak of an African knowledge, and in what sense?'[42] The process of discovering or producing such an African knowledge does not *necessarily* invalidate the whole body of existing (dominant) knowledge, although it does necessarily reject its positivist and universalist claims.

Is collection development constrained by the nature of the existing literature, and if it is, should it be so? Should builders of library classification schemes make provision only for subjects that writers actually write about? This debate about 'literary warrant' dates back at least to 1911.[43] Do librarians in South Africa carry some of the responsibility for the 'reproduction of inequalities in intellectual work' because we, like other academics, have not self-consciously attempted to offset the structural effects of how universities are organised and how knowledge is socially produced?[44] The late Harold Wolpe was referring specifically to the effects of apartheid when he made this point, but it does have a more general application. A library collection is defined as much by what its builders leave out as by what they include.

What Kirk-Greene called 'the routine infrastructure of Africana books and publishing' thirty years ago has supported African studies for several decades.[45] There are different opinions about how solid that infrastructure actually is. On the one hand, at the continental, regional, and national levels, such reference works as encyclopaedias, the various types of bibliography, dictionaries, atlases, yearbooks, and of course, journals of varying degrees of specialisation, continue to appear. Thus, the infrastructure stays in place, although smaller in scale than it should be and less regular in its updating schedule than is desirable.[46] On the other hand, as William Martin has written of his experience at the University of Illinois: 'To send a student to the library serves only to confirm [that the knowledge-base on Africa is shaky]. Even in [. . .] the third largest university library in the country–we receive only a handful of daily newspapers from the whole of Africa, whereas we receive at least this many from each major European country. Africana and African studies share one room in the library, in sharp contrast to large, lending, departmental libraries for other disciplines and areas.'[47]

Gretchen Walsh has argued regarding the situation in academic libraries in the United States, that 'the choices publishers make [about what to publish] cause difficulties for librarians trying to tailor a collection to specific curriculum needs. Publishers [. . .] want sales at least big enough to break even [. . .] This has meant, for instance, more books on South Africa [. . .] and fewer intensive studies of less well-known areas or issues.'[48] If this is true in North America, how much more difficult it is in Africa itself, with tiny publishing industries operating in ex-colonial languages and largely isolated from each other and from the larger world. But despite this, Walsh also recognises the importance of building a collection that allows the frog voices to be heard, pointing out that Africans do 'study both themselves and the rest of the world,' and arguing in favour of purchasing African imprints.[49]

This is not to say, of course, that only Africans can write meaningfully about Africa. Harold Wolpe effectively dealt with this exclusivist perspective when he objected to the contention advanced by 'black and feminist movements both in South Africa and elsewhere that no adequate account of the situation of such populations [as black people or women] can be produced except by actors whose experience is conditioned by their membership of the population in question.' Such an explanation is unacceptable 'since it reduces "explanation" to "experience" and denies the importance of theory.'[50]

CONCLUSION: THE 'ADVANCE FROM NEUTRALITY'

The idea that library practice is–or can be–in some sense 'neutral' or 'value free' is extraordinarily persistent, and is just as much an illusion in our work as it ever was in the social or natural sciences.[51] Social scientific thinking begins with the recognition that social position determines the thinker's view of the world: class, gender, and race being only the most obvious aspects. The typology of problems identified in relation to African studies applies equally to the study of any subordinate social group's contribution to history and society, often lost except in the physical artifacts left behind. We see the grandest of these as the product of the architect, artist or even patron, rather than of the workers who built them, *vide* Bertold Brecht. In the meantime, librarians grudgingly classify the less grand–posters, broadsheets, picture postcards, comic books, and all the other extraordinary signifiers of popular culture–as mere 'ephemera.'[52]

Commentators operate–in an extreme form in the colonial case–from particular class, gender, and race positions, separating, differentiating, and theorising the socially inferior other–and library collections constitute commentary. Recognising this, librarians in Africa can work to transform African studies collections developed under colonial or *apartheid* domination, applying a critical gaze, periodising the collections' history as social structures and beginning to ask what are the missing and oppressed voices? Broadly understood, archaeology, for instance, has an important role as a means of recovering the history of the oppressed, the forgotten and the lost. Libraries can cease to be mere warehouses and become living, ongoing celebrations of culture, comprehended as the material and ideational representation of human interactions. Such a library genuinely stands at the centre of the academic project and helps direct it, reworking history, reconstituting archaeology, collaborating with popular organisations to collect 'ephemera'–the visual, written, sung, and pictured representations of local struggles and concerns.

In Africa, and especially in South Africa, we work with collections shaped by the changing academic and political interests of the academy. They are framed by such crudely physical expressions of unacceptable attitudes as the tableaux of the Khoi San in Cape Town's Museum of Natural History, or human crania in the Anatomy Museum of the Cape Town Medical School. We must accept and openly confront the challenges that the new era poses to such *existing* collections. Librarians must engage with such questions as whether 'African' is an essential category or a social and socially fluid definition? How will we construct a new South African identity? What does it mean to celebrate diversity? How has colonial and independent Africa been constructed, politically and historically, and how do such constructions cut across older formations, with what consequences? What voices are excluded, and how can they be recovered, collected, and preserved in order to pose sharper questions in the present?

Empiricists have traditionally believed that researchers create knowledge through observation and the testing of data, which are objective and free of theoretical assumptions. The critique of this view in modern social science argues that researchers select data from the very beginning, basing decisions not only on explicit research values, but also on unexamined suppositions arising from the individual's socialisation (the most obvious of which are race, class, and gender). Librarians have perhaps been slower than academic colleagues in recognising that what D. J. Foskett ironically termed the creed of the librarian, namely 'no politics, no religion, no morals,' is empty idealism. Even such an eminent figure as a recent president of the [British] Library Association can argue that libraries should be value-neutral institutions.[53]

The tradition of the opinionated librarian is also long and honourable. Half a century ago, Ernest Savage was enthusiastically recommending that librarians practice 'attentive, critical, imaginative, retentive perusal' of their stocks, adding that 'any criticism [. . .] is of value [but] as a pointer, not as a verdict.'[54] A few years ago Peter G. Underwood questioned the ethical basis of this kind of positivist library practice in a short piece significantly called 'The advance from neutrality.' Underwood argued that the traditional assumption that 'libraries are neutral agencies, outside the struggle for democracy and redress' simply did not hold water in the South African context (and by extension of the argument, probably nowhere else either). He argued that 'information services should be aligned to the aspirations of the community they serve if they are to be effective,' and that what was needed was 'the evolution of an information science model which reflects cultural diversity.'[55] Although he was referring mainly to community-based resource centres, it is not hard to see that an analogous argument can be made regarding academic institutions. Underwood's attack on the positivism of library practice in South Africa was empirically based, not theoretical. But such writers as Froehlich have pointed out that it has long been held that information professionals need to be value-neutral, but that this has led to confusion over professional ethics. He contends that librarians in fact share a range of harmonious and consistent ethical values.[56]

At the beginning of this essay I posed two questions, namely whether we need to have African collections in African libraries at all, and if so, how to write collection development policies for them that make sense. In the light of the rest of this text, the answer to the first question may be a qualified and hesitant no, at least theoretically. But for many compelling reasons, we are likely to continue with our special institutes, centres and foundations–if on no other grounds than that the dispersal of an existing collection is an enterprise to be undertaken only in the most exceptional of circumstances.

But separate collections have different rationales. The African Studies Library at the University of Cape Town, for example, is a dedicated research library, defined primarily although not exclusively by its *research* function rather than its subject coverage. There is considerable African material in the main collection, too, for undergraduate use, a circumstance that may not prevail elsewhere. Such items may, in fact, attract more active use when categorised by subject matter in the general collection–teaching in rural Africa sitting with teaching in rural China, rural Paraguay, or rural Sri Lanka.

The second question is more complex. I have argued that librarians have a responsibility to recognise that their practice cannot be value-free, and that their collections are biased by the choices made by writers, by publishers, and lastly by themselves. The duty, especially in Africa itself, is to ensure that African voices, frog voices, the voices of the self, are not drowned out by the dominant voices. This requires of librarians, I believe, a recognition of the existence of what Ngũgĩ wa Thiong'o characterises as the three traditions of 'literature' from Africa–orature, Africans writing in European languages, and Africans writing in African languages.

Oral tradition is the 'most ancient and the richest [tradition] in the African heritage.'[57] Typically, librarians think in terms of recording, transcribing, translating, and fixing this tradition, but there may be alternatives. Academic institutions provide the economic foundation for thinkers and knowledge producers in the Western tradition, and there seems no good reason why this support could not be extended to those working in other traditions as well. A *griot* as a library staff member–well, why not? As librarians, we need to give voice through our collections policies to those Africans who write in and transform–even make African–European languages, including French and Portuguese as well as English. There is a sense in which these languages are no longer the exclusive private property of the metropole. Similarly and lastly, library collection policies in Africa–and above all in African studies collections–must firmly and actively support the development of writing and publishing in African languages.[58]

NOTES

1. Not just the United States, in other words. Canada, Mexico, Cuba, and Brazil, at least, have all had significant political and hence academic interest in Africa at various times.

2. It remains unclear whether there is any logical or theoretical difference between African studies in Africa, and African studies elsewhere in the world.

3. Patricia Alden, David Lloyd and Ahmed I. Samatar, 'African studies within US liberal arts education,' in Alden, Lloyd and Samatar, eds., *African studies and the undergraduate curriculum* (Boulder: Lynne Rienner, 1994), p. 2.

4. It is unclear whether this is the cause or the outcome of the parlous state of African publishing.

5. Specialisation in African library collections in African institutions is commonly national or regional rather than continental in focus and scope. Thus, for example, the library of the Institute of Ethiopian Studies at Addis Ababa University, the resource centre of the Centro de Estudos Africanos and the library of the Arquivo Histórico in the Universidade Eduardo Mondlane in Mozambique, or the East Africana collection in the main library at the University of Dar es Salaam, all carry out to a greater or lesser extent the functions of national library collections. This does not affect the main line of my argument.

6. For a discussion of this, see my 'The Alexandrian library, digital resources, and the shrinking public domain: a critique of the current model for delivering academic information in Africa,' *University of Dar es Salaam Library Journal* vol.3, no.1-2, (2001), p. 25-39. A preprint is available at http://www.imaginet.co.za/liasa/DARCH2001.rtf.

7. Mafeje makes the point that '. . . Euro-Americans can easily talk and write about 'African studies' but not 'African anthropology.' The difference in connotation is not in the phraseology itself, which is perfectly symmetrical, but in the noun agency. In 'African studies' Africa is unambiguously the object, whereas 'African anthropology' could, among other things, refer to a specific claim by Africans.' 'Who are the makers and objects of anthropology? A critical comment on Sally Falk Moore's Anthropology and Africa,' *African Sociological Review* 1 (1) 1997:2.

8. Mahmood Mamdani, 'Is African studies to be turned into a new home for Bantu education at UCT?' in *Teaching Africa: the curriculum debate at UCT* (Cape Town: Centre for African Studies, University of Cape Town, s.d.) p. 42.

9. William G. Martin, 'Deposing Tarzan, or teaching about Africa in the post-Cold War era,' in Alden, Lloyd and Samatar, eds., *African studies and the undergraduate curriculum*, p. 91.

10. Ronald Inglehart and Marita Carballo, 'Does Latin America exist? And is there a Confucian culture?' *PS: Political Science and Politics* 30 (1) 1997: 34, quoted by Jeremy Seekings, 'Logics of comparison and the construction of area studies: comparative politics, African studies and South African exceptionalism' (S.l., s.d.), p. 12. This unpublished paper is available in the African Studies Library, University of Cape Town.

11. Seekings, 'Logics of comparison,' p. 6.

12. Paul Gilroy, *The black Atlantic: modernity and double consciousness* (Cambridge, Mass.: Harvard University Press, 1993).

13. Tanzania's politico-military role as the rear base for FRELIMO in the independence war in Mozambique (1964-1974), and its subsequent close involvement (1975-1980) in what became the Frontline States, both led logically to its inclusion in the originally anti-apartheid SADCC organisation set up in 1979-1980.

14. Seekings, 'Logics of comparison,' p. 25.

15. C. Tsehloane Keto, *The Africa-centered perspective of history* (Blackwood NJ: K.A. Publications, 1989), p. 1, quoted in Bayo Oyebade, 'African studies and the Afrocentric paradigm,' *Journal of Black Studies* 21 (2) December 1990: 233. Emphasis added.

16. Afrocentrism in U.S. and Brazil has as much to do with domestic political issues around race as it has to do with African reality. Michael Turner of Hunter College is quoted as asking 'Afrocentrism in relation to which Africa–the one with problems, or the one with kings and queens?' Elio Gaspari, 'As vozes da África,' [The voices of Africa], *Veja* [Rio de Janeiro] 25 September 1991: 126.

17. Fabrice Hervieu Wané, 'Cheikh Anta Diop, restaurateur de la conscience noire,' *Le Monde Diplomatique* January 1998: 24-25, available at http://www.monde-diplomatique/fr/1998/01/HERVIEU_WANE/9787.html, accessed 14 March 2001.

18. Mamdani, 'Teaching Africa at the post-apartheid University of Cape Town: a critical view of the 'Introduction to Africa' core course in the Social Science and Humanities Faculty's foundation semester, 1998,' in *Teaching Africa*,' p. 5.

19. Peter Duignan and L. H. Gann, *A bibliographical guide to colonialism in sub-Saharan Africa* (Cambridge: Cambridge University Press, 1973), p. 8.

20. E.g., Yohanna B. Abdallah, *Chiikala cha waYao* (Zomba: Govt. Printer, 1919) and reprints.

21. The quoted phrase is theirs. Duignan and Gann, *A bibliographical guide*, p. 8.

22. Duignan and Gann, *A bibliographical guide*, p. 9.

23. Duignan and Gann, *A bibliographical guide*, p. 11.

24. Sally Falk Moore, *Anthropology and Africa* (Charlottesville: University of Virginia Press, 1994), p. 19-20, quoted by Mafeje. 'Who are the makers?'

25. A. H. M. Kirk-Greene, 'The scramble for Africana,' *African Affairs* (278) 70, January 1971: 77.

26. Of course, the political and intellectual work of W. E. B. DuBois in the series of Pan African Congresses between 1900 and 1945, and in such texts as *The world and Africa* (New York: The Viking Press; 1947) was immensely important, but belongs to a different and more honourable tradition than the British colonial one.

27. Mahmood Mamdani, 'Teaching Africa,' p. 5.

28. Duignan and Gann, *A bibliographical guide*, p. 12.

29. Adam Kuper, *The invention of primitive society: transformations of an illusion* (London: Routledge, 1988).

30. A recent example of the profession's ongoing capacity for self-immolation has been the *Darkness in El Dorado* uproar: for more details see http://www.anth.uconn.edu/gradstudents/dhume/index.htm, accessed 25 January 2002.

31. Dell Hymes, ed., *Reinventing anthropology* (New York: Vintage, 1974 repr.); Talal Asad, ed., *Anthropology and the colonial encounter* (London: Ithaca Press, 1973).

32. Kathleen Gough, "Anthropology: child of imperialism," *Monthly Review* 19 (11) 1968: 12-27.

33. Mafeje, 'Who are the makers?' p. 13.

34. E. E. Evans-Pritchard, *Social anthropology* (London: Cohen and West, 1951), p. 11.

35. 'Nzagwalu is an Igbo word meaning answering back–when you have suffered an insult, you have to answer back.' Ifi Amadiume, *Reinventing Africa: matriarchy, religion and culture* (London: Zed Books, 1997), p. 4.

36. Amadiume, *Reinventing Africa*, p. 2.

37. E.g., Henrietta L. Moore and Megan Vaughan, *Cutting down trees: gender, nutrition, and agricultural change in the Northern Province of Zambia, 1890-1990* (Portsmouth, N.H.: Heinemann, 1994).

38. Richard Wright, *White man, listen* (Garden City NY: Doubleday, 1957), p. 27-29, quoted in William S. Willis Jr., 'Skeletons in the anthropological closet,' in Hymes, ed., *Reinventing anthropology*, p. 121.

39. François Bontinck, 'Voyageurs africains en Afrique équatoriale,' *Zaïre-Afrique* [in at least 16 parts]. The earliest I have seen was no. 3, published in *Zaïre-Afrique* no. 114 (1977), p. 223-243, and the most recent no. 16, published in issue no. 158 (1981), p. 513-527. Most of the series was indexed in *Africa Index to Continental Periodical Literature* no. 3 (1980) to no. 6 (1985). Gerhard Liesegang, 'Achegas para o estudo das biografias de autores de fontes narrativas e outros documentos da história de Moçambique,' [in 4 parts in 3], *Arquivo*, no. 3 (April 1988), p. 12-34; no. 8 (October 1990), p. 61-141; and no. 10 (October 1991), p. 49-82.

40. Knicole Dominique Smith, 'Georgetown protest supports African studies,' *Black Issues in Higher Education* 16 (7) 27 May 1999: 21; Alison Schneider, 'Students accuse Georgetown of ignoring African studies,' *Chronicle of Higher Education* 45 (37) 21 May 1999: A14.

41. Harold Wolpe, Response to a letter to the editor, *Southern African Review of Books* 3 (2) December 1989-January 1990: 24.

42. V. Y. Mudimbe, *The invention of Africa: gnosis, philosophy and the order of knowledge* (Bloomington: Indiana University Press, 1988), p. ix.

43. E. Wyndham Hulme, 'Principles of book classification,' *Library Association Record* 13, 1911: 445-447.

44. Wolpe, Response.

45. Kirk-Greene, 'Scramble,' p. 77.

46. The Library of Congress reported that it catalogued 1,648 monograph titles with U.S. imprints in 1990-1991 (Walsh, 'Information dynamics for African studies: resources in libraries and beyond,' in Alden, Lloyd and Samatar, eds., *African studies and the undergraduate curriculum*, p. 217).

47. I do not read this as a criticism of the library service. Martin is making two key points: there is a racial hierarchy in area studies, and the literature is underdeveloped in any case. (The number of African studies majors may also be a factor, of course). 'Deposing Tarzan,' p. 96. For later views, see William G. Martin and Michael O. West (eds.), *Out of one, many Africas: reconstructing the study and meaning of Africa* (Urbana: University of Illinois Press, 1999).

48. Walsh, 'Information dynamics,' p. 217.

49. Walsh, 'Information dynamics,' p. 217-218.

50. Wolpe, Response. There are other arguments against exclusivism, of course.

51. I do not attempt in this piece to deal with the large question of digital resources on Africa available within Africa. See my discussions of some aspects of this in 'Copyright, contract law and digital information resources: changing library practices and the changing information environment,' paper presented to the Conference on "National Libraries in an African Renaissance" National Library of South Africa, Pretoria, 31 October-2 November 2000, available at http://www.nlsa.ac.za/nlar/darch1.pdf, accessed 27 March 2001; and 'The unsustainable library: does the Internet really help us in Africa?' *Progressive Librarian* (17) Summer 2000: 35-43.

52. For example, the late Pierre Bourdieu viewed cultural taste as an important determinant of social class; most library collections can thus be seen as the expression of a dominant aesthetic based on class.

53. G. Cornish, 'Would a rose smell as sweet?' *Library Association Record* 102 (12) December 2000: 680. See also his argument that libraries are neutral intermediaries between creators, owners and users of intellectual property 'Looking both ways: the challenge to the intermediary in an electronic age,' in Pauline Connolly and Denis Reidy (eds.), *Digital library: challenges and solutions for the new millennium* (Boston Spa: IFLA, 2000), p. 29-37.

54. Ernest A. Savage, *A librarian looks at readers: observation for book selection and personal service* (London: Library Association, 1950), p. 234, 235.

55. Peter G. Underwood, 'The advance from neutrality,' *Library Association Record* 98 (3) March 1996: 147.

56. T. J. Froehlich, 'Rethinking ethical issues in an online environment,' in David I. Raitt and Ben Jeapes (eds.), *Online Information 94* (Oxford: Learned Information Europe, 1994), p. 415-422.

57. Ngugi, 'Return of the native tongue,' *Times Literary Supplement*, 14-20 September 1990: 972.

58. The argument justifying the assertion that librarians in Africa should support the development of writing and publishing in 'African' languages, I save for another essay. Nor do I intend here to enter the debate about what constitutes an 'African' language.

Library Capacity Building in Africa or the Exportation of Technolust? Discerning Partnership Models and Revitalization Efforts in the Age of Globalization

Deborah M. LaFond

SUMMARY. Africana librarians in the United States work to sustain a larger dialogue, one that contributes to democratic futures in Africa through the support of libraries and indigenous publishing in Africa. Yet we are also products of colonial legacies which have engendered Western domination to the detriment of Africans. Can librarians from the West contribute to sustainable democratic futures by supporting the cat-

---

Deborah M. LaFond is Social Sciences Bibliographer, University Libraries, University at Albany, UL205, 1400 Washington Avenue, Albany, NY 12222 (E-mail: dlafonde@albany.edu).

For their patient perusals of my drafts, their scholarly engagement, and the subtle education on editing I received in this process, I am deeply grateful to Karen L. Starr and Gretchen Walsh. This inquiry and conversation could not have occurred without support received from the United University Professionals and the University at Albany Libraries, the inspiration of the authors listed here, ASA/ALC members, friends and family who offered support, shared my absence and stories of this journey, and those in Africa who welcomed my questions, modeled resilience, and shared their concerns as well as their hospitality and care. I dedicate this work to all the above but in particular to the memory of Kenyatta University Reference Librarian, Alice R. Bulogosi (February 8th, 1950-April 10, 2003), who shared her warmth and determination to meet scholarly needs and build support for library organizations within Kenya, regardless of all obstacles. In memoriam http://www.albany.edu/~dlafonde/Africana/bulogosimemorial2.htm.

[Haworth co-indexing entry note]: "Library Capacity Building in Africa or the Exportation of Technolust? Discerning Partnership Models and Revitalization Efforts in the Age of Globalization." LaFond, Deborah M. Co-published simultaneously in *The Reference Librarian* (The Haworth Information Press, an imprint of The Haworth Press, Inc.) No. 87/88, 2004, pp. 209-272; and: *Research, Reference Service, and Resources for the Study of Africa* (ed: Deborah M. LaFond, and Gretchen Walsh) The Haworth Information Press, an imprint of The Haworth Press, Inc., 2004, pp. 209-272. Single or multiple copies of this article are available for a fee from The Haworth Document Delivery Service [1-800-HAWORTH, 9:00 a.m. - 5:00 p.m. (EST). E-mail address: docdelivery@haworthpress.com].

http://www.haworthpress.com/web/REF
© 2004 by The Haworth Press, Inc. All rights reserved.
Digital Object Identifier: 10.1300/J120v42n87_09

alytic role of librarians in Africa who strive to support African-centered scholarship and struggles against legacies of colonialism? Or will we re-inscribe colonial legacies through our partnerships and promotion of Western centered models? Based upon the author's tour of selected higher education settings and academic libraries in Kenya and South Africa in 2001, the author reflects upon libraries in the context of "development" in Africa. The author begins to discern potentially viable models and develop criteria for partnerships by comparing methods of advocacy, collaboration and projects for information and digital futures. Descriptions of efforts to "build capacity" within African librarianship include those of African librarians and their associations, The Association of African Universities (AAU), The Africana Librarians Council (ALC), The World Bank, and The International Network for the Availability of Scientific Publications (INASP). The author observed the marketing of technology in Africa and characterizes some of the privileged dialogue on Information Communication Technologies (ICT) as the exportation of "technolust" which the author argues, contributes to increased privatization and the sacrifice of support to public universities. Such privatization reduces the broad social role of librarians and further marginalizes reference services. The author identifies critical literacies and sharing of cross-continental experience as essential in creating "mutually beneficial partnerships" to support cooperative, sustainable, democratic, information futures. In an effort to continue this important conversation and develop "true partnerships," the author shares her experience and reflection. Calls for dialogue throughout the African diaspora and beyond to promote community-based, democratic education and a sustainable intellectual, reading culture in Africa are recommended. *[Article copies available for a fee from The Haworth Document Delivery Service: 1-800-HAWORTH. E-mail address: <docdelivery@haworthpress.com> Website: <http://www.HaworthPress.com> © 2004 by The Haworth Press, Inc. All rights reserved.]*

KEYWORDS. African publishing, libraries, higher education, aid and development discourse, models for sustainable digital futures, partnerships

MARGINALIZATION OF LIBRARIES, LIBRARIANS, AND SCHOLARSHIP IN AFRICA: INTRODUCTION AND LITERATURE REVIEW

The underpinning of success in the achievement of Vision 2010 for creating an African Information Society will depend on a thorough understanding and internalization of the human right to information by African leadership and communities. The development

> of an information society should not be seen simply as a means to an economic end, but as a mechanism for empowerment out of which human dignity is derived. . . . Specifically the library and information service providers have a catalytic role to play. . . . (Raseroka 1997, 15-16)

Ms. Raseroka, a respected African leader in librarianship, asserts that librarians have a "catalytic role" to play in the development of an information society in Africa. According to Raseroka, librarians can make important contributions toward an ethical and democratic information society. Despite Raseroka's vision, librarians continue to be marginalized by the development of Information Communication Technology (ICT). The link between publishing, scholarly production, and library development in Africa may seem obvious to librarians, however, in Africa, as well as in the United States, that link is not obvious to many administrators. As in the United States, African higher education administrators laud libraries as the metaphoric heart of the university, while simultaneously they seek smaller and smaller library budgets. One increasingly attractive approach is to displace physical academic libraries in order to afford the more idealized "virtual libraries" of the future (Deegan and Tanner 2002), creating less need for buildings, books, print journals, and staff. The author observed the exportation of "technolust" to African administrators responsible for directing university resources in the development of Information Communication Technology for Africa.

> The high expenditure on information technology in educational institutions is occurring too often for political reasons, driven by technolusts; a quest to be perceived at a technological cutting edge which will always be a mirage; and commercial interests which have fostered information technology anxiety and competition within, and between, countries. (Bundy 1999, 1)

In the process of investigating tensions and trends that may explain how marginalization of librarians and scholars continues to occur in Africa, the author found technolust (Crawford and Gorman 1995) to be a powerful and complex contributing factor.

"Brick or Click" Libraries and "Leapfrogging": Dilemmas for Africa

In February 2001, the author attended the Association of African Universities meeting in Nairobi Kenya. The following statements were made to the author by African administrators at this meeting.

"Libraries are no longer necessary since information can be retrieved from the Web."

"Everything is on the Web."

"There is no longer need to allocate huge amounts of resources to libraries and buildings."

Where did these notions come from? Rosenberg finds it "unfortunate that ICTs are often seen as an alternative to the provision of print material, rather than as a supplement. For many user needs (e.g., students' textbooks), print is still the best solution" (Rosenberg) [an unpaginated electronic work]. The costs associated with ICT and the "leasing of information" from the West to support research at African Universities is a major dilemma for libraries and scholarship promotion within Africa, as it is to a somewhat lesser degree in the West. Despite the lack of clear evidence supporting the contention that virtual libraries will save money and promote scholarship within public universities, this notion has made significant headway in the United States, and now in Africa. The premise of virtual libraries as cost-effective rests upon a belief that institutions can "trade infrastructure for information," and transform "from bricks to clicks to embrace disintermediation" (Gherman 2000, 50). The advantage for Africa?–less infrastructure to trade and more information to purchase, thereby "leapfrogging" ahead into virtual reality. Nassimbeni points out that African countries vary in their ability to benefit from leapfrog theories. Fueled by dramatic predictions these theories "should not be taken to mean that people can by-pass the so-called traditional literacies of reading, writing, numeracy. . . . " Nassimbeni reminds her readers that libraries can make a particular contribution . . . not only by making information and ICTs available "but [by] also empowering citizens to take up and use the resources . . ." (Nassimbeni 1998) [an unpaginated electronic work].

Leasing of Information

Keeping the costs of electronic resources hidden until dependence is created, is key to creating profit margins necessary to develop a new market of dependence. This market-driven cycle now threatens the sustainability of libraries and impacts upon public education in the United States and in Canada, leading scholars and administrators to consider alternatives as discussed by the Association of Research Libraries' Create Change project.

> The higher education systems and the governments of the U.S. and Canada spend billions of dollars a year to support research by scholars that they then pay billions of dollars to buy back in the form of published scholarship.
>
> Scholars give away their written work by assigning copyright to publishers; they can then be restricted in the use they make of their own work, even in their own classrooms. (University of California Berkeley Libraries, n.d. under "Scholarly Publishing") [an unpaginated electronic work]

Leasing information is not ownership and does not necessarily provide access to CD-ROM downloads. Instead, leased information continues to be available only on a contract basis. Although databases that represent scholarly association indexing selection still occur, this is changing. Selection criteria for research databases are largely determined by the seller of the information and, to a lesser degree, customer input. This encourages growing uniformity of collections (Quinn 2000, 2002; Schaffner 2001). The information within databases can be re-sold to a variety of publishers and consequently libraries purchasing more than one database can be purchasing the same information over and over (LaFond, Van Ullen and Irving 2000). If a library has to drop a subscription one year, the library may lose access to all the years previously paid for. License agreements and contracts determine who uses the information, how information can be shared, or whether the information can be copied. Back files, though sometimes available for a fee, may be in a format that is inconsistent with current technology, making the files potentially inaccessible. For many libraries, access to this information is, as a result, out of reach.

If libraries in the West are finding it difficult to afford and manage market-driven knowledge, what does this mean for libraries in Africa? Many academic libraries in Africa still rely on donated books. How can African administrators recognize what may be neo-colonial methods of technology transfer when they are not familiar with the intricacies of leasing schemes, trying to be open to ICT possibilities, and are courted by database firms with the alluring promise of overall cost reduction? Just when librarians and faculty in the United States and Europe are uniting against high costs of aggregator databases and control of journal selection in these database packages, it appears that some donor agencies are uniting with vendors to market databases in Africa. In 2002, the World Bank promoted Elsevier electronic journals through the African Virtual University (Wolff 2002, 25). Publishers who offer lower prices for online contracts in Africa recognize that a new market is better than no market and stand to gain in the West from a reputation of "offering deals to Africa." But even at lower prices, is the dependence on Western, market-driven access to information a sustainable future for Africa?

Based on comments heard by the author at the 2001 AAU meeting, few participants seemed to have complete understanding of how mainstream Western database vendors operate. Many assumed that "brick" libraries in Africa need no longer be supported in light of full-text database access. Donor agencies and ICT developers were on hand at the AAU meeting to share information with administrators regarding potential access to full-text databases purchased from the West (Levy 2000), but no discussion of digital dilemmas or other critical dialogue from librarians' points of view were offered to African administrators. The Association of African Universities and donor developed Dissertations and Theses in Africa Database (DATAD) model is one response to this dilemma, for indexing to African scholarship can be accessed within Africa free of charge to participating universities. AAU plans to export this resource and preserve African ownership of information while promoting indigenous scholarly production.

Association of African Universities (AAU) Meeting, 2001

The General Conference of AAU is held every three to four years and provides declarations of priorities and directives for African Universities facing several challenges (Sawyerr 2002). The primary focus of the 2001 meeting was devoted to ICT and its importance for Africa. The AAU's theme, *African Universities and the Challenge of Knowledge Creation and Application in the New Century* was exactly on point for the author's investigations. The theme was chosen by the AAU "in view of the rapid growth in the global rate of knowledge creation, management, dissemination and application in the 20th century" (http://www.aau.org/). The inherent understanding of poverty (Heeks 1999) and the impact of the "digital divide" in Africa (Ogbu and Mihyo 2000; Nelens, Hafkin, Van Audenhove, and Cammaerts 2001) though not specifically stated, was implied through discussion on how ICT could benefit countries in Africa (Partnership for Higher Education in Africa 2003).

In 2001, four plenary sessions were devoted to the following subthemes of the meeting:

1. African Higher Education Management and Leadership in the Information Age
2. Quality of Training and Research: Towards a Dynamic Process of Curricular Reform and Innovations in African Tertiary Institutions
3. Information and Communication Technologies: Building Capacity in African Universities
4. Women in African Tertiary Institutions.

Poster sessions and parallel programs were advertised on the Web site in 2000-2001. Parallel programs announced included presentations on African digital libraries and on the Dissertations and Theses in Africa Database (DATAD)–an AAU and Ford Foundation initiative.

The author was pleased to see the topics knowledge, libraries, women in higher education, and indigenous database development integrated in the context of the program. There was an expectation on her part that discussion would emerge that might inform policy, and outline context-specific initiatives. Empowerment of women is critical in higher education, but specifically impacts the predominantly female library profession. The author, at that time, in search for potential authors for this publication, assumed she would meet African librarians wanting to contribute a paper for this special issue. The AAU and the Ford Foundation had provided partial funding to develop DATAD. The Africana Librarians Council, of which the author was a member, had also been supportive of DATAD since the early phases of the project. The author was certain that discussion of DATAD would lead to discussion about other databases developed by Africans and about libraries and the integration of librarians into ICT development. Perhaps new initiatives to support library capacity building would also be encouraged and partnerships formed.

AAU–Who Attends?

What the author did not know, and what was not apparent from the AAU registration Web site in 2000, is that rather than being a meeting where faculty, librarians, and administrators discuss issues, AAU meetings are primarily designed for high level university administrators–

Vice-Chancellors and Rectors of Universities within Africa. Donor agencies are also important participants of the conference.

While the author's e-mailed request to attend the conference received immediate acceptance, it is important to emphasize that this meeting is not a conference open to all faculty and librarians within Africa. Though perhaps, an unintended guest, this author was welcomed and hosted as if one of the elite, intended participants. Based on her interactions, and because there were only a handful of librarians out of two hundred participants, the author wondered if she was, more often than not, mistaken for a donor representative, rather than a librarian. However, her interest and questions about African scholarly production and promotion through libraries, and her interest in social transformation were welcomed. As a result, she found herself engaged individually and in sessions. Unfortunately, the DATAD presentation did not happen and, apart from a poster session on the African digital libraries, the future of African libraries and the role of librarians was not specifically addressed in any of the main plenary sessions.

Noted Constraints of African Libraries at the AAU–Integration of ICT and Libraries

A written paper by G. Olalere Ajayi, on "Information and Communications Technologies: Building Capacity in African Universities," was distributed to each participant at the meeting. Ajayi states that "it is necessary to realize that the old 'ivory tower' concept of the university has given way to the 'market type-information age' university concept, which is open to the outside world, and open internally" (Ajayi 2001, 80). Although there was no public discussion on the role of librarians and libraries in Africa at this meeting, the following constraints related to libraries were cited in his paper.

- "Lack of access to relevant materials."
- "Libraries at African universities do not stock enough materials, largely due to budgetary inadequacies of libraries."
- "The high price of printed books also makes access to, and ownership of such material, well beyond the reach of the average student and faculty members."
- "Many community libraries do not keep texts that meet the academic needs of students and faculty of universities " (Ajayi 2001, 69).

Ajayi, an ICT expert, appears certain that the continued existence of higher education institutions in Africa is linked to the development of ICT facilities. However, he states, "The funding of the library can no longer cope with the cost of acquisition and maintenance of ICT facilities." Ajayi believes a new outlook for library and archival services is necessary and notes the following:

i. Transformation of the library from its traditional book-oriented and often inward looking to the outward looking attitude with emphasis on information handling.
ii. Instead of cataloguing information alone, library must lay emphasis on collection process, compiling and disseminating it in support of students and researcher both inside and outside the institution.
iii. Transformation of the library into a new Information Services Unit.
iv. New outlook, structure, skills, and attitude which some library staff cannot easily adapt to.
v. Removal of the artificial dividing line between the library and the teaching, learning, and research functions.
vi. Generally there is need to integrate technology into library functions.

He also suggests "libraries should endeavor to generate funds from specialized services for financial sustainability" (Ajayi 2001, 81-82). Emphasis on attitudinal shifts are suggested in this document as well as the inclination toward "virtual libraries" and the move away from a "conventional book based institution" (85). Ajayi's assessment of libraries in Africa was provided at this AAU meeting but no other view of the role of the librarian was represented, particularly none by librarians.

As professionals, librarians have adapted to many currencies of the day and are aware that when terminology is replaced, new ideologies accompany them. When terminology is legitimated, it often matters little if the underlying assumptions are understood. Bundy argues that "librarianship is *not* synonymous with information management–it is much broader in principle, practice and potential. Librarians are much more than information professionals, however that trendy term is given definition" (Bundy 1999).

"Plucking Rhetorical Feathers": Marketing of Ideology and Critical Literacies

> Even senior educational administrators are vulnerable to the siren sounds of the technolusts and their proffering of an educational panacea and change agent through information technology. This is a danger in developed countries. It is much more so if developing countries conclude that information technology is the solution to their educational deficits. . . . There has been a massive misjudgment that the key educational issue of the information age is information technology, rather than information literacy. The consequences of that assumption have been evident for some time. (Bundy 1999, 1)

Librarians today are gaining more experience at reading between the lines of marketing rhetoric and reality, since we must make selection decisions comparing advertising with evaluation of database trials and mediate license agreements and contracts with vendors. It is especially important that we share our questions, concerns, and methods. Communication theory and analysis offered by Melkote and Steeves offer insight into the allure of technolust, helping to discern how this may impact persuasion strategies used in development dialogue.

> Communication in the form of market research can assist in decisions about development goals and communication strategies. Persuasive or marketing communications subsequently "sell" development ideas and associated technologies to target audiences. In this sense, development communication under the modernization framework is often viewed as a process of persuasive marketing. In contrast, critical frameworks reject marketing models that aim to spread and support Western technologies and economic and political values. Critical perspectives also view persuasive campaigns as manipulative and potentially harmful, with inadequate attention to the larger cultural context in which people live. (Melkote and Steeves 2001, 38)

Explaining why rhetoric on technology is so persuasive, Barbara Warnick, Professor of Speech Communication at the University of Washington, Seattle, paraphrases Cynthia L. Selfe and Robert W. McChesney in her book:

> Among scholars who have studied public discourse on and about new communication media, some have identified its rhetorical attributes, and in particular the narrative that threads together public beliefs about technology. Selfe (1999) and McChesney (1999) noted that the major elements of this narrative are faith in science, emphasis on U.S. pre-eminence, and reliance on unregulated free market forces as a solution to most of the world's economic problems. Selfe argued that this narrative grows out of modernism's view that science and technology, grounded as they are in systematic observation and rigor, and technological tools, will yield a better world for human species and emphasizes the importance of "a belief in science as a progressive force in modern society" that characterizes Western thinking in general. (Selfe 1999, 115)

This belief is closely associated with the view that new technologies enable the United States to maintain its role as global leader (Warnick 2002, 8). McChesney, identifies "hypercommercialism and cooptation of journalism by media conglomerates as major causes of the public's lack of awareness about the concentration of media ownership and control" (Warnick 2002, 9).

> . . . The market has assumed mythological status, becoming a totem to which all must pledge allegiance or face expulsion to the margins. . . . As this mythology is the foundation for almost the entire case for the absence of any public debate on the course of the Internet, and therefore in favor of privatization and commercialization of the Internet, it demands very careful scrutiny. (McChesney 1999, 137)

World Bank Vision of Virtual Libraries: Universities and Libraries as Obsolete?

Emphasizing the need for ICT development and distance education, William Saint, a lucid researcher and writer for the World Bank, also cites the need to support research in Africa and gives special significance "to University libraries (and librarians) [who] will be key actors in efforts to raise the quality of higher education and research through the application of new electronic technologies" (Saint 2000, 9).

The World Bank's vision for African universities as reported by William Saint, is to transition universities to virtual reality, where the university campus is obsolete. This necessitates the focus on the "application of technology" and distance education as stepping stones. Articulated here is an example of the leap of faith that university administrators in the West, and now universities in Africa, are encouraged to make.

> New technologies will make university campuses obsolete. Students will use asynchronous multimedia communications delivered by the Internet and receive learning support through virtual libraries and online video conferencing. (Saint 2000, 28)

> Research will no longer be primarily the domain of universities, and it will diverge increasingly from the structures of university education. It will become an interactive undertaking involving many types of knowledge producers who work together "virtually" in networked teams that form, dissolve, and regroup as necessary to tackle complex trans-disciplinary problems. Disciplinary science will gradually give way to "research in the context of application" aimed at understanding and manipulating complex systems. (Gibbons 1998, 42)

Knowing the World Bank envisions that "university campuses [will become] obsolete," might explain some of the Bank's projects, but it also raises questions about the future of academic libraries.

For example, the World Bank premise that universities are key to "achieving increased participation in the global knowledge-based economy in the 21st century" (Saint 2000, 1) could lend support to the goal of indigenous knowledge creation and the development of a "reading culture" in Africa, but does not necessarily reveal the Bank's well-recognized motivation to establish "stable" environments for business.

Saint, following Gibbons and Peters, indicates that "tertiary education in the future will be based much less on academic disciplines and more on cross-cutting topics or trans-disciplinary issues." . . . "The goal will be to prepare students for the knowledge economy where they will work in 'virtual' companies, organizations, committees and project teams" (Saint 2000, 28).

According to Boyer, "in such models, 'knowledge' is invariably depoliticised into technical or pragmatic forms that fit rationalizing, neo-liberal development agendas; critical knowledge is seen as a luxury commodity ill-afforded African economies of information" (Boyer 2002, 211; Nyamnjoh and Jua 2002; Nandy 2000, 118).

The World Bank also prescribes the future role of libraries and librarians to African administrators, utilizing language, which, on the surface, appears to be premised on promoting equality.

> For this transformation to occur, managers of tertiary education institutions and library administrators will need to understand and support the evolution of library roles from handmaiden to full partner in the academic enterprise. (Saint 2000, 10)

William Saint contrasts "handmaiden" and "partner" roles, seemingly to invite librarians into full partner status. However, the reference to "handmaidens" characterizes historically, unequal power relations for women within the librarian profession. It does little, however, to acknowledge the local, indigenous knowledge, and work of these "handmaidens" whose partnership in knowledge creation and scholarship has been essential.

Despite the appeal of equity, associated with virtual libraries and distance education by Saint, it is difficult to see how this transformation of librarian to "partner" would occur, when the broader mission of librarianship is subverted by ICT and technology dominance. Faculty roles have also been diminished as witnessed by the "less dollar for scholar" phenomenon associated with distance education projects. If universities are to become obsolete, it appears that librarians are useful only to the extent that they abandon their broader mission and assist in this transition. It is more likely that Saint's statement will justify perceptions of librarians as outmoded, giving support to stereotypes of librarians as clerks and gatekeepers, further distancing librarians from their broader educational roles. Granted, with the integration of computer technology, professional librarianship has acquired a more solidly male status as the number of males within the profession has significantly increased. However, the predominantly male composition of the computing technology profession suggests that gender equity is not its highest priority. Many librarians have found that the "new" virtual reality brings no guarantee of equality–leaving librarians to wonder, "Are librarians to become 'handmaidens' to technology and to the entrepreneurs who benefit from this new 'academic enterprise'?"

In spite of the World Bank's vision for virtual libraries and distance education, many librarians and scholars of education (Solely 1995; Readings 1996) from the West continue to warn about technocratic assumptions in education and learning. For example, Wisner, a male reference librarian from the United States, calls for closer scrutiny of technology and its impact on libraries, teaching, learning, and knowledge.

> We are now downwind, however–by a mere 40 years–of an invention which has done more, since its advent, to diminish reading, dumb down a populace, distract young minds, hobble their imagination at its root and claim their souls than any other in civilized human history. . . . There's just too much money in it for it to be allowed to disappear. (Wisner 2000, 50)

Wisner argues that technology, despite its potentially useful contributions to libraries, must dominate, and therefore, is not controllable. Wisner asserts his role as educator and remains suspicious of concepts that promote efficiency in learning.

> Technology now drives the budget. And it drives the cataloguing, acquisitions, circulation, interlibrary loan and reference function as well. Technology dominates the journal literature in our field and the curricula of the graduate programs that train librarians. (Wisner 2000, 59)

Wisner, passionate in his view, articulates the sentiments of many reference librarians in the United States who wonder why they spend more time fixing printers and question if, somehow, they foolishly accepted the terms of a false bargain. Wisner describes what will be lost should this trend succeed.

> Sadly the loss of tememos, the library's space, the building itself, will, I think be as profound a loss as anything. The civic benefits of people pursuing knowledge in a public space will be a diminishment to our cities.
>
> And another significant symbol of democracy will have vanished–at a time when . . . it is being undermined everywhere by a host of baleful forces more dangerous for their subtlety. (Wisner 2000, 50, 72)

In such an environment, will the catalytic role which Ms. Raseroka envisioned, include the active role librarians have historically played in supporting free inquiry and teaching scholarly process? And will the important democratic tradition of librarians providing free and equitable access to information be criteria for librarians and ICT partnerships? Unfortunately, visions for future librarianship by those at the AAU meeting did not include this kind of dialogue or questioning.

Dependence on Donors and Foreign Assistance

There are a number of donor agencies working in Africa reflected in some of the literature (USAID 1992; Saint 1992, 1996; DeStefano, Hartwell Tietjen 1995; Van Audenhove 1999; Devarajan, Dollar, Holmgren 2001; Evans n.d.). Some offer strategies and solutions to develop autonomy within universities by supporting projects which lessen dependence on politically corrupt elites, support curriculum innovation, and encourage social transformation. However, donors also often work in concert with governing structures. Klopp and Orina suggest that in Kenya, "World Bank policies for solving education crises pay little or no attention to how structural adjustment gets implemented by the highly repressive state." They argue that at a moment when political liberalization was occurring, President Moi wielded structural adjustment as a "deliberate tool against politically active and oppositional students" (Klopp 2002, 64).

One donor told the author of this paper that evidence of strategic planning (Farrant and Afonso 1997) on the part of universities is a pre-requisite for funding consideration, since this might indicate a process of democratic participation within the university. Some donors interviewed in Kenya stated that they are reluctant to fund projects based within universities in Kenya since corruption is well-known and they feared funding would not be spent on the project receiving the award. On the other hand, Rosenberg reports an example where Kenyatta University (KU) and the donor did not work effectively to address the local need or manage funds appropriately.

> The World Bank Universities Investment Project (UIP) was an example of badly managed assistance. Although 20% of the total loan was to be spent on university libraries, there would be little to show for it. Because of red tape and bureaucratic procedures, the Librarian felt that only 50% of book orders were likely to arrive and it seemed as though all equipment would be lost. There was slowness and apparent misuse of the money in the Kenyan office; procedures for the consolidation of orders and the evaluation and award of tenders were not suited to the purchase of books. If KU had been able to manage the money, all would have already been

> spent and the books received. The loan could not be used for journal subscriptions–which was what KU most wanted. It appeared that the terms of the loan and the procedures laid down for its expenditure were determined at a level way above the Library. (Rosenberg 1997, 2: 190)

World Bank Critics: Are African Administrators Caught in a War for Ideological Dominance?

Key critics of the World Bank argue that the purpose of the organization is to maintain ideological dominance, preventing any other interpretive framework from developing. For example, Sogge suggests that the Bank attempts to create an appearance of being non-ideological but that "once plucked of their rhetorical feathers," it is not difficult to discern that "the World Bank is positioning itself as the world's mightiest think tank" (Sogge 2002, 1). Sogge states that "interest in higher education, the seedbed of intellectual and political leadership" is key to creating the "leading paradigm," an instrument of control, which promotes "a knowledge and idea market resembling the highly skewed, monopoly-centered capitalism." Sogge and others argue that a primary World Bank objective is to remove any competition for influence, particularly in the minds of future leaders that might be found on university campuses. Sogge also suggests that these donor agencies utilize emancipatory themes such as "empowerment" or "sustainability" in their rhetoric, "plundering ideas of rivals and critics," whose "ideas sprang from the emancipatory camp of social movements" (Sogge 2002, 4).

While many Africans are aware that their countries are placed within ideological dominance wars, it is understandable, given such colonial legacies as economic underdevelopment, disease, and corrupt government, that many do not raise critical questions. As Sogge notes: "Jobs, contracts, and careers [may] depend on funding by Bank-led donor consortia, the audience and users of this knowledge have little choice but to go along quietly" (9). Clearly such relationship is no basis for partnerships on library development and scholarly production in Africa.

Although African scholars and administrators depend heavily on external support, they must often rely upon information synthesized from research done by international development agencies and donors. These organizations have their own interpretive frameworks, agendas, and considerable resources and power to implement projects that meet their goals. How can this kind of power imbalance be beneficial? Acknowledging that partnerships to work toward library capacity building are necessary, definitions of partnership need to be addressed if the goal of actualizing librarians' "catalytic role" in democratic education in the Information Age is to be realized. Being in the position of needing assistance is not enviable. Although support for education and knowledge creation in Africa is clearly needed, what philosophy of partnership will we choose in forming alliances with African librarians, educators, and donors? How will these partnerships be formed?

Revitalizing Libraries: Promoting a Reading Culture

A recent Carnegie Corporation of New York report, *Revitalizing African libraries: The challenge of a quiet crisis* (2000), states that "Books continue to be a critical key to solving a nation's problems and learning remains a critical element in a nation's arsenal of strategies for survival." Establishing a "reading culture" and "launching African literacy" is seen as a critical step. "The importance of books and libraries in the life of nations and their people resonates just as strongly in Africa" (Marton 2000, 1). Discussion of African university libraries in the Carnegie report relied upon the publication, *University libraries in Africa: A review of their current state and future potential* (1997), a two-year study of eighteen university libraries in eleven Sub-Saharan countries, edited by Diana Rosenberg who states:

> Most of the books and journals acquired by all libraries surveyed are published in the First World. Yet undue dependence on foreign sources of information is an unhealthy situation for a country to be in. The high prices of this material coupled with the decreasing purchasing power of local currencies puts great strain on already inadequate acquisition budgets and result in an outflow of badly needed foreign exchange. (Rosenberg 1997, Vol. 1 and 2: 19)

The Carnegie conference participants echoed a key dilemma for libraries in Africa. University libraries do not receive what is needed to support scholars and therefore, scholars do not view libraries as sources of support, leading to ". . . the loss of faith on the part of students, teachers, academic leaders in university libraries."

> The problem is one that seems to feed on itself: in past years, as university libraries failed to meet the needs of academia, in part because of lack of funds, a failure to anticipate future needs and keep pace with technology, their constituencies turned to their

> own departments and to faculty libraries for needed resources. Now main university libraries have, in many instances become marginalized in the academic community and are not seen as a center of learning to be enhanced and expanded. (Marton 2000, 4-5)

Librarians the author interviewed in South Africa, and particularly in Kenya in 2001, supported this view. How to address revitalization, as well as who should participate in the discussion, are the subjects of this paper. The Carnegie conference participants forwarded ideas that they claim will,

> [C]reate a vision of future libraries that depart significantly from current models designed by British and American colonial powers, models now crippled by a lack of funds, leadership and political clout. Libraries of the future will instead provide innovative and self-sustaining services designed to meet the particular needs of local populations, 80 percent of which are still rural. (Marton 2000, 1)

The Carnegie Corporation challenge to revitalize libraries in Africa is one among many donor-assisted projects designed to support libraries. The Carnegie report notes as problematic, the extreme reliance and dependence upon government and donor support to maintain libraries and urges the self-generation of funds and other alternative funding strategies. The challenge proposed in the report is to "develop true partnerships between donors and African leaders who can identify strategies that will point the way toward revitalizing both public and university libraries" (Marton 2000, 7). The Carnegie report notes as positive signs, the Association of African Universities' (AAU) promotion of Information Communication Technology (ICT) and the establishment of a clearinghouse for the dissemination of information concerning library management.

Reading Culture: Social Contract for Books and Publishing

Although considerable growth has occurred, the fact that there are relatively few publishing venues in Africa has been recognized as an important contributing factor to the lack of indigenous African knowledge creation. At the same time, beliefs that African publishing "could never replace that coming from the First World" persist, presenting an obstacle to development. As Rosenberg reports, "Only a quantum leap in African publishing and distribution could reverse attitudes to local and African published material" (Rosenberg 1997, 2: 20).

Social Contract for Books in Africa

Similar to the Carnegie report, which also encourages a reading culture in Africa, Zeleza argues for "a social contract for books, [and] for the development of a vigorous reading culture" stimulating new markets for reading and writing for children and adults in rural as well as urban settings (Zeleza 2003, 374). In his book *Rethinking Africa's globalization: The intellectual challenges* (2003), Paul Tiyambe Zeleza asks "Where does Africa fit in the international political economy of knowledge production, dissemination and consumption?" (Zeleza 2003, 368). One of the few to analyze libraries within this broader context, Zeleza considers the important role of African libraries in his analysis. He eloquently articulates the impact of political economy within the social context of higher education, particularly within Kenya. Zeleza relies on his readers to advocate for more African published materials, at costs that are affordable within Africa. In addition, he argues that the "development of a sustainable reading culture requires well-financed schools that produce literate students inculcated with the love of learning" (Zeleza 2003, 387). This author agrees, but asks, "How could this happen without support to libraries and librarians in Africa?"

Libraries could provide needed spaces and resource support in the promotion of indigenous scholarly production. Support to libraries and librarians would encourage capacity building if institutions affirmed the important role libraries and librarians could play as partners in ICT development and in the development of a "reading culture" as both the Carnegie Corporation and Zeleza call for.

WHAT DOES "TRUE PARTNERSHIP" MEAN?

Capacity, Agency and Partnership: Re-Inscribing Colonial Relations of Dependence?

Capacity building is defined as the enhancement of ability to undertake certain activities, solve problems, and achieve objectives. Building capacity assumes that there is something preventing an individual or group from either developing or utilizing their ability. For example, high on the list of priorities addressed by the AAU is the problem of "brain drain," the loss of the most educated and skilled, who leave Africa, succumb to illness, or become demoralized by lack of support to scholars. "Brain drain" is an example of how human capacity development can result in the loss of organizational capacity.

Interpretations of loss or need and the formation of partnerships to marshal capacity may be well-intentioned, but may also be influenced by other agendas. How does one identify these?

> Greater private-sector investment will improve Africa's demand for expertise and help to reduce "brain drain." Appropriate organizational arrangements and incentives including research networks and regional cooperation could enable Africans *in diaspora* [author's emphasis] to contribute to geographic information activities in their home countries. (National Research Council of the National Academies 2002, 117)

Here we see greater private-sector investment, a trend throughout Africa, proposed as a solution to African brain drain. This same solution is proposed in several documents discussing capacity building and the funding of higher education in Africa (Goodall, Brophy 1997; World Bank 2001). Some provide case studies to show that a balance of private and public institutions may address needs more appropriately (Olowu and Sako 2002). Critics (Samoff 1995, 2001) question the underlying motives of designs for capacity building projects and characterize assumptions as arrogant perspectives, which presume that "what is best" for one country is best for African countries in general. For example, Bethwell Ogot, a strong critic of the World Bank, argues that private universities cannot replace public universities. He also points out that World Bank regional comparisons to countries outside of Africa are used as models for Africa, but do not accurately portray specific African context (Ogot 2001). Therefore, for Ogot, World Bank assumptions about Africa's ability to generate income do not offer sustainable futures for African universities.

Meanwhile, Samoff is concerned by the "limited research capabilities within most of Africa" but argues that prescriptions to privatize education are based upon policy advice and studies informed by aid agencies who assert a dominant role in research on the "higher education sector," in order to set the course for education in Africa. According to Samoff, these same studies are rarely shared within Africa, remaining within agencies. This might tend to keep African administrators, who need to weigh options, effectively in the dark. Samoff argues that the course of education charted by most aid agencies he investigated focus little on learning and mostly upon "what was perceived to be the mismatch between curriculum and labor market needs" (Samoff 1999, 252). He argues that while these studies describe educational settings, they remain diagnostic and prescriptive, but do not provide analysis informed by those directly involved. Few exceptions aside, "their purpose is to support decisions about allocations in specific settings at specific times" (Samoff 1999, 252-253).

Formation of Partnerships

In the case of the Carnegie conference, partnerships are being formed to address what are considered areas of needed development to further the capacity of Africans. Raising the concern of "true partnerships," as the Carnegie conference has, invites our professional reflection.

> Partnership is an ambiguous word, even if all call themselves partners . . . I remember how Sir Roy Welensky, leader in Southern Rhodesia in colonial times, defined partnership as the relationship between the rider and his horse. If practice proves that it means 'relationship between equals' that is something new however. (Ehnmark, *Expressen*, 1997-06-24, translated by Dahl) (Dahl 2001, 17)

Dahl's discussion paper aptly describes the dilemma this author discovered when studying "capacity building" dialogue and examining her own assumptions about how to form partnerships. Citing the importance of "agency" as a concept in contemporary political discourse, Dahl indicates that agency, a term similar to capacity, is "morally loaded." These terms generally refer to an individual's or group's "will to act." Those "worthy" of receiving aid are those who have been prevented from utilizing their own agency. For example, "resource deficits" often make assistance morally acceptable. When lack of agency is identified, help, aid, or assistance is seen as legitimate. Interrogating conceptual differences between charity, co-operation, partnership, solidarity, and friendship, Dahl discusses the current evolving nature of relationship constructs within Swedish assistance discourse (Olsson 1992).

> Policy is overtly directed against what it argues to be an earlier way of conceptualising development assistance–in terms of do-

> nors and recipients, patrons and clients. This has been replaced by a model, which defines it as a relationship built upon a mutual contract, recognizing both partners as agents with self-interest. (Dahl 2001, 14)

Dahl cites a current framework–an attempt to frame dialogue using "principles of rightful sharing in a collective versus exchange between independent units" (Dahl 2001, 15). This is a good example of the level of complexity involved in discussing the meaning of "true partnerships" in realistic social terms. Such careful examination of terms and relationship are imperative to identifying and accomplishing emancipatory capacity building.

In December 2002, the African Studies Association planned a panel and discussion of a commissioned paper documenting further, the dependence on external support for higher education, its implications, and the possibilities for the creation of knowledge and partnerships. The authors outline several forms of partnership and note that ". . . the key issues here are responsibility and accountability, which insist on the engagement of those involved and permit control to be visible and public" (Samoff and Carroll 2002, 43).

If partnerships are to define future roles for librarians, and in particular, Africana librarians, how do we ensure that whatever language we use or whatever action we take, we do not re-inscribe colonial relations through our own work and through the models of librarianship that are exported to Africa?

Manthia Diawara graphically describes how constructions of Africa are both exported and imported through the media, inhibiting communication among Africans and forcing Africans to negotiate through artificial realities.

> A globalized information network characterizes Africa as a continent sitting on top of infectious diseases, strangled by corruption and tribal vengeance and populated by people with mouths and hands open to receive international aid. The globalization of the media which now constitutes a simultaneous and unified imaginary across continents, also creates a vehicle for rock stars, church groups and other entrepreneurs in Europe and the United States to tie their names to images of Afro-pessimism for the purpose of wider and uninterrupted commodification of their name, music or church. Clearly, the media have sufficiently wired Africa to the West, from the public sphere to the bedrooms, to the extent that

> Africans are isolated from nation to nation but united in looking toward Europe and the United States for the latest news, politics and culture. (Diawara 2003, 64)

As Diawara suggests, defining our roles in relation to Afro-pessimism or creating new forms of justifications to "save" Africa do more to promote a Westward focus, not necessarily to support African capacity. Critically examining how portrayals of Africa may influence our ideas of partnership is a step towards challenging colonialism and cultural hegemony. Urgings to "re-vitalize" using terms such as "crisis" (Altheide 2002; Zack-Williams, Tunde, Frost, and Thomson 2002; Zeleza 2003) could be a conscious or unconscious desire to create the picture that suits us, rather than promoting indigenous conversation and capacity.

TENSIONS, TRENDS, AND POSSIBILITIES

Observations made within Africa, reported in this article led the author to a deeper understanding of the complexity of libraries and higher education in Africa, the important role of librarians, and provided insight into barriers to the scholarly research process for Africans who study in Africa and the United States. The author is aware of the Western tendency to generalize about Africa and would like to remind the reader that the author speaks with specific reference to her own observations and reflections of trends witnessed during her travel in Kenya and South Africa in 2001.

Growing up in a multicultural society within the United States can encourage the desire to appreciate and learn about difference and similarity across cultures. Inspired by overwhelming positive interactions as an Africana librarian and close contact with scholars' pursuits to articulate vision and agency for Africa, the author is guided by the conviction that indigenous knowledge creation is essential to African studies everywhere, but is especially important for building democracy and community within Africa. The author traveled to Africa as participant observer in an attempt to find possible solutions for two areas of concern:

- Build capacity of scholars, librarians, and libraries to support indigenous knowledge production and democratization in Africa
- HIV/AIDS prevention in Africa.

For this author, education and library development in Africa holds hopes for strengthening African scholarship and enhancing democratization and citizen empowerment. But what does the "peripheral role" of scholarship in Africa suggest? What kind of knowledge will be produced and how will technology be used to inform this process?

Though the author had interest in Africa, African libraries, and development studies since early days of a graduate school internship on Africana librarianship at UC Berkeley (1980s), the author had not had the opportunity to visit the African continent beyond Egypt (1989), until becoming a Social Science Bibliographer for the University at Albany (1996) for six subject areas, including Africana Studies. In 1996, the author joined the Africana Librarians Council (ALC).

Africana Librarians Council (ALC)

The Africana Librarians Council (ALC), is an active working body within the African Studies Association (ASA). ALC projects listed here can be found on the ALC Web page accessed at: (http://www.loc.gov/rr/amed/9asa.html). Membership in ALC is open to any member of the African Studies Association. However, most attending members of the ALC work as librarian subject specialists in larger academic African studies centers or libraries. ALC promotes cooperative attitudes and specifically encourages African membership. The group meets twice per year and serves as both mentor and network for new and continuing Africana librarians at a wide range of institutions. Book vendors and representatives from agencies or other library and publishing projects also attend. The group maintains Web manuals on acquisition procedures and vendor contacts. Reference queries are shared and researched over an active listserv. Promotion of indigenous scholarship in Africa through collaborative projects is a consistent theme. For example, ALC has sponsored conferences and panels (Schmidt 1998) and also publishes the *Africana Librarians Newsletter* (*ALN*). Print copies are sent free of charge to libraries around the world, including Africa, and it is also available free on the Web. Long before discussions of "open access" scholarship, this resource specifically addressed promoting access to research on Africa and has been shared with librarians in Africa. African Librarians interviewed during the author's travel noted the importance of this resource as a network tool and a source of support. The *Electronic Journal of African Bibliographies* (*EJAB*) is an ALC affiliated project. *EJAB* is a freely available electronic journal featuring bibliographies on Africa and is hosted on the University of Iowa Web page.

Two other examples of ALC projects are the annual ASA Conover Porter Award for best reference sources on Africa and the ASA Book Donation Award. The ALC Book Donation Committee reviews applications for the African Studies Association Book Donation Award. The annual award provides funds to ship books to libraries in Africa upon evaluation of proposals where donors of books have been matched with African libraries who have requested books. The annual list of Africana bibliographies and reference works in the quarterly *African Book Publishing Review* (*ABPR*) is compiled by an ALC committee. The Cooperative Africana Microform Project (CAMP) is part of the Center for Research Libraries (CRL). The African Newspapers Union List (AFRINUL) is a union list of African newspapers held by research libraries in North America (Europe and Africa to be added in the future) and is a special project of the ALC of the United States and the Cooperative Africana Microform Project at the Center for Research Libraries (CRL). Another cooperative microfilming project, based at the National Archives of Senegal, is an example of an ALC partnership supporting the preservation of knowledge on or by Africans.

The ALC does not charge for their work and membership is based upon organizational membership within the African Studies Association. Informal partnerships occur regularly. Networking among librarians, sharing information and experience within the group as well as within Africa, serve as valuable forms of partnership. This network of committed librarians offered opportunities for this librarian to consider development studies and cooperative projects in a concrete way. However, this paper is not an official statement of the Africana Librarians Council (ALC). Any views, comments, errors made here should reflect solely upon the author, not upon the ALC.

METHOD

The author's research leave (2001) was intended to invite African reference librarians to articulate their own experience of reference service in Africa for this special issue on Africana librarianship, as well as to document potential future and ongoing cooperative library projects within Africa. As we have seen, trends in higher education are increasingly transnational and impact upon libraries in both Africa and the United States.

In an attempt to understand the context and contrasts observed, the author spoke with librarians, administrators, and scholars making an effort to observe and document her own assumptions and raise questions throughout the process.

Throughout the author's travel, attempts were made to interact with local contacts both as a visiting librarian and co-editor of this volume. Tangential to the main purpose of the trip, and not discussed in this paper, involvement in a U Albany campus "Save Africa From AIDS" (SAFA) campaign encouraged investigation into potential SAFA partnerships in Africa. The author accepted invitations to South African and Kenyan academic libraries and universities, library associations, and AIDS prevention projects. In addition, the author attended the 2001 Association of African Universities AAU meeting. Interviews and travel were not pre-arranged by an official agency. One-to-one contact was based primarily upon introductions over e-mail. These connections were mostly made through individuals, rather than through organizations. Though membership in the Africana Librarians Council (ALC) was recognized, the author did not present herself as an official representative of either the ALC or the University at Albany.

Forty-five librarians were interviewed: twenty in Nairobi, Kenya; ten in Cape Town; fifteen in Pretoria, South Africa. Interviews generally consisted of approximately two hour meetings both in groups and on a one-to-one basis. Questions varied and no survey instrument was used. One- or two-day orientations and discussions also occurred. University libraries, organizations, and sites in *Kenya* included: Association of African Universities, University of Nairobi, Kenyatta University, African Virtual University (Nairobi), American Reference Center Library, United States International University (USIU-Alliant International University), National Library of Kenya, Library of Congress Field Office, USAID.

University libraries, organizations, and sites in *South Africa* included: University of Cape Town (UCT), UCT African Studies Library, African Gender Institute (UCT), South African Women's Graduate Association, Clarke's Bookshop, District Six Museum, Robben Island Museum, The Slave Lodge, The Mayibuye Center, National Library of South Africa, Cape Town Public Library, University of the Western Cape, University of South Africa (UNISA) in Pretoria, Africa Institute of South Africa, and the Library and Information Association of South Africa (LIASA) in Pretoria.

Questions

- Would revitalization of publishing venues and libraries in Africa reverse brain drain in Africa?

- Will libraries in Africa serve as democratic symbols and become vital resources for strengthening and building communities, or will libraries be viewed as institutions symptomatic of "destructive colonial legacies" which some argue need to be dismantled?
- How can institutions value librarians so that they can be participants informing the education and learning process which integrates sustainable ICT development?
- What does reference service look like in Africa?
- How do social factors impact upon the goals of reference librarians?
- What is the role of the African librarian in the context of higher education today?
- What is the role of "First World" Africana librarians in supporting librarians in Africa? How do we work toward library development in a way that does not contribute to a new world order premised upon Africans as targets of colonialism and cultural hegemony?
- How do librarians in Africa define themselves in relation to their circumstances and what opportunities exist to set agendas or alter the environment toward information literacy service and their own self-definition?
- How can librarians share methods across continents to inform institutions to support creative, indigenous, democratic, and equitable community relationships?
- What is the difference in impact between donor-led partnership initiatives and those of independent scholarly or professional organizations in achieving library capacity?
- Can theory on gender inequality better inform dialogue and practice in forming equitable partnerships?
- Will new technologies make libraries, librarians, and universities obsolete?
- What forms of technology (van der Veur 2002) currently contribute toward democracy in Africa?
- How did the AAU address library capacity building, the impact of privatization on education and indigenous knowledge production?
- How has language of desire characterized as technolust penetrated African higher education consciousness?
- How can Africans insure that ICT and systems technology will not re-inscribe repressive control, dominance, and inequity within African society?
- What are the implications for academic libraries and academia in Africa if knowledge is imported from the West and purchased

through contracts with Western companies producing information databases? Will Africans mirror this same structure and promote commodification of knowledge instead of knowledge for the public good?

- Has the prominence of ICT already been marketed in such a way as to have a more disadvantageous impact on libraries and the production of knowledge in Africa?

The author frames this article as a reflection upon her own education and experience as a North American, female traveler to the African continent and works from the following assumptions.

Assumptions

Assumption 1

Increasing globalization creates a deeper sense of isolation threatening human ability to construct paths out of crisis situations. Harnessing the capacity of librarians by building cross-continental partnerships can support librarians within institutions where knowledge and potential may not be understood or valued. Utilizing existing capacity and resources should be the goal of cooperative projects. To promote ICT development and indigenous African scholarship, librarians need to be strategically placed in order to effect change in decision-making bodies within universities and policy-making bodies. Trends to dismantle reference service in the United States could detract from the goal of cultivating scholarly inquiry and production in Africa.

Assumption 2

The historically gendered role and consequent stereotypes of librarians in both the United States and Africa have had negative impacts upon professional agency. The re-framing of librarian roles must also address the gendered aspects of roles within higher education. This must be done by librarians, administrators, and scholars. Characterization of librarians as "handmaidens" does little to accurately depict the historic and varied roles or the intellectual nature of librarianship, but is often used to justify "virtual libraries" where ICT leads librarianship–not the other way around. Why not support librarians to lead the ICT development instead of librarians becoming "handmaids" to ICT?

To equate the capacity of librarians with the currently deteriorated state of some libraries in Africa, is to apply further negative stereotypes of librarian agency. Building library capacity will necessarily include librarians both female and male in a more central role of translating and designing how ICT should be integrated with teaching and knowledge production within African universities. Librarian involvement is key, as librarians are, in general, more focused upon the local needs of their communities and constituents. If any meaningful "leap-frogging" is to occur, critical reviews of ICT development experience in the West are important to consider in decision making, particularly regarding the impact upon libraries and scholarship in the United States.

Assumption 3

Democracy is not an exclusively Western concept. In order to map out democratic and sustainable societies, cogent theory and critical literacies are necessary. Ample evidence that Africans are capable of creating their own destinies should inform dialogue on capacity building. Stereotypes of Africa as the "dark continent" dependent upon the West to "develop" must be critiqued and reflected upon if mutually beneficial partnerships are going to emerge. Dialogues on building capacity must come with recognition that efforts to "save Africa" have also been used as justifications to "underdevelop Africa."

Assumption 4

Intra-continental and cross-continental networks of scholars interested in knowledge on Africa can work together to distinguish patriarchal, cultural imperialist, missionizing, or benevolent based constructs. First-world librarians who are committed to promoting knowledge creation in Africa can assist in creating formal and informal mutually beneficial partnerships.

Assumption 5

Donor funding that promotes mainstreaming of African universities into Western database consumption is not necessarily a capacity building measure. Donor funding to support indigenous indexing, database development, and the documenting of African scholarship can make positive contributions. We would go farther if both scholars and librarians were invited into conversations and forums where they are asked,

"What are the next best steps to promote scholarship and how could these steps also build stronger capacity for librarians?"

The earlier section of this paper introduced African capacity building within the context of development discourse and practice. The next portion of the author's paper integrates the author's observations in Africa (2001) and discusses models of capacity building offered by donor agencies and library centered organizations. Both sections compare partnership and "capacity building" models in order to identify elements of, and possible criteria for, relationships that promote capacity of Africans, nurture African knowledge production, and utilize technology in support of paths to democratic and sustainable higher education futures.

To understand the twin objectives of revitalizing libraries and promoting indigenous scholarship in Africa, one must have some sense of the state of libraries, university governance and how they do, or do not, support research and scholarly inquiry.

UNIVERSITIES AND LIBRARIES IN SOUTH AFRICA: OBSERVATIONS

South African visions for libraries are very broad and do promote and support research and scholarly production with particular emphasis upon addressing the historic imbalance in education.

> The existing higher education system, shaped by colonialism and exploitation, perpetuated an inequitable distribution of access and opportunity for students and staff along the lines of race, gender, class and geographic location. . . . While South Africa's higher education could claim academic achievement of international reknown, it was still characterized by teaching and research policies that favored academic insularity, with little response to the needs of South African society and the challenges and problems of Africa in a broader context. (Green Paper on Higher Education Transformation, 1996)

> In prevailing South African conditions, the non-elite, lower status institutions tend to be the historically disadvantaged black institutions. (Subotzky 2001, 2-3)

The Higher Education Act, passed by the South African Parliament in 1997 encouraged discussions of library cooperation, technology, cost effectiveness, on the part of consortium planners such as GAELIC (the largest South African library consortium formed in 1996), in order to advocate for libraries, be consistent with national policies on information provision, and utilize technological infrastructures to support libraries (Subotzky 2001). Based upon the institutions visited within South Africa and the contacts the author met at the AAU it was clear that South Africa has inherent economic and political advantages in comparison to other African states. Social transformation efforts overall have much to do with the integration of ICT into library and community development. This emphasis was impressive. Long-term planning integrating community development appears key to agendas for leadership and was perceived as a welcome benefit to other African countries.

Collections documenting the African National Congress, and an audio and video library of the resistance movements which brought about Nelson Mandela's presidency in 1994, are being developed and preserved at the University of the Western Cape (UWC), a historically Black university. Robben Island is the prison where Nelson Mandela and other dissidents were imprisoned. It is now a museum and a library. Previous political prisoners now serve as guides on daily tours of the museum, giving witness to their experiences there. UWC is working with the Robben Island Museum to build another museum planned for the waterfront in Cape Town.

University of South Africa (UNISA) has developed impressive outreach and distance learning programs to both urban and rural communities which harness technological developments to support education, not steer it. Reference librarians appeared to play an active role in providing resource packets for online courses to rural constituents who received education through innovative distance learning programs. Due to time constraints, the author did not interview students involved in distance learning. Public library efforts have also focused on the development of local and rural libraries. Public libraries (Issak 2000) are very popular and continue to play a role in creative information dissemination through collections, displays, and the distribution of health alerts. Networks of librarians and consortia (Edwards 1999) work together on a variety of information literacy initiatives and the librarian organizations continue to develop. For example, INFOLIT is a group of staff at the five higher education institutions in the Western Cape working on information literacy goals. While visiting South Africa in 2001, a newly formed Library and Information Association of South Africa (LIASA) was in the process of being formed. (For more discussion of the history of these organizations, see Kagan 2003,18-19.)

In general, the author observed that South Africans welcomed travelers, respecting the potential benefits from building cross-continental partnerships, and appeared to be very conscious of their potential leadership role in Africa. Without knowing whether the ranks of librarians have increased overall, the author did not observe a large number of librarians of color in the historically white universities visited (Kagan 2003). The author received a CD-ROM copy of the 2001 World Bank initiative to create the online African Digital Library offering net-Library access of online electronic copies of books throughout Africa. This was developed in concert with the Tecknikon South Africa. Book selection at the time seemed very limited and did not appear to focus on indigenous African scholarship, though it may have augmented collections or provided access to books for some who had electronic access but had no access to books.

Sustaining Reference Service and Collections: South Africa

As a visitor from the United States, university libraries in the Cape Town area seemed familiar. Libraries appeared to be arranged similar to academic libraries within the United States. Many of the materials purchased originate in the West. The author observed one method academic institutions used to obtain indigenous publications within Africa. Manuscripts, documents, and publications from Africa are delivered to universities from bookstores which regularly acquire sources from publishers and vendors throughout Africa. These organizations play an important role in delivering African indigenous materials to academic libraries in Africa and the West. Henrietta Dax from Clarke's Bookshop in South Africa toured the author through the Bookshop and discussed some of her acquisition trips throughout Africa and methods for locating reports, documents, and materials published in Africa. These suppliers are relied upon to supply subject-specific material to major Africana collections in Africa, the United States, and Europe as well. The Library of Congress field offices in Africa also supply African documents to libraries in the United States.

Africanization of Collections: "What Is African Culture?"

Within the context of social transformation and developing collections, discussions on Africanization and indigenous culture (Odhiambo 2002) and its meaning for libraries was very active (see Darch in this volume). Africanization of collections necessitated tough choices for future acquisitions and collection building. Whether to focus collection development efforts on relevant collections which document culture and experience of indigenous South African groups (previously not collected), or to preserve historically held collections, sometimes referred to as "colonial archives" (Desai 2002), or whether to focus on both, were among conversations. In addition, standard Western indexing sources and full-text databases consumed a larger portion of the acquisition budget.

At the University of Cape Town, database selection in public areas included the African Journals On-Line (INASP database), an electronic index and abstract tool for African-produced publications, in addition to Western-derived disciplinary databases which index scholarship, primarily from the West. However, even with the status of premier-elite university within South Africa, and the relative abundance of resources as compared with Kenya and other universities within South Africa, the University of Cape Town acquisition librarians found that the price of journals and "leased information" through databases and full-text packages purchased from the West threatened their ability to sustain subscriptions and maintain their goal of access to a variety of collections and full-text resources. Commodification of knowledge and collections through access to leased subscriptions was a concern addressed in South Africa. If this was true for the University of Cape Town, how might other libraries in comparatively lesser positions throughout Africa fare?

Shared Experience and Partnerships: Integrating Reference and ICT

A librarian from Pretoria traveling to the United States (1999) phoned a librarian to visit the University at Albany Libraries. This meeting led to the development of several connections and interviews made at the UNISA library where the author was welcomed and hosted in 2001. The author subsequently visited the University of Cape Town, where an active ideological debate on whether to dismantle the African Studies Library, a separate library of the University of Cape Town system, was in progress. Should the collection be integrated into the main collection or was there value in keeping a separate African Studies Library within the library? Although, the "African Renaissance" debate discussed in Darch's paper in this volume had influenced the need for this discussion, from the author's observation, it appeared that part of the issue had also to do with whether the library could afford to offer in-depth reference service provided at this library as well as new initiatives that promoted technological access. This impression came from interviews with librarians of the African Studies Library at UCT and comments from a University of Cape Town administrator who asked this author her opinion of the University's *Knowledge Commons*, a fully equipped technologically advanced resource center located at the entrance of the University of Cape Town (UCT) main library. He noted that the university had "sunk" a lot of money into its development. The Commons operates similar to "Information Desks" within the United States, featuring at least twenty computers in a room sending a clear message that the University of Cape Town is a leader and recognizes the importance of integrating ICT tools in research. Interestingly, the University of Cape Town Library *Knowledge Commons* integrates reference service and access to technology without diminishing the importance of the library and the librarian.

As a result of the author's interviews with librarians at the African Studies Library, the author observed a dedicated reference posture where scholars found a space to focus, concentrate, and dialogue with subject specialist librarians. Through these interviews and invitations to these librarians to visit other libraries on the author's itinerary, an informal connection was formed. The author also extended an invitation to librarians to attend the ALC meetings. The librarians of the African Studies Library of UCT, in the process of "making a case" not to dismantle the library were able to dialogue with members from the ALC to discuss this issue. Intelligently, the University Library Director of UCT sent one of the librarians interviewed from the UCT African Studies Library to the United States and other South African libraries to visit and study libraries and African Studies collections (Spring 2001). This librarian traveled with the author to libraries in Cape Town and Pretoria and subsequently visited the United States on an independent tour to interview major African Studies libraries. Ultimately, the decision was made not to dismantle the African Studies Library collection at the University of Cape Town.

DISMANTLING REFERENCE COLLECTIONS AND SERVICE: TRENDS IN THE UNITED STATES

One of the key issues discussed in technology transfer contexts is the importance of opportunities to see the 'plus and minus' of situations by those who are not necessarily selling the technology. Perhaps the librarian traveling to the United States from South Africa was apprised of some of the decisions made and lessons learned in the United States.

"Handmaidens" to Technology?

As a librarian working at the Information Desk for many years at the Reference and Collection Development department of the University of California at Berkeley in the mid 1990s, the author recalls similar issues to those described at the University of Cape Town in 2001. A decision at UC Berkeley was made to develop a new Information Center located near the entrance of the Doe Library featuring access to fully equipped study/research spaces. Since it was thought impossible to maintain both the "Reference and Reading Room," and the new "Doe Information Center," one had to go. The decision to dismantle the historic Reference and Reading Room of the Doe library encountered significant resistance. Despite the resistance, the reference collection developed over thirty years was "sacrificed" in favor of a larger, technologically equipped Information Center. This extraordinary, internationally recognized reference collection was integrated into the main stacks of the collection. Reference librarians, and other staff members who had worked at the smaller Information Desk, now worked at the new Information Center with a skeleton set of reference tools. While the new space increased access to technology, it did little to integrate the reference tools, research perspectives, and provided less access to subject specialists. Librarians became "handmaidens" to machines, assisting access to printers, databases, and e-mail, instead of providing in-depth research service previously offered to scholars and students. After approximately seven years, this policy was re-evaluated and rated a failure. According to reports by staff, the University of California Doe Library is now in the process of attempting to recreate the historic Reference and Reading Room collection which was earlier so disdained.

South Africa: Selective Decisions About What to Import

This trend in the United States to "downsize" reference collections is but one example of the demise of reference service and the "disembodiment of the librarian" (Martell 2000). Interestingly, the University of Cape Town did not appear to import this trend. Instead, the University of Cape Town Knowledge Commons is staffed with reference librarians. Africanization of collections is continually being addressed within all libraries at UCT and service has increased in the UCT African Studies Library, creating a greater need for material on Africa and reference service to support this research. The library has been involved with the Digital Imaging of South Africa (DISA) (Peters, Pickover 2001) project as a satellite site scanning journals from the Anti-Apartheid years and is planning two digital projects–one a poster project and the other a political ephemera project of leaflets handed out in the 1980s in the Western Cape.

Valuing Reference Service: Cross-Continental Benefits

Knowledge of the decision at the University of Cape Town Library to value reference service and find ways to support both ICT and reference is beneficial to librarians in the West as well. Sharing this experience supports librarians in developing their capacity and prevents them from being characterized as "either with technology or against," leaving room for librarians to assert their expertise and broader role within the Information Age. This example of a mutually beneficial partnership included a common interest and goal of supporting scholarly assistance to African scholars. Librarians can value and share methods that offer support to librarians in the process of becoming players who argue for the integration of technology–but not at the expense of reference service and collections. Taking interest in library development and making person-to-person connections can prove effective. This proactive approach also combats the negative, isolating tendencies of globalization. As Diawara suggested earlier, the tendency to "look toward the West" is cultivated and can easily become unconscious. However, in this case, social costs were considered as well and the "invisible labor" of librarians participating in the cultivation of scholarship appears to have been valued. Despite the apparent favor of virtual libraries, public spaces (Äng, Das, Dobbie, and Kent 2001; Jones 2001; Miller 2002) where access to materials is combined with research assistance from librarians appear to be necessary, particularly in the case of Kenya.

OBSTACLES TO INDIGENOUS KNOWLEDGE CREATION: CENSORSHIP, CRISIS, AND CAPACITY IN KENYA

Collections and Library Facilities in Nairobi: Observations and Interviews

Library systems in Africa expanded rapidly on the heels of explosive growth in education after independence, but since the onset of

> the economic crisis and structural maladjustment in the 1980s in many countries, funding for education in general and libraries in particular declined sharply, necessitating severe cuts in the acquisitions of books, journals and other materials. (Zeleza 2003, 372)
>
> North American libraries, for example, started facing continuous cuts in their budgets, a situation made worse by escalating costs of books and serials which forced many of them to reduce their serials holdings by canceling journals that had weak support among faculty or were little used by students.
>
> If the libraries in the North were suffering from fiscal cold, those in Africa were reeling from pneumonia. (Zeleza 2003, 398)

University libraries in Nairobi appeared to be active study halls. Each library carrel and study space was filled by a student. From this image, one could guess that the students took their studies seriously, that libraries were either accommodating increased enrollments of students, or that students found it difficult to find access to study space due to increasingly insecure housing and crowded domestic spaces. All of these explanations appeared to be true.

Condition of the Library and Donated Materials

The author was shocked by the condition of the Kenyatta University Library. Card catalog drawers were stacked all over the room. Although shelving and shelf reading in the main collection appeared to have been largely abandoned, there was evidence of current acquisitions.

Among other libraries identified in Africa in 1996-97, Rosenberg rated Kenyatta University's building and facilities as "totally inadequate." Her 1997 description and findings (Rosenberg 1997, 2:182-194) of Kenyatta University Library largely concur with statements from staff during the author's visit in 2001. However, in 2001, new library space was in the process of being constructed. The African Virtual University had also been added to the campus.

At the time of this writing, many public university libraries in Kenya relied upon donated materials. Zeleza acknowledges this reliance on donations as a response to the crisis of libraries in Africa but notes that "book aid is episodic . . . and it reinforces Africa's dependency on Western intellectual paradigms, problems and preoccupations" (Zeleza 2003, 372). Rosenberg reports, "apart from local newspapers and magazines, all serials are donated; donated books make up between 30% to 50% of all acquisitions" (Rosenberg 1997: 2, 189). Donations, the author observed, appeared to have been unpacked and unprocessed for a long period of time. Interviewees indicated that this was due to a lack of consistent and reliable staffing to catalog materials.

Indexing and Impact on Creation of Knowledge

Unlike South Africa, examples of indexes documenting indigenous knowledge were not observed in the Kenyan libraries visited. Despite the successful use of CD-ROM technology in Africa, which has been a positive factor, the author found that CD-ROM indexes to literature were very "hit or miss" in terms of coverage dates. In fact, often no subscription existed and the CD-ROMs were donated, or purchased when funds were available. This translated into incomplete holdings of indexing tools, leaving a scholar to wonder what was missed in the review of his or her topic. Since many of these tools are developed in the West and indexed in the West, this poses added problems for scholars who wished to create a literature review on a particular topic. In addition to the acknowledged lack of publishing venues in Africa, relevant literature reviews are more difficult to develop with hit or miss indexing and lesser access to current literature. It is likely considered a source of embarrassment to base a work on "dated sources" and therefore, authors may not want to risk their reputation by focusing on possibly "outdated" information. Access to current information in Nairobi was dependent upon utilization of other sources.

Dissertations

Interested to know how the *Dissertations and Theses in Africa Database* (DATAD) project was perceived by librarians in Kenya, the author raised questions about dissertations. In general, librarians interviewed looked forward to its development and stated that they had been queried for the project. The author asked, "Was there was a record of dissertations and abstracts for students who had graduated or completed their research?" In some cases, the author was shown a catalog drawer with a sketchy list. For most of the Kenyan libraries visited, there was no procedure that made it mandatory for students to register the dissertation with the library. Dissertations are not submitted on a regular basis particularly when Kenyans go outside the country. Some librarians felt that dissertations completed outside the country should also be included and that signed agreements should be made before traveling, particularly when an African university sponsors such travel and research. The focus on documenting African dissertations was mentioned as a key concern. However, it was also mentioned with some frustration that the capacity of librarians within institutions had not been tapped to develop collaborative projects. Librarians stated that though they had identified several indexing projects that could have been initiated, these "local" projects were difficult to match with funds from donors.

Crisis in Public Education

Librarians interviewed in Kenya cited widespread deterioration of public education in Africa as an impediment to developing indigenous scholarship. Censorship, lack of intellectual autonomy, and academic freedom inhibit scholarly production in Kenya.

> In a growing number of African countries, scholars and writers had to negotiate carefully between the impulses and demands of their intellectual calling and the crippling surveillance of both state power and civil society. Scholarly research and production was ensnared in a stifling web of censorship. Monitored especially closely were research and publications in the social sciences and humanities, with their propensity for deflating the inflationary rhetoric of development and national unity proclaimed by the new political class. (Zeleza 2003, 398)

There appeared to be consensus that a correlation exists between low rates of publication in African universities and the increasing demoralization faced by scholars who encounter surveillance and censorship described above. In addition, faculty reported that they do not receive support or are unfairly compensated for research. Interviewees also stated:

> "So many begin research but are not able to continue."
>
> "'Brain drain' results in low retention of highly qualified staff."
>
> "The student to teacher ratio is too high to manage effective education."
>
> "Equipment for students is lacking."

Citing cases of corruption within universities and governments, some spoke of grants coming into the university as a result of faculty proposals only to have funds siphoned off or used in other ways than intended.

Universities as Contested Space for Free Speech

> As in Malawi, Kenya, where I had worked for many years, permission from the government had to be sought to organize an academic conference locally or to attend one abroad. Accordingly, lists of participants or the contents of articles would be scrutinized by overzealous and obtuse bureaucrats for any potential inclusion of subversive invitees and information.
>
> Censorship sought to create a culture of silence, which was loudly enacted through open harassment, dismissals, arrests, and even death of the errant intellectual. Such conditions were obviously not conducive to critical scholarly inquiry and productivity. In the worst-affected countries, many academics and writers, if they did not flee abroad, often learned the survival arts of self-censorship and intellectual apathy and publishers kept their distance from potentially troublesome and unrewarding scholarly publishing, concentrating on the safer and more lucrative school textbook market. (Zeleza 2003, 398-399)

The author learned that several student strikes had recently occurred on the Kenyatta University campus and that the university had suspended classes on a regular basis. Students had been expelled and professors had been fired (Amutabi 2002). Complaints by students included lack of university support to students and lack of support to libraries. However, student protest was also linked to complaints about censorship, academic freedom, and the firing of professors who had voiced their opinions. In an article, Jacqueline Klopp discusses the situation of student activists who are silenced and rendered invisible because of their activism and are often expelled from the state controlled universities. Klopp describes,

> . . . how the integration of Kenya's university system into the wider system of repressive rule means that the struggle for university autonomy and academic freedom in Kenya, as in many other parts of the continent is fundamentally linked to wider struggles to democratize the state and economy. (Klopp 2002, 45-46)

Governance, Status, and Autonomy Within Universities: Impact on Agency and Gender

At the time of the author's travel in Kenya, appointment to Head the University was made by the country's president, then President Moi. The President of the country is Chancellor for all Kenyan universities. Vice Chancellors and Rectors of each university in Kenya report directly to the Chancellor. The University Vice-Chancellor in Kenya appoints University librarians for the university.

The author was told that a university library director must receive authorization from the Vice-Chancellor for any expenditure over fifty U.S. dollars. University library directors interviewed indicated that participation in academic meetings such as the Faculty Senate or other meetings that set agendas or outline the research needs of students and faculty are rare. Female library directors are also not the norm in Kenya. If the library director is a woman, and is lucky enough to be invited to meetings, gender and/or status as librarian might discourage her from speaking. The university atmosphere is highly charged by conflict. Self-identification as a contributing professional could be severely diminished in this environment because of fear of reprisal for one's views or non-compliance with authorities. Professional development for both faculty and librarians was described as inadequate. Librarians from the Kenyatta University campus were not allowed to attend the AAU meeting held on the campus.

Interviews with students and observations of interactions indicated frustration and demoralization at the hierarchical, predominantly male dominated power relations, which appeared to impact negatively upon the agency of women in Kenya. That positions within universities are often secured and maintained based upon tribal affiliations is well known in Kenya. Also common, but not openly discussed, is the experience of sexual harassment on campuses. Violence against female students, employees, or professors in the form of pressure to succumb to sexual advances by professors or administrators are marks of what some call "postcolonial phallocracy," a critique of male academics who are "protecting vested interests" through the continued subordination of women (Nyamnjoh and Jua 2002, 5). Both young men and women frequently approached the author to discuss exit plans from the country for different reasons–most reported for economic hardship. However, young women in particular indicated that they saw no future for them in Kenya.

The Forum for the Advancement of Women in Education (FAWE) tries to address these issues in several publications. FAWE drafts strategies and procedures to address sexual harassment and discrimination within educational institutions and in communities. However, as in the United States, absence of formal complaint procedures and interpretations of harassment within a male-dominated culture can make it very difficult for individuals to negotiate assistance. Interviewees suggested that education and political will to eradicate the barriers experienced by women in higher education must be addressed in active campaigns and through the development of support networks.

AAU Plenary–Women in African Tertiary Institutions: Equity, Empowerment, and Advancement

To encourage discussion on gender issues in higher education, two presenters spoke at the 2001 AAU plenary session on women in higher education: Professor Ruth Meena, University of Dar Es Salaam and Professor Pennina Mlama, Executive Director of *The Forum for the Advancement of Women in Education* (FAWE). Both presented country-specific data and progress reports on the advancement of integrating girls and women at the tertiary level, particularly in policies which redress gender inequality. Though citing some important progress, both pointed to areas of needed improvement in creating better follow-up in translating national gender policies and rhetoric into action and coherent strategies.

> We are going to argue that such discrepancies result from either lack of commitment on the part of policy planners, or lack of knowledge on how to mainstream gender in policies programs and strategies or a combination of both. It is going to be argued that some governments make gender policies as a symbolic gesture of appeasing activists and particularly feminists, or some do it as a symbol of demonstrating a commitment to the international commitments made without an intention of transforming the gender balance. And yet some do it with a genuine motive of transforming gender relations but lack the skill and capacity to mainstream gender in core country program processes. (Meena 2001, 113)

Professor Meena specifically addressed the need for more analysis on causes for the gender gap and recommended that educators revisit the "written and hidden curriculums" with a goal of empowerment and "enhanc[ing] human rights awareness."

> Education, is not empowering the African citizens, particularly women and poor men to challenge power structures including patriarchal structures that perpetuate ideologies of social exclusion. This is being attributed to two related factors. First, low participation of women in tertiary sector leads to their exclusion in decision making processes hence denial of opportunities to challenge the power structures and corresponding ideologies that continue to relegate women a low social status. Additionally, the stereotyped curriculum in all levels continues to reproduce submissive citizens and particularly women who are socialized into accepting their subordinate social positions. (Meena 2001, 127)

Despite the excellent presentations delivered by the speakers, the breakout sessions on gender did not achieve the stated goals of developing specific methods to lessen obstacles for women in education. Lack of expert gender training facilitators during these sessions prevented an appropriate level of depth to address this issue seriously. Perhaps FAWE members could have facilitated these sessions or provided mini-workshops and this could have made a greater impact. Several concerns raised did not make their way into AAU final recommendations and priorities for future objectives, including an initiative for a women's caucus within the AAU.

Librarians Interviewed on the Subject of Indigenous Knowledge Creation

When asked, "What do you think might promote indigenous knowledge production in Africa and how might library and librarian capacity be supported to further knowledge creation?" librarians responded by articulating the context of their universities, the relationship between the lack of university support to libraries and research in Kenya, as well their own status. Several librarians and faculty members interviewed in Kenya cited the trend to privatize education as problematic and told this author that it was not possible to rely on the university library to serve their patron's research needs. Once again, limited access to indexing tools, journals, current monographs, and computers was said to contribute to "peripheral knowledge production." Staff development training was cited as severely lacking within the libraries. Though librarian proposals for indigenous indexing projects had been identified and forwarded, they did not appear to receive priority. Some librarians cited the need for a stronger National Library in Kenya to initiate indexing projects. Lack of curriculum resources was raised frequently as was over-reliance upon photocopied textbooks for use by students.

Librarians Mediating Privatized Spaces

In spite of all of the difficulties faced, the author witnessed a high level of service commitment on the part of reference librarians in Kenyan public universities. Faculty lauded librarian service while they noted the conditions they faced. Librarians offered traditional reference service, utilizing local collections, orientation, user education, as well as letters of introduction and referrals to other research sources and libraries. Most importantly, reference librarians also performed extended reference service through travel to private, restricted libraries to access information for their patrons. It is widely acknowledged that faculty and students go off campus for current information sources.

Some librarians used their "official" role to assist "public university" patrons by mediating these private institutions to access, primarily, up-to-date journal articles or full-text databases. The librarian's institutional status may entitle entry to these facilities. Extended service may involve payment of annual or daily admission fees in order to access electronic or print indexes and full-text packages. Librarians the author spoke with understood that resources existed elsewhere, but were not accessible to their patrons because of their lack of financial standing or status. Librarians performing this extended service indicated that travel fees and entrance fees to these private facilities often came out of the librarians pocket. They were not subsidized for these fees or for their travel time. Traveling via "matatu" in Kenya can be a risky situation. Since little public transit exists in Nairobi, most people get to and from work by bicycle, ride-sharing, walking, or by riding an independently owned and operated "matatu" van service. This service is known more for the entrepreneurial benefit to individuals managing the service than for the safety of its passengers. Therefore, extended reference service in this context is what most would consider, "above and beyond the call of duty." This is but one example of time and energy investments made by librarians who attempt to bridge the many infrastructural, digital, and development divides in Kenya. As with reference librarians the world over, commitment to the patron often comes first for these African librarians. Though conscious and mindful of the importance of developing self-sufficient users as discussed in professional librarian literature, librarians in Kenya noted that it was difficult to establish information literacy goals in these conditions.

Private, often restricted institutions, are often donor-funded initiatives or private universities funded by organizations outside the country. NGO settings and non-profit-based centers play an important role in stimulating knowledge production. However, librarians reported that access to the African Virtual University, located on their own campus at Kenyatta University, was not accessible to them.

THE AFRICAN VIRTUAL UNIVERSITY (AVU): PRIVATE EDUCATION ON A PUBLIC UNIVERSITY CAMPUS

Information Communication Technology (ICT) in Nairobi

Upon visiting public university libraries in Nairobi in 2001, one might get the impression that ICT connectivity is not possible. However, computer access at the University of Nairobi's library faired better than at Kenyatta University. At the Kenyatta University library, only one patron-accessible computer was available. This computer was located in the reference area of the library and was used primarily by reference librarians and students to search CD-ROM subject indexes.

In sharp contrast to both universities, Nairobi's city center sports many privately owned e-cafes with high-speed connections and up-to-date software and computers. These cafes operate night and day and are filled with people queued to use computers for e-mail at a charge of approximately two to three dollars every half hour. Further examples of this contrast were observed upon visits to private, restricted libraries and private universities which operated in quiet, almost unutilized spaces. ICT connectivity was clearly possible, so why had there not been a greater effort to connect public university libraries?

Ajayi stated earlier that the cost of ICT is one of the major obstacles to creating sustainable futures for libraries. The African Virtual University (AVU) is promoted as a capacity building initiative by the World Bank, a partnership claiming to develop and promote access to ICT on university campuses while building "world-class degree programs for the education of scientists, technicians, engineers, business managers, health care providers, and other professionals." The goal of AVU is to "offer university degree programs in science, technology, and medical fields; noncredit training and seminars; remedial instruction; and electronic library services" (http://www.avu.org/). Supplementing public university course offerings through AVU courses could be an advantageous relationship for public universities. It is presumed that the receipt of technology will place universities in a better position to attract local business partners who benefit from this mission and also help to sustain the project. "Sharing quality academic faculty, library resources and laboratory experiences available" is to come from participating African Virtual University sites, which reportedly include the University of Massachusetts, the New Jersey Institute of Technology, Indiana University, and others. Lectures by professors in the United States and Europe are purportedly sent by satellite to African universities through the AVU. This project, formerly led by the World Bank, is now an independent project. The Vice-Chancellor of Kenyatta University now has stewardship of the project in Kenya. The question "for whom" is absent from much of this advertisement.

Virtual Libraries: Marginalization of Librarians in Public Universities?

In 2001-02, the *African Virtual Library Initiative*'s (AVL-I) stated mission is to:

> [Facilitate] the provision of bibliographical and other information online services that meet the needs of educational, research and development work in Eastern Africa, with a view to developing linkages with other regional initiatives to create a truly African virtual library. (http://www.avli.org/People.html)
>
> The goal of the AVL-I is to influence all types of libraries in Africa to place their holdings on the World Wide Web for global access and to achieve full online status before the end of the first decade of this century. For Kenya where the AVL-I was launched in April 1999, the progress towards the goal of attaining online status by the year 2004 is on full steam and is achievable. (http://www.kabissa.org/lists/newsletter-submissions-l/1037.html)

The AVLI's intention, as stated, is to offer consultancy on knowledge management projects. The African Virtual University has also been developing its online virtual library. As of August 2003, electronic resources such as EBSCO (through INASP PERI), Gale, and World Bank databases and other resources feature prominently on the AVU digital library site (http://www.avu.org/online/section/library/index2.htm). However, based upon interviews with librarians from Kenyatta

University, librarians on site were not involved in the development or design of either of these virtual library models.

AVU in Kenya: Who Attends?

Upon first approach to the campus of Kenyatta University (2001), there are signs directing visitors to The African Virtual University and the Cultural Center nearby. One of several satellite sites of the AVU in Africa resides on Kenyatta University campus in Nairobi in a pastoral setting. It is important to note that although access to the physical AVU site is restricted to those paying to attend AVU, the private nature of the AVU is not immediately obvious and it is not described to visitors as private or separate from the public university. The AVU is housed in a separate structure on the university grounds so most visitors to the Kenyatta University campus would assume that the AVU at Kenyatta University is part of the public university campus.

An investigation into who is eligible to attend AVU revealed that this information is difficult to obtain; it is not clearly stated on the main AVU Web site. In 2001-2002, there was no description of the fees to attend AVU. Advertisement is vague on the issue of access–who attends, what the cost is, or what the benefit is to Kenyatta University, a public higher education institution where the AVU is housed. However, a follow-up search in June 2003 notes that, although no description of fees is available on the main AVU home page, the AVU page for Kenyatta University had recently added information on courses and fees.

Inside AVU: Restricted Use at Kenyatta University

The author's foreign, "possible donor" status, enabled her entry inside the AVU. The absence of computers in the Kenyatta University Library stood in sharp contrast to the array of computers sitting in the AVU labs. The author observed a small class of eight to ten students, reading from several video monitors displaying videotapes of printed pages, which had been videotaped from a hard copy computer manual. The author wondered if little access to print materials may have been the rationale for this type of instruction.

- Was this an example of curricular innovation?
- If textbooks are difficult to acquire, is reading from a videotape a better solution?

- Was this a temporary solution or a model for a sustainable information delivery?
- What were the costs as compared to the cost of purchasing manuals?
- How did this impact on learning and what message does it send to students who are aware of the more advanced equipment available?

AVU Benefit to Kenyatta University? Commentary on AVU from Interviews

Librarians interviewed indicated that one possible income-generation benefit could be associated with the AVU fee-based e-center. It was reported in 2001 that no other access to e-mail or Web service existed on this campus, situated outside of central Nairobi by about twenty miles. The AVU technology reportedly provided the basis for the development of this e-center which provided access to Internet and e-mail services for students and faculty at Kenyatta University for a fee. The commercial fee-based e-center model observed in downtown Nairobi was clearly imitated on the campus. However, this income generation from students already paying tuition was seen as problematic. According to interviewees, fees collected from the campus e-center are deposited back into the AVU account, not to the university or the library or the overall campus budget. Confirmation of this by the Kenyatta University director for the AVU was sought. Despite four attempts to visit the office of the AVU director, the door remained closed with no indication of hours listed.

Kenyans who spoke about AVU raised several concerns. Some charged that the AVU received public university funds to develop and sustain this project, thereby further draining resources for public higher education funding. Others suggested that the AVU could be an attempt to bypass some of the political structures in Kenya to introduce curricular reforms. This is questionable since the Vice Chancellor of the University, appointed by President Moi, backed the project. Overwhelmingly, those interviewed in Kenya questioned the capacity building nature of the project or perceived the African Virtual University (AVU) as a usurper of financial resources from the public education mission of the university.

If students paying public university fees are denied access to the AVU, as was stated in interviews, it is easy to imagine how this might be perceived as an unjust inequity leading to an obvious site of activism.

This trend of privatised corporate/public university "enclaves" also exists in the United States. However, it was easy to see how impressions of the demise of public education would logically follow. Would this also interrupt any chance for Kenyans to develop education which supports free and democratic inquiry? Or was technical training the most important goal here? The observations made here did not offer a positive view of education and did not appear to encourage indigenous scholarship or support the "local," "existing capacity" of libraries or local academic librarians.

More questions emerged on the author's part.

- "What is promised to the students at the public university for this exchange?"
- "How does AVU benefit and support the campus library?"
- "Whose agenda was this?"
- "Did AVU represent the World Bank's intention to have more control over the kind of education delivered in Kenya?"
- "Why weren't librarians from Kenyatta University involved in the library project?"

World Bank Panel: Questions and Responses on the AVU

The author posed some of these questions directly to AVU and World Bank representatives at the World Bank's panel during the question and answer period at the African Studies Association in December 2002, Washington, D.C. The author specifically asked, "Why does the World Bank want to further marginalize librarians in Africa through the African Virtual University?"

In response, according to the World Bank and AVU representatives, results from a 1997 pilot study showed that there was "growing readiness to pay for higher education in Africa" proving that the concept of paying for education was acceptable within Africa. Based upon the findings of the World Bank pilot study, the African Virtual University was sustained. The criticism that "existing capacity" had not been effectively utilized was noted. How could that have been overlooked?

Experience in the Street in Kenya: School Fees

The finding of the World Bank seemed to contradict the author's experience of what appeared to be common dilemmas for Kenyans. In addition to daily encounters of needy refugee "street children" in Kenya, the author could not go a day without at least two people (often off the street, but more commonly from wait-staff in restaurants, hotels, and e-centers) inviting her to send money to assist in paying school fees for their children. Often, parents or relatives carried pictures of children with documentation of their school fees with hope of receiving support from "wealthy" foreigners. Most Kenyan librarians interviewed confirmed the reality of this problem and indicated that the ability or inability to pay education costs determine the fate of many children. Kenyan children could not receive primary level public education without paying the equivalent of two to three thousand dollars per year in public school fees. Typically, Kenyans with steady jobs are offering support to family members who cannot afford this expense.

Citing "governmental interference . . . and the predatory encroachment of neo-liberal paradigms of international development organizations and their pressure toward greater privatization of higher education," Dominic Boyer also articulates this situation and suggests that privatization of education is problematic.

> Seen from the perspectives of the authors, African universities appear to be facing the worst of both worlds. The universities have at best indifferent and at worst hostile relations with political power, yet the only financial recourse is linked to raising fees beyond the circumstances of most citizens or to international development agencies and multinational corporations, each of which have their own agendas for and models of higher education which potentially threaten a new cycle of intellectual dependency. (Boyer 2002, 211)

According to Joel Samoff, the following are standard policy objectives of the World Bank:

- "Reduce the central government role in providing education;
- Decentralize;
- Increase school fees;
- Encourage and assist private schools;
- Reduce direct support to students, especially at the tertiary level;
- Assign high priority to instructional materials;
- Introduce double shifts and multigrade classrooms; Favour in-service over pre-service teacher education; etc." (Samoff 1999, 251).

World Bank Panel and Dialogue at ASA–2002

During the author's presentation of parts of this paper at the ASA conference in December 2002, ASA participants from Ghana and other countries within Africa who experienced the AVU model in their countries, stood up and cited similar scenarios as articulated by the author's experience in Kenya and also questioned the efficacy and the notion of capacity building in this model. The only positive statements made were by a representative of AVU who attended the session.

In what could be seen as an oblique response to similar criticisms of AVU, Graham Till, Principal of Barnham Business College (where tuition cost for the online degree program is 7,495 pounds per year, approximately $12,241 U.S. dollars), admits that the AVU has not reached the goal of sustainability. In a recent document, Till states that while the AVU did not reach the goal of sustainability,

> The objective is still to enable greater access to higher education for African students using modern ICT's but the approach will be more gradual and cautious and will involve finding the best ways to overcome the constraints that limit access to quality tertiary distance learning opportunities in Africa, whilst better harnessing the local skills and contributions of African faculty. [To further AVU,] . . . Universities will offer certification for groups of courses including AVU delivered elements rather than accrediting the latter separately. (Till 2003, 31-32)

However, the reasons cited for AVU's "failure" are not its privatised access structure, marginalization of existing capacity, or the importing of Western databases which support Western capacity, or the potential use of public university infrastructure to support private education. None of these were found to be problematic. Instead, the AVU's future success is now seen to be dependent upon a board of trustees, the inclusion of business representatives and a council of vice-chancellors, as well as "a pedagogically more sound mix of asynchronous resources replacing much video delivery" (Till 2003, 33).

> In these ways it is believed that AVU will overcome more general acceptance problems such as its perceived stance as unnecessarily competitive with, and superior to, local provision both within and beyond participating universities. . . . Greater attention to pedagogical and programme structure issues is promised, and collabo-

> ration with the UK Open University is under discussion. More emphasis also will be given to strengthening support areas and improving access to information not only for subject faculty but also for librarians.

Perhaps Till heard the criticisms of AVU but one wonders if he grasped the meaning. Absent from this philosophy are ethics of access to information which are just as important as the medium of delivery.

INASP: A Model Which Incorporates Indigenous Knowledge Production and Sustainability

The International Network for the Availability of Scientific Publications (INASP), a project of the International Council for Science (ICSU), was founded in 1992. The primary goal of INASP is to facilitate the exchange of information between and within countries, particularly where publication and distribution is less developed. INASP's objectives include:

- Support of existing efforts to disseminate scientific and scholarly information,
- Identification and support of new projects to increase local publication and access,
- Promotion of local "capacity building in information production, organization, and dissemination" (http://www.inasp.info/info/inasp.html).

A good example of how INASP operates is their management of the online database "African Journals Online," which indexes, abstracts, and provides access to the contents of over 200 journals published in Africa. Access to abstracts is completely free of charge. Photocopies of articles are obtained through online requests at ten USD per article in the United States or five pound Sterling. Researchers from countries included in INASP's "Programme for the Enhancement of Research Information," or PERI, are eligible for photocopies at no charge. Monies received for photocopies of articles are funneled back to support ongoing journal publication in Africa. Eventually, INASP hopes to move management of the program to Africa. INASP provides a much needed model for how technology can be used to meet the needs of scholars and societies, both North and South, while supporting the production of local print media, which is still so crucial in many parts of the world. Support for INASP comes from various organizations including: Carnegie Corporation of New York, the Department for International Development (UK), the Ministry of French Foreign Affairs, UNESCO, and WHO. The creation of a sustainable journal service model that has eventual African ownership as its goal incorporates key criteria for indigenous knowledge production. Additionally, INASP provides a wide range of workshops and resources to assist librarians and administrators in managing electronic journals and resources. Given that the AAU meeting had African knowledge creation and dissemination as one of its main objectives, models such as INASP, which integrate librarian expertise, ethics of free or low-cost access, ICT expertise and support to educational goals, should have received stronger endorsement at the AAU meeting.

IMPEDIMENTS TO LIBRARIAN SCHOLARLY PRODUCTION

In contrast to the ALC emphasis of supporting and promoting indigenous scholarship published within Africa, Rosenberg reports that "Everyone [in Africa] prefers to be published in established journals; it was also a quicker method of publication than local journals, which published so infrequently and irregularly" (Rosenberg 1997, 2: 193).

This author had a different experience. While many librarians graciously discussed their concerns with the author, surprisingly, most of the librarians interviewed were reluctant to actually develop an article for publication for this volume. Out of the forty-five librarians interviewed, twenty-five in South Africa and twenty in Kenya, the editors received only one submission from an author/librarian in South Africa. In Kenya, two librarians who were interested in developing an article, drafted major concerns together with this author but neither were able to continue the work because of "several hardships" they faced.

Why was this the case?

When Will We Hear from Reference Librarians in Africa?

Despite the editor's intention to invite African librarian participation for this volume, the editors were forced to consider several environmental factors to explain why this invitation may not have been viewed as an opportunity. The author had hoped librarians would contribute to the collective understanding of librarians supporting African scholarship and scholarship about Africa. However, she learned that her invitation to contribute a manuscript to a Western publication might be viewed with skepticism.

Intellectual Theft Impacting Partnerships?

Conversations with Africans alluded to an unfortunate history of Westerners who come to Africa to mine knowledge from Africa but do not credit Africans for their ideas, which are then published within Western journals. This type of theft may be virtually impossible for the creator of intellectual work to detect without the requisite access to information, particularly access to complete ranges of Western indexing tools.

While visiting in Nairobi (2001), Kenyan news reported claims that Kenyan university research on AIDS at the University of Nairobi had been lifted by major United States universities (in connection with pharmaceutical companies). This scandal aired on several local news broadcasts in Kenya, but received little coverage in the United States.

A longstanding tradition of expropriation of African cultural artifacts and knowledge by the West, with little criticism from librarians and scholars, may also engender distrust and lack of credibility in developing partnerships.

Who Publishes Library Literature in Africa?

Another possible reason for reluctance to take on writing an article for this volume could be an issue of status. Was it generally true that library practice was documented and published primarily by librarian administrators? Was this perception or reality? What might make it difficult to take on this project?

Finding workspace to support research activity proved to be difficult in Nairobi. Librarians from Kenyatta University and the University of Nairobi endeavored to locate a space with access to a computer for these interviews but collaborative research space for reference librarian use was not generally available.

The author also found that in Kenya, even asking librarians to state their practice or voice their concerns in the form of an article assumes that "telling the story" is a legitimate and safe thing to do. Impediments to librarian publishing may also include a host of potential reprisals librarians may face by attempting to address needed structural changes. Appearance of critiquing or reporting scenarios that may be perceived as having political implications could mean loss of job or life. In contrast to many students and several independent scholars in Africa, librarians receive a salary. However, librarians also face similar conditions of insecure infrastructures and must extend energy to respond to the hardship of others, further limiting their energy to devote to scholarship.

Multiple factors appear to intersect here. Scholarly activity is not only demonstrated by publications. However, the author had a strong sense that it was a rare case where a reference librarian is invited or encouraged to author a work, and rarely do positions afford the time and energy.

Despite these conditions, librarians' organizations, such as the Kenya Library Association are active and pursue grants from agencies to host programs and workshops for librarians. The author accompanied two librarians who received a grant from an international agency to develop ICT training workshops for Kenyan librarians. Librarians are active in and maintain connections with the International Federation of Library Associations (IFLA) (Musisi 1998; Bulogosi 2003). Rosenberg acknowledges the important role of librarians and library associations as well as the need for librarians to be visible in order "[to] win back government funding and to prove the crucial role of libraries in national development." Training for librarians (Ocholla 2000) and promotion and support for national library or local library associations like the Kenya Library Association, or other regional associations, can do much to engender capacity of libraries and librarians. Rosenberg lists several important organizations in an essay on the Web site accessed at: (http://www.inasp.info/pubs/bookchain/profiles/rosenberg.html).

CONCLUSION: CONSCIOUS PARTNERSHIPS FOR DEMOCRATIC INDIGENOUS EDUCATION FOR AFRICA

> What is remarkable, however, is not the continued submission by some scholars to the silences imposed by the state and elements of civil society, but the courage of many others who continued to research, write and publish, both at home and abroad, at great personal and professional risk. Together with the ever restive students, they turned many universities into sites of prodemocracy struggles that began sweeping African countries from the 1980s. Theirs was a fight against the erosion of resources and the erasure of their voices, which undermined their production and reproduction as intellectuals. (Zeleza 2003, 398-399)

Clearly, the expanded role of ICT in Africa is beneficial. However, depending upon the design of virtual futures, Africa could, once again, become dependent if technology and motives are not critically examined and questioned. This is where external experience and partnerships could be most beneficial.

Granted, African universities cannot afford to be ivory towers, isolated from communities who face consequences from development and democratic divides. Neither should universities become "service parks for private capital" (Zeleza 2003, 400). Reliance on donor-assisted privatization, structural adjustment programs and development agendas or prescriptive pedagogy will not meet the needs of African societies, nor will they revitalize them if underlying goals are to create market dependency.

A University campus can model community building even when pro-democracy struggles are part of that community. Large numbers of Africans continue to die from HIV/AIDS, lack clean water, and have many other problems. Africans must decide if virtual space will enhance or further distance the divides that many communities face, and they must know all of the costs.

Librarians and scholars in Africa and the West are among those calling for a "global conversation of universities and scholars in which Africa participates on its own terms, with the interest and concern of ordinary Africans as its guiding principle" (Nyamnjoh and Jua 2002, 1). Whether it be through discussion of "postcolonial phallocracy" or Eurocentric education, these critical dialogues continue with recognition of the transnational and local dimensions. Examination of "epistemological orders of the West" (Zeleza 2003, 393) may also produce analysis of virtual futures which may differ from those described here. South Africa continues to provide leadership in the development of libraries and education throughout Africa. Fortunately, South Africa's emphasis on social transformation and equity has, in a number of instances, encouraged critical analysis of promises made in the name of technology. Kenyan vision, resistance, and resilience, as articulated by authors cited in this paper, provide ground upon which to build future indigenous and democratic roles for librarians and scholars in Africa. Many of these authors have demonstrated critical analysis on this path. It is within the context of emerging local examination of education that librarians can position themselves. Librarians in Africa continue to emerge as partners in building educational foundations that consider what is best for Africa, while transitioning from entrenched inequalities to pedagogies of liberation (Meena 2001). Scholars and administrators in higher education might do well to invite this participation. Reference librarians who have face-to-face dialogue with scholars and communities are among those best positioned to understand the needs of their communities. Promoting librarian capacity within Africa could be maximized at this critical juncture if scholars and librarians were able to take more active roles as participants in this collective agency and could insert themselves into transnational conversations. Critical perspectives, true participation, and inclusion of scholars and librarians should be encouraged in organizations such as the Association of African Universities. Much more could be done to integrate the voices of women and the agency of librarians in these settings, drawing on both internal and external experience of committed educators.

Alternative visions of education center on the creation of a reading culture in Africa. The need to develop networks of scholars who envision democratic futures is a collective act. Zeleza's motivation to create a "cultural economy" of reading, publishing, and dissemination of books, appears to be based upon the painful circumstances he has experienced in Kenya and the desire to provide avenues for creating dignity and sustained community.

> To read is in a large sense to partake in collective intellectual conversation crystallized over many generations, to claim and perhaps to contribute to, the immense heritage of social thought. That is why illiteracy is so debilitating, so destructive, so dehumanizing for the illiterate, who whatever their abilities and ambitions, wiles and wisdom, are cut off from the written dialogues and endowment of humanity. (Zeleza 2003, 369)

Zeleza encourages African capitalists to support the development of a reading culture by offering book prizes and notes that the Zimbabwe International Book Fair (ZIBF) is a step in the right direction. However, he also decries "the ravages of structural adjustment" policies promoted by the World Bank (Zeleza 2003, 386). Therefore, Zeleza might find it difficult to consider a "mutually beneficial partnership" with the World Bank.

The ALC and INASP are models of partnership that are not driven by market motivation. They utilize existing librarian capacity, and work from the principle that knowledge is a part of the "public good," which must be affordable. The free flow of information necessary for cultivating scholarship is hampered by mirroring market motivation and contributes to "tendencies to convert every bit of information into a piece of marketable intellectual property" (Darch 1998, 6). When information and knowledge become commodified, they reflect the economic and social framework within which they are exchanged. Commodification of knowledge and information impacts upon the development of publicly available and free information to support democracy, as well as possibilities for developing effective and equitable partnerships. Open source options present possibilities for alternative constructs. Free and open access to information and education is key to the North American Library Bill of Rights and the ethic of librarianship, despite "virtual futures" that do not include these principles.

As we participate in our own efforts to build democratic education and "global consciousness" (Pala 1995; Robertson 2003), librarians in the West who see the need to develop cross-continental, formal, and informal partnerships, face several challenges. To form equitable partnerships with African librarians, reflection upon assumptions and agendas of librarians and donors must continue to be examined. Criteria and methods for engaging in partnerships will require willingness to hear, listen, and design strategies together, in a sustained manner. This necessitates honesty and learning about our histories–a conscious effort not to re-inscribe, but to understand the "complex workings" and interests of colonial models (Desai 2001, 174) and how these may inform our relationships. As Nyamnjoh and Jua argue:

> Only the forging of this mutuality will help re-energize African scholars and allow for a building of a genuinely international and democratic community of researchers. (Nyamnjoh and Jua 2002, 21-22)

WORKS CITED

African Studies Association. 2002. Program: African Studies Association 45th Annual Meeting. Africa in the information and technology age. Washington, D.C., 5-8 December 2002.

African Virtual University. www.unesco.org/iiep/eng/focus/elearn/webpub/pdf/avu.pdf.

Africana Librarians Council of the African Studies Association. http://www.loc.gov/rr/amed/9asa.html.

Ajayi, G. Olare. Information and communications technologies: Building capacity in African universities. Paper presented at the 10th Association of African Universities (AAU) General Conference, Nairobi, Kenya, February 2001.

Altheide, David L. 2002. *Creating fear: News and the construction of crisis*. Hawthorne, NY: Walter de Gruyter.

Amutabi, Maurice N. 2002. Crisis and student protest in universities in Kenya. *African Studies Review* 45, no. 2: 157-177.

Äng, Conny, Henk Das, Allison Dobbie, and Susan Kent. 2001. *The public library–idea, cyberplace, physical presence*. Gütersloh: Bertelsmann Foundation. http://216.239.39.104/search?q=cache:CsaKJxIgXSwJ:www.bertelsmann-stiftung.de/documents/Cyberplace_physicalpresence.pdf++site:www.bertelsmann-stiftung.de+The+public+Library-idea,+cyberplace,+physical+presence.+&hl=en&start=4&ie=UTF-8.

Association of African Universities (AAU) and Ford Foundation. Dissertations and Theses in Africa Database (DATAD). http://www.aau.org/datad/.

Association of Research Libraries, Association of College and Research Libraries, and SPARC. n.d. Putting scholars back in control. http://www.arl.org/create/librarians/issues/putting.html.

Boyer, Dominic. 2002. The African crisis in context: Comparative encounters with educational rationalization. *African Studies Review* 45, no. 2: 205-218.

Bulogosi, Alice R. 2003. The Kenya Library Association. In *The Encyclopedia of Library and Information Science*. ed. Miriam Drake. Avaiable from Dekker.com. http://www.dekker.com/servlet/product/productid/E-ELIS/toc.

Bundy, Alan. Challenging technolust: The educational responsibility of librarians. Paper presented at the annual conference of the International Association of Technological University Libraries (IATUL) held at the Technical University of Crete, May 1999. http://www.library.unisa.edu.au/papers/techno.htm.

Centre for Information Literacy, University of Cape Town. n.d. INFOLIT. http://www.adamastor.ac.za/Academic/Infolit/committees.htm.

Crawford, W. and Gorman, M. 1995. *Future libraries: Dreams, madness and reality*. Chicago: American Library Association.

Dahl, Gudrun. 2001. *Responsibility and partnership in Swedish aid discourse*. Discussion Paper 9. Uppsala: Nordiska Africainstitutet.

Darch, Colin. The shrinking public domain and the unsustainable library. Cape Town, South Africa: University of Cape Town. Paper presented at an invitational conference on "The Electronic Library: Gateway to Information." Lund, Sweden: June 2-6, 1998. Sponsored by the Swedish International Development Cooperation Agency and Lund University.

Deegan, Marilyn and Simon Tanner. 2002. *Digital futures: Strategies for the information age*. New York: Neal-Schuman Publishers, Inc.

Desai, Guarav. 2001. *Subject to Colonialism: Self-fashioning and the colonial library*. London: Duke University Press.

DeStefano, Joseph, Ash Hartwell and Kren Tietjen. 1995. *Basic education in Africa: USAID's approach to sustainable reform in the 1990's*. United States Agency for International Development. Technical Paper No. 14.

Devarajan, Shantayanan, David R. Dollar, and Torgny Holmgren, eds. 2001. *Aid and reform in Africa: Ten lessons from ten case studies*. Washington, DC: The World Bank.

Diawara, Manthia. 2003. Toward a regional imaginary in Africa. In *World Bank literature*, edited by Amitava Kumar. Minneapolis: University of Minnesota Press.

Edwards, Heather M. 1999. South Africa's GAELIC: The Gauteng and environs library consortium. *Information Technology & Libraries* 18 (September): 123-128. Database online. Available from ABI/Inform Full Text.

Electronic Journal of African Bibliographies (EJAB). University Libraries, University of Iowa. http://sdrc.lib.uiowa.edu/ejab/.

Evans, David R., ed. n.d. *Education policy formation in Africa: A comparative study of five countries*. Washington, DC: U.S. Agency for International Development; Division of Health and Human Resources; Office of Analysis, Research, and Technical Support; Bureau for Africa.

Farrant, John H. and Lioudmila M. Afonso. 1997. Strategic planning in African universities: How relevant are northern models? *Higher Education Policy* 10, no. 1: 23-30.

Gherman, Paul M. 2000. Found Money: Trading infrastructure for information. *Journal of Library Administration* 31, no. 2: 49-62.

Gibbons, Michael. 1998. *Higher education relevance in the 21st century*. World Bank contribution to the UNESCO World Conference on Higher Education. Washington, DC: World Bank. Quoted in William Saint. *Tertiary distance education and technology in Sub-Saharan Africa*. Washington, DC: World Bank. Education and Technology Technical Notes Series Vol. 5, 1, 2000.

Goodall, Deborah and Peter Brophy. 1997. *A comparable experience? Library support for franchised courses in higher education*. Centre for Research in Library and Information Management, University of Central Lancashire. British Library Research and Innovation Report 33 RIC/G/176.

Green paper on higher education transformation. 1996. Department of Education, Pretoria, South Africa. http://www.polity.org.za/html/govdocs/green_papers/hegreenp.html?rebookmark=1.

Heeks, R. 1999. Information and communication technologies, poverty and development. *Development Informatics*. Working Paper Series, No. 5. Manchester, UK: Institute for Development and Policy and Management.

Hyden, Goran, Michael Leslie, and Folu Ogundimu, eds. 2002. *Media and democracy in Africa*. New Brunswick, NJ: Transaction Publishers, Inc.

Issak, Aissa. Compiler. 2000. Public Libraries in Africa: A report and annotated bibliography. International Network for the Availability of Scientific Publications (INASP). Oxford, United Kingdom.

Jones, David J. 2001. People places: Public library buildings in the new millennium. Hong Kong: Library Development in the Millennium Seminar, 2001. http://www.slnsw.gov.au/plb/publications/papers/peopleplaces.cfm.

Kagan, Al. 2003. The transformation of South African librarianship: Survey results and analysis of current opinions. *Progressive Librarian: A journal for critical studies & progressive politics in librarianship* 22 (summer): 1-37.

Klopp, Jacqueline M. and Janai R. Orina. 2002. University crisis, student activism, and the contemporary struggle for democracy in Kenya. *African Studies Review* 45, no. 1: 45-46.

LaFond, Deborah M. and Mary K. Van Ullen, and Richard Irving. 2000. Diversity in collection development: Comparing access strategies to alternative press periodicals. *College and Research Libraries* 61, no. 2: 136-144.

Levey, Lisbeth A. 2000. *Journals on the web: What's out there? What does it take? How can Africa jump on board?* Nairobi, Kenya: Project for Information Access and Connectivity. *Library and Information Association of Africa.*

Martell, Charles. 2000. The Disembodied librarian in the digital age, Part II. *College and research libraries* 61, no. 2: 99-119.

Marton, Betty A. 2000. *Revitalizing African libraries: The challenge of a quiet crisis.* New York: Carnegie Corporation of New York.

McChesney, Robert W. 1999. *Rich media, poor democracy: Communication politics in dubious times.* Urbana: University of Illinois Press. Quoted in Barbara Warnick. *Critical literacy in a digital era: Technology, rhetoric, and the public interest.* Mahwah, NJ: Lawrence Erlbaum Associates, Publishers, 2002, 8-9.

Meena, Ruth. Women's participation in higher levels of learning in Africa. Paper presented at the *10th Association of African Universities (AAU) General Conference*, Nairobi, Kenya, February 2001.

Melkote, Srinivas R., and H. Leslie Steeves. 2001. *Communication for development in the Third World: Theory and practice for empowerment.* 2nd ed. Thousand Oaks, CA: Sage Publications, Inc.

Miller, William. 2002. The library as a place: Tradition and evolution. *Library Issues: Briefings for faculty and administrators* 22 (January); http://www.libraryissues.com/pub/LI220003.asp.

Musisi, Jafred S. 1998. The standing conference of Eastern, Central and Southern African Librarians (SCECSAL): It's impact in the region. *Maktaba: Journal of the Kenya Library Association*, (July) Special Issue, 9-15.

Nandy, Ashis. 2000. Recovery of indigenous knowledge and dissenting futures of the university. In The university in transformation: Global perspectives on the futures of the university, ed. Sohail Inayatulla and Jennifer Gidley. London: Bergin & Garvey. Quoted in Dominic Boyer. The African crisis in context: Comparative encounters with educational rationalization. *African Studies Review* 45, no. 2: 2002, 205-218.

Nassimbeni, Mary. 1998. The information society in South Africa: From global origins to local vision. *South African journal of library & information science* 66 (December) Database online. Available from Ebsco Academic Search Premier.

National Research Council of the National Academies. 2002. *Down to earth: Geographic information for sustainable development in Africa.* Washington, DC: National Academies Press.

Nelens, Gert, Nancy Hafkin, Leo Van Audenhove, and Bart Cammaerts, eds. 2001. *The digital divide in developing countries: Towards an information society in Africa.* Brussels: Brussels University Press in cooperation with SMIT (Studies on Media Information and Telecommunication) and UN-ECA (United Nations Economic Commission for Africa).

Nyamnjoh, Francis B. and Nuntang B. Jua. 2002. African universities in crisis: The political economy of violence in African educational systems. *African Studies Review* 45, no. 2: 1-26.

Ocholla, Dennis N. 2000. *Training for library and information studies: A comparative overview of LIS education in Africa. Education for Information* 18, no. 1:143-167.

Odhiambo, E.S. Atieno. 2002. M.K.O. Abiola distinguished lecture: The cultural dimensions of development in Africa. *African Studies Review* 45, no. 3: 1-16.

Ogbu, Osita and Paschal Mihyo. eds. 2000. *African youth on the information highway: Participation and leadership in community development.* Ottawa: International Development Research Centre.

Ogot, Bethwell. 2001. *Selected essays, 1961-1998.* Trenton, NJ: Africa World Press (forthcoming). Quoted in *Paul Tiyambe Zeleza. Rethinking Africa's 'globalization': Volume 1, the intellectual challenges*, Trenton, NJ: Africa World Press, 2003.

Olowu, Dele and Soumana Sako. eds. 2002. *Better governance and public policy: Capacity building and democratic renewal in Africa.* Bloomfield, CT: Kumarian Press.

Olsson, B. 1992. *The ownership and cultivation of knowledge: The rationale for Swedish support to universities in developing countries.* Swedish Agency for Research Cooperation With Developing Countries.

Pala, Achola O., ed. 1995. *Connecting across cultures and continents: Black women speak out on identity, race, and development.* New York: United Nations Development Fund for Women.

Partnership for Higher Education in Africa. 2003. *Securing the lynchpin: ICT for teaching, learning, and research–a workshop for African universities, 29 July-August 1, 2002.* United Nations International Conference Center Addis Ababa, Ethiopia. New York: Partnership for Higher Education in Africa.

Peters, Dale and Michele Pickover. 2001. DISA: Insights of an African model for digital library development. D-Lib Magazine 7 (November); http://www.dlib.org/dlib/november01/peters/11/peters.html.

Quinn, Brian A. 2000. The McDonaldization of academic libraries? *College and Research Libraries* 61, no. 3: 248-61.

Quinn, Brian A. 2001. The impact of aggregator packages on collection management. *Collection Management* 25, no. 3: 53-74.

Raseroka, Kay. Leapfrogging into the third millennium: Opportunities or a mirage for Sub-Saharan academic communications. Paper presented at the Proceedings of the 40th anniversary conference of the Africana Librarians Council Schmidt held in Columbus, Ohio November 13, 1997. In *Africana librarianship in the 21st century: Treasuring the past and building the future. Edited by Nancy Schmidt*, Bloomington, IN: Indiana University, African Studies Program.

Raseroka, Kay. 1997. *The role of university libraries.* Association of African Universities 1997 Accra-North Ghana; http://www.aau.org/english/documents/librole.htm.

Readings, Bill. 1996. *The university in ruins.* Cambridge, MA: Harvard University Press.

Robertson, Robbie. 2003. *Three waves of globalization: A history of developing consciousness.* New York: Zed Books.

Rosenberg, Diana. 1997. *University libraries in Africa: A review of their current state and future potential.* Vol. 1, Summary; Vol. 2, Case studies: Botswana, Ethiopia, Ghana, Ivory Coast, Kenya; Vol.3, Case studies: Mozambique, Senegal, Sierra Leone, Sudan, Tanzania, Zimbabwe, donor policies and practices. London: International African Institute.

Rosenberg, Diana. n.d. Current issues in library and information services in Africa. http://www.inasp.info/pubs/bookchain/profiles/rosenberg.html.

Saint, William. 2000. *Tertiary distance education and technology in Sub-Saharan Africa.* Washington, DC: World Bank. Education and Technology Technical Notes Series Vol. 5, 1.

Saint, William. 1992. *Universities in Africa: Strategies for stabilization and revitalization.* Washington, DC: World Bank Technical Paper 194, Africa Technical Department Series.

Samoff, Joel and Bidemi Carrol. The Promise of partnership and continuities of dependence: External support to higher education in Africa. Paper presented at the 45th Annual Meeting of the African Studies Association, Washington, DC, December 5-8, 2002.

Samoff, Joel. 2001. Knowledge banks and gateways: The changing of forms of foreign aid and influence. *NORRAG News* 30. (Northern Policy Research Review and Advisory Network on Education and Training); http://www.norrag.org/db_print_article.php?id=812.

Samoff, Joel. 1999. Education sector analysis in Africa: Limited national control and even less ownership. *International Journal of Educational Development* 19: 249-272.

Samoff, Joel. 1995. Troublesome issues in the structural adjustment of educational research. *NORRAG News* 18. (Northern Policy Research Review and Advisory Network on Education and Training); http://www.norrag.org/db_print_article.php?id+274.

Sawyerr, Akilagpa. Challenges facing African universities: Selected issues. Paper presented at the 45th Annual Meeting of the African Studies Association, Washington, D.C., December 5-8, 2002. http://216.239.39.104/search?q=cache: gurb3bIc4D0J: www.aau.org/english/documents/asachallenges.pdf+Sawyerr,+Akilagpa.+Challenges+Facing+African+Universities.+&hl=en&start=1&ie=UTF-8.

Schaffner, Bradley L. 2001. Electronic resources: A wolf in sheep's clothing? *College and Research Libraries* 62, no. 3:239-49.

Schmidt, Nancy J. 1998. *Africana librarianship in the 21st century: Treasuring the past and building the future.* Proceedings of the 40th anniversary conference of the Africana Librarians Council held in Columbus, Ohio November 13, 1997. Bloomington, IN: Indiana University, African Studies Program.

Selfe, Cynthia L. 1999. *Technology and literacy in the twenty-first century: The importance of paying attention.* Carbondale: Southern Illinois University Press. Quoted in Barbara Warnick. *Critical literacy in a digital era: Technology, rhetoric, and the public interest.* Mahwah, NJ: Lawrence Erlbaum Associates, Publishers, 2002, 8.

Sogge, David. 2002. Give & Take: What's the matter with foreign aid? Zed Books. Quoted in "Money Talks." 1-16. http://www.nu.ac.za/csds/Publications/donor_3.PDF.

Solely, Lawrence C. 1995. *Leasing the Ivory Tower: The corporate takeover of academia.* Boston, MA: South End Press.

Subotzky, George. 2001. Quality of training and research: Towards a dynamic process of curricular reform and innovations in African tertiary institutions-the Moroccan experience. Paper presented at the 10th General Conference of the Association of African Universities, Nairobi, 5-9 February 2001. Photocopied.

Till, Graham. 2003. *Harnessing distance learning and ICT for higher education in Sub-Saharan Africa: An examination of experiences useful for the design of widespread and effective tertiary education in Sub-Saharan Africa.* Burnham, England: The Training Store Limited.

United States Agency for International Development. 1996. *Making a difference in Africa: A report on USAID assistance to Africa.* Washington, DC: USAID.

United States Agency for International Development. n.d. *Africa: Growth renewed, hope rekindled. A report on the performance of the development fund for Africa, 1988-1992.* Washington, DC: USAID.

University of California Berkeley Libraries. n.d. Scholarly publishing: What faculty can do. http://www.lib.berkeley.edu/Collections/publishing.html.

Van Audenhove, Leo. 1999. *Development co-operation in higher education: A strategic review of international donor policy and practices.* Brussels: Belgian Administration for Development Cooperation.

van der Veur, Paul R. 2002. Broadcasting and political reform. In *Media and democracy in Africa*, eds. Hyden, Goran, Michael Leslie, and Folu Ogundimu, 81-105. New Brunswick, NJ: Transaction Publishers, Inc.

Warnick, Barbara. 2002. *Critical literacy in a digital era: Technology, rhetoric, and the public interest.* Mahwah, NJ: Lawrence Erlbaum Associates, Publishers.

Wisner, William H. 2000. *Whither the postmodern library? Libraries, technology, and education in the information age.* Jefferson, NC: McFarland& Company, Inc., Publishers.

Wolff, Lawrence. 2002. The African virtual university: The challenge of higher education development in Sub-Saharan Africa. *TechKnowLogia* (April-June); http://www.techknowlogia.org/.

World Bank. 2001. *Private solutions for infrastructure: Opportunities for Uganda. A country framework report.* Washington, DC: World Bank.

Zack-Williams, Tunde, Diane Frost, and Alex Thomson. 2002. *Africa in crisis: New challenges and possibilities.* London: Pluto Press.

Zeleza, Paul Tiyambe. 2003. *Rethinking Africa's 'globalization': Volume 1, the intellectual challenges.* Trenton, NJ: Africa World Press.

Index

© 2004 by The Haworth Press, Inc. All rights reserved.